PAUL MARTIN

WORLD ENCYCLOPAEDIA *of* COCKTAILS

CONSTABLE · LONDON

This book is dedicated to

Kenneth Forbes

He backed our visions and ideas and continued to support them during the bleakest of hours. Without Kenneth I would surely never have had the opportunity to produce this volume.

First published in Great Britain 1997 by Constable and Company Ltd
3 The Lanchesters, 162 Fulham Palace Road, London W6 9ER

ISBN 0094755302

Printed in Great Britain by St Edmundsbury Press Ltd, Bury St Edmunds, Suffolk.

A CIP catalogue record for this book is available from the British Library

CONTENTS

APERITIF

▼

When starting to put together this book, I had three specific goals in mind. The first was to pass on the wealth of factual information and inspired conjecture that I have correlated over the years about the history of the top classic drinks. The second was to supply a recipe section large enough to provide a representative collection of popular cocktail recipes spanning a hundred years of *mixology*. The third was to create a truly authoritative guide to the mixed drink, a reference work of both domestic and professional appeal that was also readable and entertaining.

World Encyclopaedia of Cocktails is the result of my endeavours.

I subconsciously commenced my cocktail apprenticeship during my early teens. Inspired by the continental concept of constructing bed frames from masonry, I set about building just such a bed for my personal use. Incorporated in the design was a shrewdly camouflaged cabinet, with access gained via the foot of the bed. It occurred to me that this was an ideal location to conceal the various bottles of illegally purchased *Malibu* in my possession. No sooner had the first of my school friends discovered this domestic speakeasy than the 'Bar Bed', as it came to be known, adopted the idiosyncrasy of alcoholic safety-deposit box for the entire class. My parents never could understand why upwards of fifteen kids would spend the entire evening in a room that measured ten foot by six.

In retrospect I can see that I was destined to pursue a profession where alcohol played a fundamental role. During the early 'eighties I began my career in earnest, gaining invaluable experience working for a number of popular central London cocktail establishments. However, as my thirst for knowledge increased, I discovered that those I had previously believed were fountains of information were actually "drought-ridden", to coin a phrase. Few displayed more than the most rudimentary understanding of the subject. Inspired by the challenge and fuelled with a desire to chronicle the fascinating history of the finest of all mixed drinks, I initiated a campaign of investigation that will no doubt continue to occupy me in my ceaseless quest for historical enlightenment. A quest, I am thrilled to add, that steered me towards many kindred spirits, who have been a great inspiration to me. I now find myself in an entirely different world to the one I first perceived, one where I have made the acquaintance and friendship of other like-minded maniacal cocktail fanatics.

There are over 2500 cocktail recipes to be found within these pages. Selection was remarkably difficult. In 1990 the United States Bartenders Association listed over 10,000 officially recognized recipes, and each day bartenders continue to create new concoctions with the most animated titles, so selecting a *mere* 2,500 was no easy matter.

I have given proper coverage to the old favourites, the drinks that have continued to be popular, in some cases for over a hundred years. Their survival is the endorsement of their quality. Drinks invented more recently also feature prominently, though national or international popularity is a prerequisite to their inclusion. New cocktails that have the potential for longevity are also included. I describe in some detail the multitudinous variety of cocktail styles, including Slings, Sours, Shooters etc., and finally, I include over three hundred of my own creations. When I know who invented a particular cocktail I provide his or her name. However, I believe that the thousands of cocktail bartenders the world over are equally deserving of recognition, as each individual *mixologist* plays an essential role in perpetuating the popularity of the cocktail.

The cocktail has the unique capacity, because of its variety, to satisfy any taste for alcohol, with flavours ranging from sharp, sour and bitter to sweet, fruity and creamy and with alcohol bases covering the entire spectrum of the distillers' array. In the hands of a skilled mixer these constituents are transformed into elixirs. With this book the reader has the benefit of an entire career's-worth of cocktail knowledge, and with a little practice can become a skilled exponent.

CHAPTER ONE

Equipment and Mixing

GLASSWARE

The selection of suitable glasses is a subject of importance, deserving a separate book of its own. No host, be he professional or otherwise, can be expected to provide the correct receptacle for every drink, so for the purposes of this guide I have selected eighteen universal styles of glass. This decision is designed to complement the characteristics of each cocktail and is based on the extensive availability of such glassware. But nevertheless, it is perfectly acceptable to serve a cocktail in whatever glass you have at your disposal. Though the styles marked with an asterisk are the absolute fundamentals for the domestic bar.

martini* (5oz)
highball* (10–12oz)
old-fashioned* (8–12oz)
wine glass* (5–7oz)
goblets large, medium and small* (6–12oz)
liqueur (3oz)
shot 2-2½oz)
pousse café (2–3oz)
salude grande (7oz)
Napoli grande (14oz)
coupette (6oz)
sour glass (3–5oz)
deep dish champagne saucer (4–7oz)
champagne flute (4–6oz)
Pilsner/beer (10–12oz)
brandy balloon (10oz+)
tankard (12–20oz)
liqueur coffee (8oz)

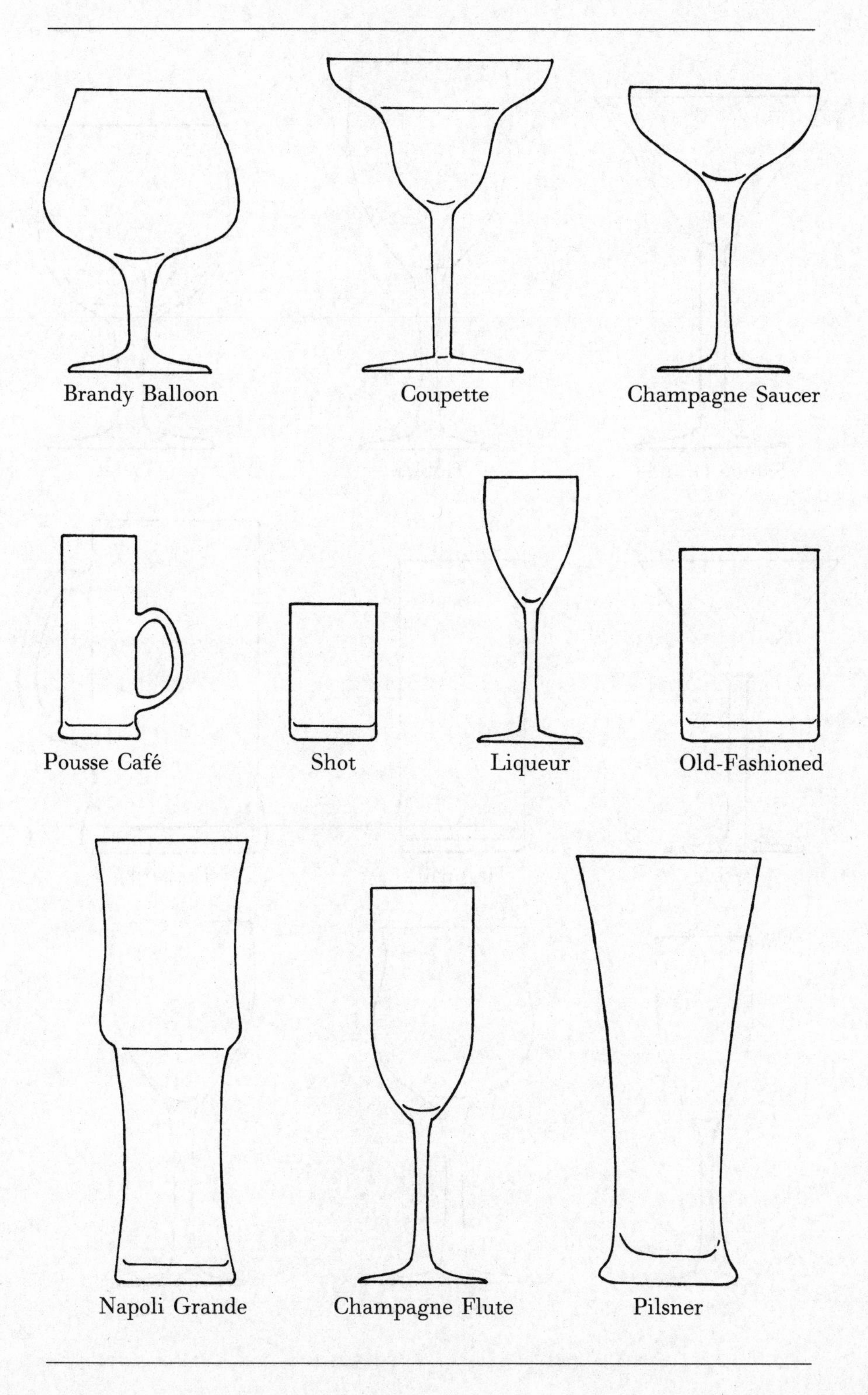
Brandy Balloon
Coupette
Champagne Saucer
Pousse Café
Shot
Liqueur
Old-Fashioned
Napoli Grande
Champagne Flute
Pilsner

Salude Grande
Goblet
Goblet
Martini
Highball
Tankard
Sour
Liqueur Coffee
Wine Glass

MIXING EQUIPMENT

There are three basic forms of mixing a cocktail other than pouring it straight into the glass. The principal method is to shake. Early examples of cocktail shakers were of elaborate and ornate design but they lacked practicality and became effectively redundant for mixing drinks. In contrast, the modern shaker is an example of precision and efficiency.

There are two forms of shaker in use today, the two piece Boston shaker and the more common three piece shaker. The Boston shaker is formed by slotting together the mouths of two beaker-shaped containers one smaller than the other, to create a canister.

To allow this, the beakers are different sizes. The smaller half is often made from glass. The Boston can be a very awkward utensil to operate. It is difficult to separate smoothly and impractical to strain from. However, the three piece is a model of simplicity. Shaped as a tall beaker, the lid has an opening with a straining device over which there is a cap. If you wish to strain, you simply remove the cap and pour, whereas if you wish to dispense the entire contents, you remove the lid and cap together.

The second method of mixing a cocktail is to stir. In general, any glass jug will suffice, its major prerequisite being a good lip to pour through. The ingredients are combined with ice, stirred together with a long-handled barspoon and strained into the glass, retaining the ice with a spring-loaded Hawthorn strainer. The strainer is spring-loaded, allowing it to adapt to the circumference of most openings.

The critical difference between shaking and stirring is that while the shaker is more effective in chilling a cocktail, it dramatically erodes the ice, creating a higher water content in the cocktail. However, there are certain ingredients that require the energetic action of the shaker in order for them to unite.

The final method – blending – does away with any difficulty in combining ingredients. The blender has extended the previously limited range of compatible cocktail ingredients. We can now liquidize most natural products and consequently develop an unlimited range of alcoholic concoctions. There are a number of professional bar blenders on the market. They are designed for sturdiness and longevity, a fact that is reflected in the price. A domestic blender will not endure the same rigorous use. Therefore, if you use it often make sure that you crush the ice-cubes before adding them to the blender; this will significantly reduce the stress on the motor and prolong its life.

Most bars will have an electric ice crusher. For domestic use there are various manual crushers on the market, most of them at reasonable prices. However, if you do not wish to spend money on a machine for crushing frozen water, simply wrap the ice-cubes in a clean tea-towel and bash them a few times with a rolling-pin or other blunt instrument. This technique is most effective.

MEASUREMENTS

The measurements in this book are all based upon the fluid ounce. When mixing a cocktail it is essential that you maintain the ratio between the ingredients; you can happily adjust the quantity of alcohol without affecting the character and quality of the cocktail as long as the ratio is preserved.

oz. = 1 fl.oz or approximately 28ml
tbsp. = level tablespoon
tsp. = level teaspoon
dash = 1/4 teaspoon
dash of egg white = level tablespoon
splash = 2 drops
dot = 1 drop

EXPLANATION OF TERMINOLOGY

Throughout the book I will be providing simple instructions for mixing and presentation. Below is a list of terms and a detailed explanation of what is to be understood by each.

Mixing the Drink

Shake and strain
Using a cocktail shaker, shake the ingredients together with a regular scoop of ice-cubes (normally six to eight) and pour the contents into the recommended glass, retaining the ice in the shaker.
Shake and pour
This time shake the ingredients together with a regular scoop of ice-cubes and pour the entire contents, including the ice, into the recommended glass.
Stir and strain
Using a glass mixing jug, stir the ingredients together with a large scoop of ice-cubes (normally ten to twelve) and strain into the recommended glass, retaining the ice in the jug.

Stir and pour
This time stir the ingredients together with a large scoop of ice-cubes and pour the entire contents, including the ice, into the recommended glass.

Blend until...and pour
Blend all the ingredients together with ice-cubes in a liquidizer or food processor until smooth or frozen (I will indicate which). If smooth, use a regular scoop of ice-cubes, if frozen, use a large scoop. This usually takes between ten and twenty seconds. Pour the entire contents into the recommended glass.

Build
Add a regular scoop of ice-cubes to the recommended glass and then pour the ingredients over the ice in the order given. Stir before serving.

Layer
This will apply to cocktails that have one spirit or liqueur floating on another. Slowly pour the ingredients, in the order given, into the glass. Use the back of a spoon to control the flow. Each ingredient will float on the preceding one. The order is intended to take advantage of the various original gravity ratings.

Muddle
Muddling is the crushing or mashing of a number of specified ingredients. A pestle is the most effective tool for muddling although many use the back of a barspoon.

Top, Topping etc
This instruction is given only when a specific measurement is not quoted. In this instance, fill to the top of the glass with the ingredient required.

In the event that the method for a particular cocktail requires more detailed instruction, I will provide it at the time.

Garnishes

I never garnish my cocktails unless the garnish is specified in the recipe. I have nothing in particular against garnishing cocktails, but always prefer to concentrate my efforts on creating a sublime drink rather than making it look like an entry for a flower show. I have therefore only suggested a garnish where I think it is advisable. If however you wish to dress your cocktails further, there are no hard and fast rules, although the flavour of the ingredients usually points towards the recommended garnish (e.g. lemon juice, twist of lemon, etc.)

Garnish with...

This either means that you drop the suggested garnish into the finished cocktail or, in the case of sliced fruit, make a cut towards the centre of the fruit and then slide the garnish on to the rim of the glass.

Add a twist of...

Unless otherwise stated, cut a thick slice of peel from the citrus fruit referred to, squeeze the zest from the skin on top of the finished cocktail and drop the peel into the drink. Only the dry martini and a few others dispense with the peel after using the zest.

Frosted glass

A frosted glass is one that has spent a minimum of ten minutes in the deep-freeze. Exposure to the air leads to an opaque frost covering the surface area. It does however, rapidly warm up. So, it is a good idea to remove the glass from the freezer immediately before dispensing the drink and no earlier.

Salt-rimmed glass

To salt rim a glass, run the lip of the glass through the flesh of a citrus fruit (whichever one happens to feature in a particular recipe), and then dip the damp rim into a shallow saucer of salt. Shake off the excess and the glass is ready. It is important to avoid salt adhering to the inside of the lip so attempt to wet only the top and outer lip.

Sugar-rimmed glass

As above, only using granulated sugar.

CHAPTER TWO

Spirits and Liqueurs

This chapter provides the reader with information on the spirits and liqueurs used for this book. It is not intended to be a catalogue of the boundless range of products on the world market, but rather a comprehensive guide to what is required to create the range of cocktail recipes in this book. I have gone into some detail about the production and distillation of the major spirits, and provided a guide to the production of liqueurs. This is followed by a glossary of the remaining ingredients.

GIN

▼

The origin of gin can be traced back to a Dutch apothecary named Franciscus Sylvius. During the late sixteenth century he ran a series of experiments, flavouring 'aqua vitae' with the juniper berry. He christened this brew 'genievre', which also became known as geneva or genever, the Dutch word for juniper. This original concoction was a product of purely medicinal inspiration. It successfully alleviated a variety of ailments in addition to imparting a sense of contentment. Indeed, it was the inebriating effect on many a British soldier that gave rise to the expression 'Dutch courage'.

When William of Orange became William III of England in 1689, gin recieved a great boost in its popularity. The new monarch effectively banned the import of French wines and brandies by raising the duty. In addition, he passed an act of state decreeing that the masses be encouraged to consume domestically distilled grain spirits to discourage further the import of French spirits into England. The king led by example, installing gin as the palace pouring-spirit at Hampton Court. The banqueting hall became known as the 'gin temple'.

The popularity of gin advanced unimpeded, by 1736 when measures were introduced in an attempt to curb expenditure the average consumption per head of population was just short of one gallon.

The disastrously high tax of 1736 was repealed in 1743, having failed to slow the increasing production and widespread use of gin.

The consumption of gin continued to survive various acts of parliament and periods of prohibition. Despite being held as the root cause of national dissension and insobriety, gin eventually shrugged off its tarnished image as a lower-class tipple and began to establish itself as a respected and high-calibre product.

Eventually government restrictions imposed to regulate production opened the door to many of the great gin 'houses' and paved the way for the spirits of outstanding quality we have become so familiar with today.

Gin is created from neutral grain spirit which is double distilled in a continuous-still, producing a clean, pure and tasteless grain spirit of high alcohol content. The selection of grain and water for the pure spirit is very important. The quality of the spirit will substantially influence the character of the gin produced. The 'botanicals' are what flavour the gin. The juniper berry must be the predominant ingredient but others include; caraway, angelica root, orange and lemon peel, coriander seed, orris root and cassia bark. The distiller will possess the secret formula for his gin and will source botanicals of the finest grade.

There are a number of methods for producing gin. The first and cheapest is to flavour the grain spirit with oils of the various botanicals normally used in the distillation process. This method is called 'cold compounding', and produces a product of gin character but of less depth and dimension than a distilled gin.

One method for a distilled gin is 'racking'. This involves placing the botanicals in racks within the neck of the still. As the grain spirit is heated, the vapour rises through the racks, removing the essential oils from the ingredients. Thereafter it condenses and drops into a receiving-still as gin. The other method is 'steeping'. In this instance the botanicals are steeped in the grain spirit, allowing the flavours to infuse fully. A gentle heat is then applied to the still and the distillation process occurs. Again the vapour rises, condenses and is collected as gin. In both methods the distiller must recognize at which point the 'middle cut', which is the purest part of the spirit, should be made. The gin will take a while to reach the required flavour and alcohol content, accordingly the early portion of the distillation known as the head, is redirected for use in a future distillation. At the optimum moment the gin is chanelled in to a receiver. Constant checking will alert the distiller as to when the character of the gin is no longer suitable and the flow should be stopped. At this point, the final part of the distillation known as the tail is also redirected to join the head for future use. The gin is finally diluted to the required strength with the use of distilled water and bottled. Gin is rarely matured.

London Dry Gin: This was originally the term for a 'dry' (unsweetened) gin distilled within the London area. It has become a generic term for any dry gin of a similar style. The only remaining London distilled dry gin is Beefeater gin from James Burrough Ltd.

Plymouth Gin: This was originally a more aromatic gin than the dry product produced by the London distillers. The production of this local Devon gin came to a halt during the Second World War. Although resurrected after the war, the market for this fragrant gin had all but disappeared. Plymouth gin is now a much drier product than its charismatic predecessor, although it retains its historical standing. Plymouth gin was the original gin used in 'pink gin'. With both products being of significant medicinal consequence for the naval town, the marriage of bitters and gin was inevitable.

Geneva/Genever: This product, also known as 'hollands', is made by compounding juniper berries with *moutwijn* (malt wine). This is a strong grain spirit made from malted barley. The two versions of geneva are *oude* (old) and *jonge* (young). These are often diluted with a corn grain spirit, the *oude* containing a higher percentage of *moutwijn*. The final product is significantly more aromatic than London gin.

Old Tom Gin: This is a rarely produced sweetened gin. The name is credited to a Captain Dudley Bradstreet who is said to have used a container carved in the shape of a tom-cat to dispense this gin. Payment would be inserted into the cat's mouth whilst the gin would be served through the cat's paw via a tube.

TEQUILA

▼

Tequila is created from the blue Mezcal, a member of the Agave family otherwise known in America as the century plant. The mezcal resembles a tall cactus and produces elongated blooms that can take up to twelve years to appear. At the heart of this matured plant lies the key to the tequila – a huge fruit resembling a pineapple and weighing between 75 and 150 pounds. The fruit, known as a *pina*, is stripped and sent to the distillery for production. The juice of the pina is extracted by various methods of compression and then left to ferment for three to five days. The resultant alcoholic mash then starts a pot-still double distillation producing a colourless tequila at approximately 50% alcohol. It is aged in white-oak barrels, the variety of tequila dictating the style of barrel. For a white or silver tequila the barrel will be lined with wax to prevent the tequila from extracting colour from the barrel, whereas a gold or anejo (aged) tequila will be matured in a normal barrel so the final product receives a golden tint.

Tequila is only tequila if it is made within a specific area, namely, the village of Tequila and its environs and an additional area around Tepatitlan. In addition there are standards of excellence below which the product must not fall. Anything produced outside this area is known as mezcal.

One idiosyncrasy of the tequila drinker is the desire to swill the last mouthful in the bottle and with it the Agave worm. The significance of this worm is that it feeds exclusively on the pina of the mezcal plant. However, contrary to popular misconception, it will only be found in mezcal and never in tequila.

VODKA

▼

It is unclear whether vodka, or wodka meaning 'little water', originated in Russia or Poland. Both were known to be distilling vodka as far back as the twelfth century. As with many other distilled beverages, vodka was originally used as a medicinal product. There are no strict guidelines as to what vodka is distilled from; it can be made from any number of grains (corn, wheat, rye, etc.) or even the much loved potato. Vodka is produced using a double pot-still distillation after which the spirit is subject to a charcoal filtration process. This is intended to remove all flavour and nose, resulting in a smooth, pure grain spirit (potato vodkas are rarely made now). The key to the quality of the vodka lies in the selection of the grain and the source of water used to dilute the final product. As a general rule, vodka is not aged, thus avoiding the possibility of inheriting any unwanted characteristics from the cask. However, when producing a flavoured vodka, the use of cask ageing will benefit the smoothness of the final yield.

Zubrowka: As with all Polish vodka, this is a rye-based spirit. However, in order to impart a delicate aromatic bouquet, zubrowka grass (bison grass) is steeped in the vodka. The bottle usually contains a blade of the grass. This is also known as green vodka.

Gold Vodka: Known as *starka* in Poland, this is a vodka aged in wooden casks for between five and ten years. *Winiak* is a vodka that has been aged in old wine casks and hence is a dark golden colour.

Pepper Vodka: Known as *pertsovska*, this dark pepper vodka from Russia is infused with cayenne, capsicum and cubeb. It is said to be based on a seventeenth-century recipe created by Peter the Great.

Flavoured Vodkas

There are a variety of different flavoured vodkas on the market, many of which originate from outside Eastern Europe. They are mainly created by infusing the vodka with the fruit, spice or herb required. In this book I refer to the range of vodkas produced by Absolut of Sweden. There are many other brands that produce products of comparable quality. I have just used the Absolut range as a guideline.

Absolut Citron: Lemon-flavoured vodka. Subtle, clean and fresh.

Absolut Kurrant: Made with various berries although the black-currant dominates. Very strong fruity flavour.

Absolut Pepper: The hottest and smoothest pepper vodka on the UK market.

RUM

▼

Rum is the generic term for a distilled cane spirit that was first produced in the West Indies during the seventeenth century. This early product was a crude spirit consumed predominantly by the slave population. The name is said to have derived from either of two West Indian words in use at that time, *rumbullion* and *rumbustion*. An alternative theory is that the name derives from the Latin for sugar, *saccharum*. It was Christopher Columbus who introduced sugar cane to the Caribbean in the late fifteenth century, the cane originating from the Canary Islands.

Naturally, rum is not exclusive to the Caribbean; it can be produced wherever sugar cane grows.

Rum is considered to be the first alcoholic spirit produced in America. In 1667 a Boston distillery was known to be producing rum with molasses from the West Indies. By the mid eighteenth century, the appeal of rum in America was reflected by the existence of nearly one hundred rum distilleries.

The basic process of rum production is the same everywhere, although there are many variations between the different rum-producing countries. Initially the sugar cane is crushed to release the juices, which are then boiled to create a condensed syrup. The sugar within the syrup crystallizes and is removed to leave the molasses used for the rum production.

For a light white rum, usually of South American origin, the molasses are diluted with water and fermented using cultured yeast. This results in a weak alcoholic solution known as 'wash' which is distilled in a column-still and produces a high strength (greater than

80% alcohol) colourless rum. The purest part of the rum (the middle cut) is then matured in wooden barrels. The rum will inherit some debris from the barrel so it is filtered prior to bottling. In the event that the rum is to be sold as 'dark', caramel is added for colour.

For a full-bodied rum, Guyana, Jamaica, etc., the molasses are diluted with water, but this time a natural fermentation occurs. This can take a longer period than with the light rum (up to three weeks). The resultant alcoholic liquid is distilled in a pot-still producing a 'low wine'. This is then distilled for a second time and the middle cut is then matured in wooden barrels. After a prolonged period of maturation the rum is then coloured with caramel and bottled. A Demerera rum is produced by the same process but employing a column-still.

Jamaica: This is traditionally a dark, full-bodied rum with a deep and heavy nose. These are the most popular and effective rums for use in mixing cocktails.

Guyana: Rum from Guyana is known as Demerera rum, after the river that flows through the country. It is similar to the Jamaican in terms of body although it tends to be somewhat smoother. It can often be found as very high-proof versions.

Puerto Rico: This country produces very dry (white) light rums, by the column-still method, and now produces many popular Cuban brands. It also produces some dark rums.

Cuba: The lightest of the rums, Cuban rum is possibly the original ingredient of the Cuba libra and the daiquiri.

Haiti: These rums are produced using the French method of the cane juice rather than the molasses. A double distillation process is used and the result is similar to the full-bodied Jamaican rums, deep, rich and fruity.

Batavia Arrak: This 'rum' is produced on the island of Java employing the same method of naturally-fermented molasses. However, the addition of specially cooked Javanese red rice imparts a unique flavour. The arrak is matured in wooden barrels for up to nine years after which it is blended and bottled. It has a dry flavour and an extremely floral and pungent nose. There are many products that bear the arrak title; however, none resemble the arrak from Batavia.

WHISKY & WHISKEY

▼

SCOTCH WHISKY

Malt Whisky

Barley is malted by soaking it in water for up to two days, after which it is spread out over a concrete floor where a controlled environment causes the barley to germinate and secrete the all-important diastase enzyme. It is this enzyme that makes the starch soluble and capable of creating sugars. At this stage the germination is halted by drying the barley (green malt) over a peat kiln. The peat smoke imparts the unmistakable Scotch whisky character. The dried malt is then crushed and mixed with boiling water in a mash-tun. The mixture is agitated vigorously in order to regenerate the enzyme, the excess husks are extracted and the resultant liquid is known as wort. Cultured yeast is added to the wort and left to ferment for up to three days, producing an alcoholic liquid called wash. The wash receives its first distillation in a wash-still, creating a 'low wine' of 18–22% alcohol. The low wine then receives a second distillation in a spirit-still during which the desired middle cut is channelled off whilst the undesireable fore-shots and feints, the first and last portion of the distillation, are sent back to the wash-still for further distillation. At this stage the spirit is 69–70% alcohol and is piped into sherry or oak casks for maturation. The whisky should be matured for a minimum of three years, although few are sold at less than five. In the case of many Highland malts a period of between ten and twenty years is quite customary.

Subsequent to the maturation period, the skill of the blender comes into play. In order to create a whisky of consistent character he may employ upward of fifty whiskies in his closely guarded recipe. Once the blend has been completed the whisky is left to rest, allowing all the flavours to combine successfully. Finally, caramel is added for colour, water is added to reduce the alcohol content and the product is filtered and bottled.

Single Malt Whisky: This is the unblended product of one single distillery. Most distilleries send their whisky for blending with other malts and grain whiskies; however, more distilleries are becoming inclined to market their own product as single malt.

Blended Whisky: This is a blend of any number of different whiskies. Most grain whisky is used for blending, although the more popular blends will incorporate a high percentage of malt whisky.

Vatted Malt Whisky: This is a blended whisky using only malts. No grain whisky is used, therefore the consistent quality of these blends is almost guaranteed.

Grain Whisky

Two cereals are used for grain whiskies, barley and maize. The maize provides the bulk of the starch. First it is ground into flour, and then steam-pressure cooked. This results in the particles swelling and bursting, exposing the starch. The barley goes through the identical process as malt whisky to become 'green malt'. The maize and green malt are then combined in a mash-tun with hot water so the starch of the maize is exposed to the diastase of the barley, which turns it to sugar. The resultant worts are mixed with cultured yeast and left to ferment. After two days the wash is transferred to the stills. The still used is a Coffey continuous-still which consists of two vertical columns divided by a series of perforated plates. One is called the rectifier the other the analyser. The wash is poured into the top of the analyser whilst pressurized steam enters from the bottom. As the two meet, the alcohol is vaporized and is then condensed by the introduction of further cold wash from above, which in turn is also warmed by this process. The vapours exit from the top of the analyser as feints and pass across to the rectifier whilst the spent wash is discarded from the base of the analyser. The feints enter the rectifier at the base and are cooled and condensed at a controlled level where the resulting grain whisky is piped to the spirit-receiver. From here the over-proof whisky is run off into vats where it is diluted. Finally, it is run into casks and stored for a minimum maturation period of three years.

IRISH WHISKEY

The production method for Irish whiskey is very similar to that of Scotch malt whisky bar a few essential differences. The principal cereal is barley; however only a small amount is malted, the rest is dried and milled into a fine powder, thus exposing a huge amount of starch. In addition, a small quantity of oats is added. This is to balance the loss in yield as barley alone has a reduced efficiency in fermentation. Unlike the Scotch malt, there are three distillations and these occur in the much larger pot-stills. Finally, the Irish malt will yield a condensed product of approximately 86% alcohol compared to the Scotch malt at 69–70%. The minimum maturation period for this whiskey is five years, and is often in the region of twelve years. This is due to the increased time required for pot-still whiskeys.

AMERICAN WHISKEY

Bourbon

Bourbon is distilled in a Coffey continuous-still, utilizing the same process as Scotch grain whisky. Bourbon must contain a minimum of 51% corn with the balance being made up of both rye and barley. In practice the percentage of corn is much higher. Bourbon is matured in new charred white-oak barrels for a period of not less than a year. It is the practice of using these charred barrels that imparts the unique bourbon character and colour. The use of charred oak barrels transformed the taste, although the identity of the person who first discovered it is matter of conjecture. However, it is said that the Rev. Elijah Craig, who is credited with the invention of Bourbon, employed the process of burning out old barrels used for the transportation of fish. On one occasion he forgot to clean out one charred barrel and the resulting whiskey proved to be the best of the whole batch.

Barrels are only used once for the making of Bourbon and after use they have for many years been sold to Scotland and other places for use in the maturation of Scotch whisky.

Corn Whiskey

Like Bourbon, this is a predominantly corn-based whiskey. However, unlike Bourbon there must be a minimum of 80% corn in the mash and the ageing will take place in used or uncharred casks.

Rye Whiskey

Rye whiskey must be distilled from a mash containing at least 51% rye. Like all American whiskeys it is produced using the continuous-still. Rye comes in either straight or blended varieties. The blended can contain neutral grain spirit or other grain or rye whiskeys.

Sour Mash

Subsequent to the fermentation of the wort the alcoholic wash is separated from the spent mash. Some of this mash is then added to the next batch of mash to be fermented. The objective is to ensure continuity of flavour and character.

Light Whiskey

Introduced in 1968 to respond to the increasingly popular market for lighter Scotch whiskies, this is a mixed-grain whiskey distilled at a very high 160 proof (80% alcohol). This creates a much cleaner, lighter spirit, full of depth and character. Like the corn whiskey, it is stored in used or new uncharred oak casks. Light whiskey is generally used for blending, although straight light whiskey is available.

Tennessee Whiskey

Tennessee whiskey must be made from at least 51% of any grain spirit (usually corn or rye) and must be produced in Tennessee.

CANADIAN WHISKY

Canadian whisky is considered to be of rye base. However, in truth many brands have a higher proportion of corn than of rye. Other cereals are used to influence the flavour. Distillation is by continuous-still, employing a very similar technique to bourbon. Canadian whiskeys are generally smooth, light and full of character.

BRANDY

▼

COGNAC

Approximately sixty-five miles north of Bordeaux on the River Charente lie the towns of Jarnac and Cognac. This is the heart of Cognac brandy producing country. In 1909 the region was officially divided into seven sections to acknowledge the differences in quality of the grape yield. The key to successful grape production lies in the crumbly chalky soil around the town of Cognac. Coupled with conditions of climate and light, the type of soil distinguishes the area classifications.

Grande Champagne: This area lies within Cognac itself and produces the finest of all Cognacs. Maturation of this spirit takes a long period and results in a delicate Cognac exuding subtlety and distinction.

Petite Champagne: This area surrounds three-quarters of the Grande Champagne lying south of the Charente, and consequently enjoys soil conditions of comparable quality. However, it does not receive the same protection from the sea weather and produces spirit of similar quality but of slightly less body than the Grande Champagne. This is reflected in a reduced maturation period.

Borderies: This area borders with the Grande Champagne area, north of the Charente and north-west of Cognac. However, despite its close proximity, the soil has a considerable clay content by comparison with Grande and Petite Champagne. The Cognac produced has a full-flavoured, mellow quality and is often selected for blending.

Fins Bois: This area completely surrounds the previous three, with most of the land lying to the north and north-east. In addition there is an isolated section of Fins Bois lying to the south-west. The soil conditions here are stony and support much forestry. The Cognac matures quickly and is of fine quality.
Bons Bois: This surrounds the Fins Bois area and encompasses the isolated section of the Fins Bois along the Gironde coast. The soil here is predominantly clay. The Cognac is agreeable but lacks refinement and finesse. Most of the production makes up inferior blends.
Bois Ordinaires and Bois Communs: These areas lie in respective order to the north-west of the Bons Bois, with the majority of the Bois Communs bordering the coast. The soil has a pronounced sandy quality and the vines are subject to the Atlantic climate conditions. The Cognacs produced are crude and unrefined, and are almost exclusively employed for inexpensive blends.

After the grapes are pressed, the wine is allowed to ferment naturally for a period of approximately thirty days. During this period no sulphur dioxide is added; this would only destroy the subtle character and distinct flavour of the cognac. The distillation process takes place in the winter, to avoid a natural secondary fermentation in the Spring – a fermentation that would impair the characteristic qualities of a fine cognac. The cognac is double-distilled in a Charentais pot-still. The cold wine is fed into the pot-still from a smaller container called a *chauffe-vin*. Heat is applied directly to the base of the pot-still so as the wine enters it is vaporized. The vapours travel out through the neck of the pot-still and are channelled through the *chauffe-vin* before being collected as *brouillis* at approximately 30% alcohol. The journey through the *chauffe-vin* serves a dual purpose. The cold wine helps to condense the vapours while the heat from the vapours warm the wine prior to distillation. For the second distillation, the *brouillis* are returned to the pot-still for slow and controlled heating. The cellar master will select only the finest 'middle cut' for maturing, returning the heads and tails to the next *brouillis*. Collection commences when the cognac is at 75–80% alcohol and is cut off once it diminishes to 60% alcohol. The average strength of the cognac being in the region of 70% alcohol.

The next stage is maturing in barrels. Traditionally the oak from the Limousin and Trancais forests are used. The wood is cut into staves and then exposed to the elements for a period of four years. This prevents shrinkage subsequent to barrelling and removes any excess solubles such as tannin from the wood. The new cognac will be stored in the new barrels for up to a year. During this period it will extract tannins and other soluble extracts from the wood, becoming coloured and darker. It is important to move the cognac into an older barrel so that it does not extract too much from the new wood. It will be left to mature in a controlled environment for more than 50 years. Prior to bottling there is the blending. The cognac may be coloured with caramel and then reduced to the desired alcohol content using distilled water. After resting and filtering it is bottled, and ceases to mature.

Styles of Cognac

VS (Very Superior)/Three Star: Legal Minimum Age (L.M.A.) 2 years; usual Minimum Age (U.M.A) 3 years, Parameters (P.) usually employed 3–7 years.
VSOP (Very Superior Old Pale)/Réserve: L.M.A 4 years, (U.M.A 5 years,) P 5–15 years.
Napoléon: L.M.A 6 years, (U.M.A 6–7 years,) P 7–15 years.
XO (Extra Old): L.M.A 6 years, (U.M.A 6–7 years,) P 20-plus years.
Vieux/Vielle Réserve: L.M.A 6 years, (U.M.A 6–7 years,) P 7–40 years.
Fine Champagne: The word 'champagne' is not to be confused with the Champagne-producing region. In this instance it derives from the Latin *campania*, meaning 'open countryside'. A fine champagne cognac must posses a minimum of 50% Grande Champagne grapes with the balance coming from Petite Champagne.
Grande Champagne: This cognac will be produced exclusively from Grande Champagne grapes.

ARMAGNAC

Proclaimed as the 'Spirit of Gascony', Armagnac is understood to predate the production of cognac by two hundred years. As with Cognac, however, the wines must be produced from vines within a specific delimited geographical area. The Armagnac production area is approximately 160 miles south of Cognac, west of Toulouse, and is divided into three regions.

Bas-Armagnac: Encompassing and spreading to the west of Fauze, the sandy soil conditions here prove to be the best for producing fine Armagnacs.

Ténarèze: This is the central area surrounding Condom to the east of Bas-Armagnac. The soil here has a high clay content and produces good quality, early maturing Armagnac.

Haut-Armagnac: Surrounding the previous two areas in a clockwise direction from the north of Ténarèze to the south-west of Bas-Armagnac and stretching east of Auch. The soil here is very chalky, but unlike the Cognac region results in an inferior quality Armagnac.

Armagnac is usually distilled only once, in an Armagnac continuous-still. The wine is produced in the same manner as cognac, omitting the sulphur dioxide and avoiding the second fermentation (on the lees). Upon distillation, the wine is piped from a feeding-tank into the top of the copper-still. Heat is applied to the base of the still, vaporizing the wine upon contact. The vapour passes up through the new wine, entering the still and out through the condenser. The condenser pipe (worm) is run back through the feeding-tank, performing the same heat transferral as with Cognac. The Armagnac is collected beneath the feeding-tank. Armagnac is sometimes produced by the double distillation pot-still method, though this is not traditional. After distillation the white Armagnac is of high strength, 50–55% alcohol. Oak casks fashioned from wood from local forests have proved ideal for the maturing of the volatile young spirit. The addition of colour and the process of blending occurs under the watchful eye of the cellar master while distilled water is used to reduce the strength to marketable level (40% alcohol).

Styles of Armagnac

Bas-Armagnac/Ténarèze/Armagnac: Must be the exclusive product of the area and have remained in cask for a minimum of two years.
VS/Three Star: A minimum of three years in cask.
VO/VSOP/Réserve: A minimum of five years in cask.
Extra/XO/Napoleon/V.A.Réserve: A minimum of six years in cask.

CALVADOS

This is an apple-based brandy from Calvados in the Normandy region. Ripe apples are crushed and fermented using cultured yeast. The mash is then double distilled in a Charentais still employing a very similar technique to cognac. The high-proof calvados is then transferred to oak casks for maturation. The colour and the quality of all calvados improves with age.
Three Star: A minimum of two years in cask.
Vieux/Réserve: A minimum of three years in cask.
VO/Vielle Réserve: A minimum of four years in cask.
VSOP: A minimum of five years in cask.
Napoléon/Hors D'Age/Age Inconnu: A minimum of six years in cask.

In America there is a product called applejack. This is made by a similar process but is not subject to the stringent minimum-age requirements.

OTHER BRANDIES

The term 'brandy' comes from the German *Branntwein* meaning 'burnt wine'. In the UK brandy has become a generic term for distilled grape wine. The finest of these are produced in Cognac and the Armagnac regions. However, grape-wine brandies are produced in countries the world over. In France a grape-wine

brandy is called *eau-de-vie de vin* and referred to as *une fine.* The French employ another method of producing grape brandy, and that is to ferment the discarded pulp from the grape pressing. Brandy made from this method is called marc.
Grappa: Produced in Italy, this is a grape brandy produced by the same method as the French *marc.*
Pisco: Originating in Peru, this is distilled from the muscat wine.
Weinbrand: German grape brandy is made from the wine of other European countries.

In this book when brandy is one of the ingredients, I list cognac, as I think it makes a better cocktail. However, the use of inexpensive grape brandy is quite acceptable.

LIQUEURS

▼

A simple definition of a liqueur is a base spirit blended with a flavouring and sweetener. The flavouring is obtained by extracting the essential oils from the flavouring source. The most common group of flavourings is the herb family. However, fruits, roots, barks, seeds, spices, berries and flowers are also in abundant use. The essential oils are extracted by one of four specific methods.

Extraction through distillation: The natural products are steeped in the base spirit for a period long enough to allow complete infusion of the flavours. This is similar to the process used for the production of many gins. The spirit is then subject to a double distillation. This is undertaken in vacuum conditions thus allowing a reduced temperature and protection of any delicate product.
Extraction through pressure: This is the application of a mechanical press to remove the oils from citrus peel.
Extraction through maceration: The natural products are soaked in the base spirit and then crushed to release maximum flavour. The spirit is then filtered, providing the 'aromatic infusion' which may be condensed or used for distillation.
Extraction through digestion: This is maceration in a heated base spirit. The temperature is maintained at 40–60°C for several days. The extraction is much faster than with the cold process and can ultimately extract more flavour.
Extraction through percolation: The base spirit is passed through the product in a continuous stream. This can be performed with the base spirit either hot or cold. Alternatively the product is racked above the heated spirit. The vapours pass through the product extracting the oils *en route* and then condense in the top of the still and drop back into the percolating spirit below, completing the cycle. This can only be used for products that are stable when heated.

Liqueur production

One method of liqueur production is to flavour the selected base spirit with (ethereal) oils or herb extracts. This has become a very effective technique for creating liqueurs and has reduced the expense of distillation. But the majority of liqueurs are produced by compounding. This is the method of mixing ingredients that have been subject to previous extraction. The blender will follow a specific recipe and sequence that results in a product unique to that particular producer. After compounding, the liqueur must be rested so that the ingredients can combine. The most successful method is to mature it in oak casks. Prior to bottling the liqueur will be reduced in alcohol content with the use of distilled water and sugar, colour will be added if required; and finally it will be filtered to remove any impurities.

GLOSSARY

▼

This is not an exhaustive glossary of the world's alcoholic and non-alcoholic products. Rather it is a guide through the ingredients you will require to mix the cocktails in this book.

Absinthe: A very dry and bitter drink of high alcohol content. Originally made from aniseed, fennel, orris root, coriander, hyssop, liquorice and wormwood. Invented by Dr Ordinaire, it was sold to Henri Louis Pernod in 1797. The product was banned by France in 1915 because of the toxic nature of the wormwood. Pernod went on to market a successful substitute, replacing the wormwood with star anis.

Advocaat: A Dutch liqueur made from egg yolks, sugar, vanilla and grape brandy; 15% a.b.v.

Amaretto: An Italian liqueur made from almonds and apricot kernels. Said to have been invented and made in Saronno in 1525; 28% a.b.v.

Amer Picon: A bitter aperitif flavoured with orange and gentian; 21% a.b.v.

Angostura Bitters: Invented in 1824 by Dr J.G.B Siegert in the Venezuelan town of the same name. Now produced in Trinidad. A secret recipe based on gentian; 45% a.b.v.

Anis: A generic term applied to all aniseed-flavoured drinks, in particular sweetened liqueurs.

Anisette: A sweet aniseed-flavour liqueur. Most famous producer is Marie Brizard of Bordeaux. Marie Brizard was born in 1714 and inherited her secret recipe from a West Indian she nursed during an epidemic; 25% a.b.v.

Apfel Korn: A German liqueur made by macerating apples with grain spirit, 20–30% a.b.v.
Apple Schnapps: See Apfel Korn above.
Applejack: See under Calvados in Brandy section (p. 32).
Apricot Brandy: Most apricot brandies are liqueurs produced by one of the methods referred to previously (p. 32 et seq). Usually grape-brandy based; 20–30% a.b.v. A true apricot brandy would be distilled from the *mash* of the apricot.
Aquavit: There are many producers of aquavit although the best known are the Danish. The name is derived from the Latin *aqua vitae* meaning 'water of life'. It is a grain- or potato-based spirit, flavoured predominantly by caraway seed and then re-distilled; 40–50% a.b.v.
Armagnac: See under Brandy section (p. 35).
Arack/Arrak/Arak: See under Batavia Arrack in the Rum section (p. 25).
Archer's Peach Schnapps: A sweet peach-flavoured grain-based spirit; 23% a.b.v.
Asbach: A German grape brandy produced using the same maturation methods as cognac; 40% a.b.v.
Aurum: An Italian orange-and-herb flavoured grape-brandy-based liqueur; golden in colour; 40% a.b.v.
Bacardi: A light rum. See under Rum section (p. 25).
Bailey's: An Irish liqueur made from Irish whiskey, double cream and chocolate; 15% a.b.v.
Banana Liqueur: See Crème de Banane.
Benedictine: Created in 1510 by the Benedictine monks of Normandy. Each bottle is monogrammed with D.O.M., meaning *Deo Optimo Maximo* (To God most good, most great). There are twenty-seven secret ingredients for Benedictine, which are macerated to produce a sweet, golden, herbal liqueur; 40% a.b.v.
Blackberry Liqueur/Blackberry Brandy: See Crème de Mûre.
Blackcurrant Liqueur: See Crème de Cassis.
Blue Curaçao: See Curaçao.
Bourbon: See under American Whiskey in Whisky section (p. 29).
Byrrh: A French bitter aperitif based on quinine and orange; 17% a.b.v.

Cachaça: A double-distilled Brazilian cane spirit; 35+% a.b.v.
Calvados: See under Brandy section (p. 36).
Campari: A very dry and bitter Italian aperitif of pronounced quinine character; 24% a.b.v.
Caperitif: A wine and spirit aperitif flavoured with herbs; 20+% a.b.v.
Chambord Black Raspberry Liqueur: A french black raspberry liqueur made with honey and herbs; 25+% a.b.v.
Chartreuse: Created and produced by the Carthusian monks of the Grande Chartreuse monastery near Grenoble. Dating from the sixteenth century, this closely guarded recipe includes 130 herbs and spices. The ingredients are macerated and distilled, followed by prolonged maturation in oak casks. No artificial colours are added. Green Chartreuse is 55% a.b.v., yellow is 40% a.b.v.
Cherry Brandy: This is produced by the maceration of fruit in base spirit and is therefore by definition a liqueur. See Apricot Brandy above. Generally a sweet cherry-flavoured liqueur; 25–40% a.b.v.
Cognac: See under 'Brandy' section (p. 32).
Cointreau: A popular French brand of triple sec. Triple sec is a clear curaçao. See *Curaçao;* 40% a.b.v.
Crème de Banane: A banana flavoured liqueur made by the maceration of bananas in spirit; 30% a.b.v.
Crème de Cacao: A sweet liqueur flavoured with cocoa and vanilla; 25–30% a.b.v.
Crème de Cassis: A sweet liqueur produced from the maceration of blackcurrants in spirit. Produced in the Burgundy region; 16–25% a.b.v.
Crème de Fraises: A sweet liqueur produced from the maceration of strawberries in spirit; 20–25% a.b.v.
Crème de Fraises des Bois: A sweet liqueur produced from the maceration of wild strawberries in spirit; 20–30% a.b.v.
Crème de Framboise: A sweet liqueur produced from the maceration of raspberries in spirit; 20–30% a.b.v.
Crème de Grand Marnier: A cream liqueur flavoured with the curaçao orange and based on the Grand Marnier liqueur.
Crème de Menthe: A sweet peppermint-flavoured liqueur. Comes in green or white (clear); 30% a.b.v.

Crème de Mûre: A sweet liqueur produced from the maceration of blackcurrants in spirit; 20–30% a.b.v.
Crème de Noyau (Noyaux): A sweet liqueur flavoured with almonds, peach kernels and apricot kernels; 30% a.b.v.
Crème de Pêche: A sweet liqueur produced from the maceration of peaches in spirit; 25–30% a.b.v.
Crème de Prunelles: A sweet liqueur produced from the maceration of plums in spirit; 40% a.b.v.
Crème de Rose: A light liqueur produced from rose petals and flavoured with vanilla; 25–30% a.b.v.
Crème de Violette: A sweet liqueur produced from the infusion of violets and vanilla; 30% a.b.v.
Crème Yvette: An American liqueur made from Parma violets. Violet in colour; 35% a.b.v.
Curaçao: A sweet liqueur made by infusing the bitter peel of the curaçao orange with a grape-brandy spirit. After distillation and rectification the curaçao is colourless and is known as triple sec. It can then be sweetened and coloured (blue curaçao, orange curaçao, etc.); 20–40% a.b.v.
Drambuie: A Scotch whisky liqueur made from Highland malt whisky and honey. Drambuie is derived from the Gaelic *An Dram buidheach* meaning 'the drink that satisfies'; 40% a.b.v.
Dubonnet: A bitter-sweet aperitif with a hint of quinine. Available in 'red' or 'blonde'; 17% a.b.v.
Elixir d'Anvers: Known as the Belgian national liqueur. A green-yellow, bitter-sweet liqueur made from herbs and seeds.
Fernet Branca: An Italian herbal digestif made in Milan. Extremely bitter flavour. Known for its medicinal properties, it is often prescribed as a hangover cure, and was the only legal alcohol available during the American Prohibition; 40–45% a.b.v.
Forbidden Fruit Liqueur: An American brandy-based liqueur made from the Shaddock grapefruit with honey and orange. A bitter-sweet flavour; 32% a.b.v.
Frangelico: An Italian liqueur made from herbs, berries and hazelnuts. Sweet and nutty; 23% a.b.v.
Galliano: Named after Major Giuseppe Galliano, who defended Fort Enda during the Italian–Abyssinian war of 1896. A golden

herb liqueur, sweet with tones of vanilla. The fort is depicted on the bottle label; 40% a.b.v.

Glayva: A Scotch whisky liqueur flavoured with herbs and honey; 40% a.b.v.

Goldwasser: A caraway and aniseed flavour liqueur with edible gold flakes in the bottle. Originally produced in Danzig (Gdansk) by der Lachs. Now produced in West Berlin. There is a silver flake version called Silberwasser; 30–40% a.b.v.

Gomme Syrup: A sugar-syrup solution. To make: heat 1 pint water and stir in 2lb granulated sugar until dissolved. Allow to cool, then bottle.

Grand Marnier: A cognac based curaçao-orange liqueur. The fruit is steeped in the brandy. Two versions, Cordon Jaune at 35% abv and Cordon Rouge at 40% a.b.v.

Grappa: See under Other Brandies in Brandy section (pp 36-7).

Green Izarra: An Armagnac based liqueur flavoured with plants from the French Pyrenees; 48% a.b.v. There is also a yellow version at 35% a.b.v.

Grenadine: A sugar syrup flavoured with pomegranate. Usually non-alcoholic, although it is available at 3–5% a.b.v.

Hollands: See under Gin section (pp 18-21).

Hot Shot Tropical Liqueur: A sweet fruit 'cocktail' flavoured liqueur.

Irish Whiskey: See under Irish Whiskey section (p. 29).

Jack Daniel's: A Tennessee sour mash whiskey. See under American Whiskey (p. 31).

Geneva/Genever: See under Gin section (p. 21).

Kahlúa: A sweet rich Mexican coffee flavour liqueur; 26.5% a.b.v.

Kina Lillet: See Lillet.

Kirschwasser/Kirsch: A German cherry-flavoured brandy distilled from the fermented pulp of Black Forest cherries. Kirsch is the French version which is more fruity and less dry; 45% a.b.v.

Korn: A clear grain spirit produced in Germany. Usually drunk straight or as a chaser to beer; 35–40% a.b.v. Also flavoured versions of lower alcohol content. See Apfel Korn.

Kümmel: A digestif liqueur made with caraway seeds, fennel, cumin, orris root and other herbs. Originally developed by Lucas

Bols in the sixteenth century. It is said to have been drunk by Peter the Great who in turn took the recipe East. Kümmel is produced in Hamburg and a number of other European countries in addition to Holland, the degree of sweetness depending upon the recipe employed; 35–50% a.b.v.

Lemoncello: An Italian lemon-flavoured liqueur.

Lena Liqueur: A sweet yellow banana flavoured liqueur made by Suntory of Japan; 20+% a.b.v.

Lillet: The most famous brand is Kina Lillet. This is a light and very dry French vermouth with a subtle hint of orange; 17% a.b.v.

Madeira: A wine from the island of Madeira fortified with brandy. Generally drunk as an aperitif; 15–20% a.b.v.

Malibu: A Jamaican coconut-flavoured rum liqueur; 28% a.b.v.

Manderine Napoléon: The French mandarin is the English tangerine. The liqueur is made from the maceration of tangerines in aged cognac; 40% a.b.v.

Mango Liqueur: See Suntory Mango Liqueur.

Maraschino Liqueur: A clear Italian liqueur distilled from the maceration of crushed sour Marasca cherries; 30% a.b.v.

Mezcal/Mescal: See under Tequila section (p. 22).

Midori Melon Liqueur: A bright green, sweet melon-flavour liqueur from Japan; 20% a.b.v.

Monin Lime Liqueur: A deep green, sweet lime-flavoured liqueur based on brandy; 33% a.b.v.

Moscato di Sicilia: A sweet wine from Sicily made from the moscato bianco grapes.

Noilly Prat: A very dry French brand of dry vermouth made by steeping a combination of herbs in white wine for a period of eighteen months; 17% a.b.v.

Noix de Coco: A sweet rum based liqueur flavoured with macerated coconut; 21% a.b.v.

Old Tom Gin: See under Gin section (p. 21).

Orange Bitters: A very dry and bitter orange essence for the flavouring of various drinks in particular cocktails; 20% a.b.v.

Orange Curaçao: See Curaçao.

Orange Flower Water: A light non-alcoholic essence made from the infusion and distillation of orange blossom.

Orgeat: An almond-flavour sugar syrup, non-alcoholic.
Ouzo: A Greek *absinthe* substitute. Strong aniseed flavour, drier than the French pastis; 40% a.b.v.
Oxygenée Cusenière: An aniseed-flavoured *absinthe* substitute.
Parfait Amour: A violet liqueur, both sweet and citrus with a hint of orange.
Pastis: The best known brand of pastis is Ricard. It has a stronger flavour of liquorice than Pernod, the original *absinthe* substitute; 40–45% a.b.v.
Peach Brandy: See Crème de Pêche.
Peach Schnapps: See Archer's Peach Schnapps.
Peach Tree: A Dutch sweet grain-based liqueur with a very powerful flavour of peach. Very similar to Archer's Peach Schnapps; 25–40% a.b.v.
Peppermint Schnapps: A sweet peppermint-flavour grain based spirit; 20–30% a.b.v.
Pernod: The original *absinthe* substitute. See Absinthe; 40–45% a.b.v.
Pimento Dram: A dark red West Indian liqueur made by steeping pimento berries in cane spirit.
Pimm's: See chapter on Classics (p. 66).
Pineau des Charentes: An aperitif wine made by blending local Charentes wines with cognac and maturing for a year in oak casks; 18+% a.b.v.
Pisang Ambon: A Dutch banana liqueur flavoured with 'exotic' herbs. Emerald green in colour; 21% a.b.v.
Pisco: See under Other Brandies (p. 36).
Plymouth Gin: See under Gin section (p. 18).
Poire Williams: A pear-flavoured brandy made from the Williams (Bartlett) pear. The bottle is tied to the tree so that the young pear will grow to maturity inside the bottle. When the pear is ripe, it is picked along with the bottle and the remaining space is filled with the brandy; 40–45% a.b.v.
Polish Pure Spirit: A neutral grain spirit from Poland. Extremely strong, and usually sweetened and diluted prior to drinking; 79.9% a.b.v.
Prunelle: A purple coloured plum flavoured liqueur; 30+% a.b.v.

Punt e Mes: A bitter sweet aperitif produced in Italy. Flavoured with quinine. Means 'Point and a Half', and is traditionally drunk with a piece of chocolate; 17% a.b.v.
Quinquina: A French aperitif wine flavoured with quinine. Was used for the prevention of malaria.
Rock and Rye: Traditonally rye whiskey with rock-candy crystallized in the bottle. The modern version uses rock-candy syrup and fruit flavouring; 30–40% a.b.v.
Royal Mint Chocolate Liqueur: A sweet and creamy chocolate and mint liqueur made in England; 30% a.b.v.
Rye: See under American Whiskey (p. 29).
Sake: Although it has the appearance of a spirit and is known as rice wine, sake is neither. It is fermented from rice and is technically a beer. Sake should be drunk warm; 15–18% a.b.v.
Sambuca: A member of the family of sweet aniseed liqueurs, it is uniquely flavoured with liquorice and witch-elderbrush; 35–40% a.b.v.
Schnapps: A grain distilled based spirit. A neutral schnapps will usually be drunk chilled and straight; 40+% a.b.v. Flavoured schnapps is much sweeter and lower in alcohol content; 20–35% a.b.v.
Scotch: See under Whisky section (p. 27).
Silverwasser/Silberwasser: See Goldwasser.
Slivovitz: A plum brandy made from the Pozega plum. It has a dry and bitter quality which comes from the use of the plum kernel. Slivovitz is aged in wood; 40+% a.b.v.
Sloe Gin: Made from the maceration of sloe berries in gin. Sweet and fruity; 25–30% a.b.v.
Sour Mash Whiskey: See under American Whiskey (p. 30).
Southern Comfort: Although this is a liqueur, it is more like a flavoured whiskey. The base spirit is flavoured with peach extract, fresh peach, orange and herbs. It is said to have derived from a peach and Bourbon cocktail; 40% a.b.v.
Strega: A sweet and aromatic yellow Italian liqueur made from over seventy different herbs. Known as the drink of lovers; 40% a.b.v.
Suntory Mango Liqueur: A sweet yellow, mango flavoured liqueur from Japan; 20% a.b.v.

Suntory Strawberry Liqueur: A sweet red strawberry flavoured liqueur from Japan; 20% a.b.v.
Swedish Punsch: This is based on the arrack-type rum. A mixture of arrack, wines and neutral spirit, left to marry for a period of three to six months and then bottled; 30–50% a.b.v.
Tia Maria: A Jamaican rum-based coffee liqueur, flavoured with Blue Mountain coffee beans; 30% a.b.v.
Triple Sec: A refined and smooth white Curaçao. See Curaçao; 40% a.b.v.
Van der Hum: An aromatic South African liqueur made from the naartje tangerine; 31% a.b.v.
Vatted Whisky: See under Scotch Whisky (p. 28).
Vermouth: A flavoured and fortified wine. The majority of herbs, spices, barks, roots, berries, seeds and petals that appear in liqueurs and bitters will be found in vermouth in addition to countless others. Vermouths are macerated for periods of up to eighteen months, and in some instances are fortified with distilled spirit. The dry vermouth is a pale golden colour whilst the sweet is coloured with caramel and flavoured with sugar 16–18% a.b.v.
White Rum: See Rum section (p. 25) another term for 'light' rum.
Wild Turkey: A brand of high strength bourbon whiskey. See under American Whiskey (p. 29); 50.5% a.b.v.

CHAPTER THREE

The Classics

Of the many thousands of cocktails that exist, only a small minority have had a lifespan of any consequence. The Martinez, Pink Gin and Plaza cocktails were mixtures of unrivalled popularity during their particular eras. However, such is the fickle nature of fashion that these one-time doyens of the fifties have now faded into obscurity. Similarly, the concoctions dominating the bartenders' repertoire today had not been conceived of ten years ago and are likewise to possess the same appeal in a decade's time. Since most cocktails last for such a short time, few merit the description 'classic'.

A true classic is a drink of subtlety, combining a limited number of ingredients to inter-act, allowing the distinct characteristics of one to influence another. Very few classics contain more than two spirits, the more constituents in a drink the more muddled and confused the flavours. Fruity and flavoursome mixed drinks are not sophisticated enough to achieve long term appeal, as the continuing migration of younger imbibers to the classic cocktails demonstrates. Arguably, there are many cocktails that are borderline classics, but in my view the following fifteen are without doubt the finest examples of this genre.

THE BLOODY MARY

There is much confusion and contradictory evidence as to when, where and by whom the Bloody Mary was invented. General opinion, with which I agree, suggests that it was at Harry's New York Bar Paris, in 1921 by Pete Petiot. However, the 1940's copy of *Harry's ABC of Mixing Cocktails*, of which I am lucky enough to have a copy not only fails to attribute this drink to Pete Petiot but lists it under a different title, the Red Mary. It is possible that the credit was omitted in error; after all, Harry appears to have forgotten to credit himself with creations that feature within the same pages. Or, perhaps Harry renamed the original Bloody Mary for this 1940s publication. Perhaps the recipe came first but was not given a name for some time. I feel the most plausible explanation is that the Red Mary was simply Harry's own version of Petiot's Bloody Mary with each recipe varying the spices.

The inspiration for the title was Queen Mary I.

The following recipe differs from Petiot's original in that I have included celery salt.

3oz Vodka
6oz Tomato Juice
freshly squeezed Juice of 1/2 Lemon
pinch of Salt and Pepper
1–3 dashes Tabasco Sauce
4–6 dashes Worcestershire Sauce
1 tsp. Celery Salt

Shake all the ingredients together with a scoop of ice and pour into a 12oz highball glass.

THE BLUE BLAZER

The Blue Blazer is a classic of unique character. It is a rarely mixed cocktail. Created by Professor Jerry Thomas during the 1840s, it was so christened because of the blazing blue flame that passes between the mixing cups. It appears in the first edition of *The Savoy Cocktail Book* which has an illustration of him performing the feat at the Metropolitan Hotel, New York, during the 'Roaring 'Fifties'. The cocktail shows just how innovative Jerry Thomas was. In the 150 years since that inspired creation there has been almost nothing to rival this liquid inferno. The recipe is simple but can be quite dangerous to make. I would advise practising first with cups of water.

1 wineglass Scotch Whisky
1 wineglass Boiling Water
tsp. Sugar (to taste)
1 slice of Lemon Peel for twist

Use two silver-plated mugs with handles. Pour the water into one mug and the whisky into the other. Ignite the whisky with a match and mix the two mugs by pouring the blazing ingredients back and forth five or six times. Performed skilfully this will create a long stream of iridescent blue flame. Finally, dispense the ingredients into a large bar glass (Old-Fashioned) and serve with a twist of lemon.

THE COLLINS

John or Tom? The original Collins was the John Collins, and dates back to the latter part of the nineteenth century. Invented at the much quoted Limmer's Hotel by a London bartender of the same name, the base spirit was the prevalent Dutch genever, more commonly referred to as hollands. London distilled dry gin was yet to establish itself. The Tom Collins is a cocktail made by the same method but with a minor modification in the constituents. As a substitute for the hollands, Old Tom sweet gin was used and the Tom Collins was born. As described earlier, Old Tom was not a brand name but rather a generic term for a specific style of sweetened gin. With neither hollands nor Old Tom commonly obtainable, the John and Tom Collins have adopted a modern identity. On most British cocktails menus the Tom is a vodka Collins and the John a gin. However, across the Atlantic the John is a bourbon Collins and the Tom is the gin. The recipe itself is similar to the Gin Fizz (p. 364) and Gin Sling (p. 226) but predates both.

2½oz Gin
freshly squeezed Juice of 1 lemon
Sugar to taste (Gomme syrup dissolves more easily)
Soda Water

Place 6 ice-cubes in a 10oz. highball/Collins glass and add the ingredients in the above order. Top with the soda, stir and serve.

THE DAIQUIRI

Whilst frozen fruit-flavoured daiquiris swamp the cocktail market, these drinks owe their existence to a more established classic. The original daiquiri, similar to the other drinks in this chapter, is based on simplicity. There are two versions of its origin both centred around the Daiquiri iron mines in Santiago, Cuba. In 1898, the American engineers working on the iron mine were told that Charles M. Schwab, president of Bethlehem Steel was coming on a visit. Wishing to greet him with something original, one of the engineers recollected the cocktail invented for them at La Florida restaurant in Havana. A barrel was decapitated, and into it was poured one pound of sugar, the juice of one hundred fresh limes which grew locally in abundance, ten bottles of Bacardi Carta Blanca and a bucket of ice. This potion was hailed by Mr Schwab who drank far too many. Nowadays daiquiris are less strong, the usual ratio being the juice of 1 lime to 2oz. light rum and a teaspoon of sugar. The other version of its origin is that the local Cuban cane spirit was prescribed as a cure for malaria. So the American engineers made it more palatable by adding fresh lime juice and sugar.

2oz White Rum
freshly squeezed Juice of 1 Lime
1/4oz. Gomme Syrup (or 1 tsp. Sugar)

Shake all the ingredients together with a scoop of ice and strain into a 5oz martini glass.

A closely related variation of this drink is the Bacardi cocktail. To mix, simply substitute grenadine syrup for the sugar.

THE GIMLET

The Gimlet was named after the sharp metal utensil that was used to perforate casks and sometimes doubled as a rudimentary corkscrew. The cocktail was the product of two ingredients that came together by geographical and medicinal circumstance. The first ingredient was gin, in this instance Plymouth gin which was widely drunk in the British Navy and is the basis of pink gin. A Plymouth gin distillery was first established in 1793. However, even throughout the pinnacle of its production, during the early part of the twentieth century, it remained a fundamentally local spirit. Its highly aromatic qualities were much esteemed in spite of the overwhelming popularity of the dry London product and consequently 'Plymouth' became a generic term. The second constituent was Rose's Lime Cordial, a condensed and sweetened lime-juice product. First invented by a Scotsman named Lauchlin Rose in 1867, this cordial like many other beverages of the era had a pharmaceutical inspiration, in this case as a preventative for scurvy. Accordingly it found its way to the naval port of Plymouth, and other towns. Although I cannot accurately date this 'marriage in heaven', it certainly predates the Second World War, when the Plymouth distillery was bombed.

2oz. Gin (Plymouth if available)
1oz. Rose's Lime Cordial
slice of Lime

Shake the ingredients together with a scoop of ice and strain into a chilled 5oz. martini glass. Decorate with the slice of lime and serve.

THE KIR

Although I have very little to offer in terms of historical information, the Kir has its place among the classics simply because of its international allure. The drink is named after the Abbé, Felix Kir, Resistance hero and wartime Mayor of Dijon. I have always assumed that it must have been invented at a time when a Resistance hero could be openly honoured and therefore place its birth sometime after 1945. The original recipe hails from Burgundy and consists of crème de cassis and white Burgundy. Today, few are so pedantic as to quibble about the wine region; white and dry are the only prerequisites. The most notable variation of this drink is the kir royale using champagne. The rarely consumed red-wine version is known as a cardinal.

1 tsp. Crème de Cassis
chilled Dry White Wine

Drop the cassis into a wineglass and pour the chilled white wine over it. If mixing a kir royale, use a champagne flute.

THE MANHATTAN

More martinis and manhattans are drunk in the world than all the other types of cocktail put together. Nevertheless, the manhattan has been neglected by a number of cocktail books, most surprisingly from the *Concise Encyclopaedia of Gastronomy* by André Simon published in 1946, during what must have been a high point in the drink's popularity. Unlike the dry martini, upon which so much has been written, the manhattan has failed to inspire research. However, it is suggested that the drink was first created for Jenny Jerome (wife of Lord Randolph Churchill and mother of Winston), when she gave a banquet in honour of Samuel J. Tilden at the Manhattan Club in New York, probably in 1890.

This unique blend of rye or bourbon whiskey and sweet vermouth has spawned a multitude of equally famous cocktails, the Scotch whisky Rob Roy being the most familiar, while the substitution of gin in 1919 created the now celebrated Bronx. The manhattan can be served either straight up or on the rocks. I would however advise against the rocks, especially if you are a slow drinker. Melting ice can ruin a cocktail. The two variations on this classic bourbon drink are the dry manhattan and the perfect manhattan. Although the original is made with sweet vermouth it is simply titled manhattan.

2oz. Bourbon or Rye
1oz. Sweet Vermouth
1 dash Angostura Bitters
Maraschino Cherry

Half fill a mixing glass with clean whole ice-cubes. Add the bourbon, vermouth and bitters and stir for approximately 10 seconds. Strain into a 5oz. martini glass, garnish with the cherry and serve.

THE MARGARITA

The margarita is the archetypal South American classic and the best example of tequila's mixability. In contrast to the other drinks in this chapter it is a comparative adolescent, originating from the 1940s. There was a cocktail that predated it called a marguerite, but this was a concoction that did not include tequila. There are many stories about mythical females of Latin descent, after whom this cocktail was supposedly named. One story is from the 1930's, although I have been unable to establish whether this cocktail existed then. Another, later than my suggested date, is one of many claiming the identity of the first *senhorita Margarita.* The septuagenarian Spanish cocktail wizard Enrique Bastante Gutiérrez was the man who told me its derivation. Enrique, who is a former world cocktail champion, has served some of the great names in cinema history. One of these was Rita Heyworth, for whom this cocktail was invented. I prefer this explanation.

2oz. Tequila, 1oz. Cointreau (Triple Sec)
1oz. Freshly Squeezed Lime Juice

Shake all the ingredients together with a scoop of ice and strain into a salt-rimmed 5oz. martini glass or a coupette.

THE DRY MARTINI

It is a common misconception, especially in the UK, that a dry martini is a glass of dry vermouth with some ice and a splash of lemonade. A bartender can sometimes assess which drink is being alluded to by the age of the customer. Under twenty-one, and it is likely to be the vermouth. The dry martini was named after its inventor rather than its ingredients. If you refer to it as vermouth and not its brand name you will find the concept easier to grasp. Ironically the dry martini evolved from the gin and French (vermouth) drink and not the Italian vermouth that is the primary cause of all the confusion. There is much argument about the ingredients and proportions of the inaugural dry martini. There is a cocktail called a martinez which originated from the town of the same name just outside San Francisco. The recipe was first published in a reprint of *The Bon Vivant's Companion, or How to Mix Drinks,* in 1887, although it is said to have been invented in 1874. Some authorities mistakenly believe the dry martini evolved from this drink. The origin of the martinez actually predates the dry martini by a generation, and although it uses the same ratio of gin to vermouth it differs from the dry martini in the addition of orange bitters and a dash of maraschino. A popular theory suggests that the dry martini was invented by an Italian bartender by the name of Martini di Arma di Taggia. The mixing is said to have taken place at the Knickerbocker Hotel in New York around 1910. I have always liked this theory, especially as the recipient of the drink was apparently John D. Rockefeller. However, during some intensive research I discovered that the origin of the gibson (a dry martini with a cocktail onion and a recognized derivative of the original), actually predates these events by between seven and nineteen years. I therefore suggest that these events occurred pre 1891 and considering that Mr. Rockefeller would have been in his mid-forties, this timing is conceivable. At the time of its conception the dry martini was half each of London dry gin and dry vermouth. The 'dry' referred to the gin and so as tastes became progressively drier so the percentage of vermouth decreased to the point where today's dry martinis are so desiccated they contain infinitesimal amounts of vermouth. Techniques vary as to how to measure such a minuscule quantity. Some try to use a steady hand, extracting a single drop from the neck of the bottle; for others, more than a drop of vermouth would be considered almost tidal proportions. A common method is to pour a measure of dry vermouth over the ice in the mixing jug, briefly stir and then discard it prior to adding the gin, thus delicately flavouring the dry martini with only the vermouth that has clung to the ice.

The question of how to dispense the correct amount of vermouth has resulted in various experiments. The first is attributed to a Mr David Levy. It was due to his craving for marinated olives that he stumbled upon the idea of preserving them in dry vermouth. He mixes a naked (no vermouth) martini and then stirs the olive around the drink a couple of times just as he serves it. This is a winning formula. The second idea is more eccentric. It is the brain child of a Mr Christopher Coore, a casualty-nurse working in Jeddah. He has a medical background that alerted him to the potential of 'sustained release vermouth'. He explained to me that the whole principal was to slow down the release of the vermouth to a degree that was not possible by hand and eye alone. Thus he unveiled his secret weapon – a tray of ice-cubes. These were not ordinary ice-cubes, they were 75% bottled water and 25% dry vermouth. Instead of mixing the chilled gin over a jug full of ice for ten seconds, you stir the gin with one ice-cube until it has dissolved. Christopher admitted that this can take some time, but if you need to adjust the proportions for further attempts, you can do so to a microscopic degree by decreasing the 'mix time'. (I should point out that this meeting did not take place in the dry kingdom of Saudi Arabia).

For some, however, myself included, even this does not result in a dry enough martini. I have heard stories of bartenders bowing in the direction of France as they stir the gin and of others waving the shadow of the vermouth bottle over the mixing glass, both techniques resulting in an arid martini. But in order to create a true naked martini I simply cast all thoughts of vermouth from my head. There is a lot of contention as to whether a 'Naked' is really a martini. I will address this matter later.

So to my recommended ritual for mixing a martini, which demands close attention to detail neglecting an apparently minor element of the mixing process will result in a mediocre product.

You must have all your equipment to hand. If you have to pause midway through the proceedings in order to locate a missing stirrer you may lose the continuity so important for a triumphant conquest. You will need a glass mixing jug (preferably with a lip), a straining device such as the spring-loaded Hawthorn strainer, a stirrer (taller than your mixing jug) and last but not least, your glass. The subject of suitable glassware for a dry martini is an equally obsessive topic. I discovered my favourite glass in 1989; it is a 5oz. martini cocktail glass with a subtly inverted lip thus allowing a slightly fuller meniscus on the drink's surface. In fact, such is my fanaticism about possessing the perfect chalice for my beverage, that when I discovered the manufacturers had ceased production of this particular style, I bought up their remaining stock of forty-seven

The single most important word to remember is 'cold', this should be lodged permanently in the forefront of your mind. Everything used in the production of this drink must be chilled so that the final product has its moment of perfection frozen in time. Of course you can also, like me, chill your jug, strainer and stirrer. Although such devotion to the cause of coldness is not essential, it is fundamental that your glass should be chilled. I always keep a supply of martini glasses in the freezer in case of emergencies. But this being a logistical impossibility for most people, I would recommend at least ten minutes of chilling before mixing and serving the cocktail. In the event that access to a freezing compartment is unavailable, an effective alternative is to pack the glass with crushed ice. Next, depending upon how much I have available, I fill the mixing jug with ice. The condition of the ice is of vital importance; it must be whole unbroken cubes of clear ice. Cracked or crushed ice will over-dilute the final product, and ice with a fashionable build-up of frost can not only dilute but also cloud the drink. Clear ice normally indicates water with a natural balance of minerals unlike tap water which can include various purifying agents such as chlorine. In my 'dry martini laboratory' I use ice-cubes made only from bottled mineral water..

It is only now that I will remove the ingredients from the freezer. Keeping the gin chilled gives it a wonderful viscous quality. You may wonder why I have chilled the gin prior to stirring it over the ice. If the gin was warm it would take too long to chill the drink by stirring alone, once again resulting in over-dilution. The mixing process is a delicate balance of chilling and diluting with too much of one resulting in too much of the other.

Assuming we are following the rational behaviour patterns of a non-naked martini-drinker the time has come to add the vermouth. It is a good idea to add this first; if your enthusiasm takes over and you add too much, you will not have ruined three shots of gin. Immediately add the required quantity of gin and begin to stir in a rapid but smooth circular motion. (Try not to clatter the ice together, it is said that this will 'bruise' the gin.) After ten seconds remove the glass from the freezer and strain the contents of the jug into it, leaving barely enough room for the accompaniment. Etiquette requires that there should always be daylight of about a centimetre between the top of the drink and the lip of the glass. When I was running my bar, if I was ever even a hair short of the lip my customers would return it as a short drink. It has also been suggested that as this cocktail should be consumed ice cold it should only be served in small quantities.

Olive or Twist

The next stage is to determine what variety of martini yours will be. The two variations most popular for dry martinians are with an olive or a twist. On rare occasions martini drinkers add both to their cocktail, but it is usually one or the other. The olive should be a green, pitted, unstuffed, skewered by a cocktail stick and placed in the finished drink. There are numerous varieties of green olives, upon which I am no expert, so I will not begin to advise you as to which are the best. My personal preference is for manzanilla olives. The twist on the other hand is somewhat more technical. Although self explanatory, a lot of people seem to be baffled as to what a twist really is. The idea of the twist is to extract the zest from the skin of a lemon and leave it on the surface of the drink, giving an aroma of lemon which lasts until the drink is finished. I have seen the twist decorated in different ways, including some deftly produced knots and bows of lemon sliver dropped in to the cocktail. Whilst this may look attractive, it is completely ineffective. It is said that on one occasion when presented with a dry martini of this variety, Sean Connery exclaimed 'If I had wanted a fruit salad I'd have asked for one!'

For a quality twist you first require a ripe and fleshy lemon; these are inclined to have much more oil in their skin. Shave a slice of the skin about 1cm wide for the length of the fruit, taking care not to cut into the fleshy citrus part. Hold the piece of lemon peel a couple of centimetres above the surface of the drink with the outer skin facing down, and twist. A fine spray of the aromatic lemon zest will create a transparent film across your drink.

Assuming you have performed all the necessary preparations, the entire process from beginning to end should take no longer than one minute. The following is a summarized six-point guide:

1: Pre-chill your glass.
2: Fill the mixing jug with ice.
3: Add the pre-chilled ingredients in the required ratios.
4: Stir quickly and smoothly for approximately 10 seconds.
5: Strain contents in to your martini glass.
6: Add olive or twist and serve.

The Naked Martini

I referred earlier to the naked martini, that is, a dry martini without a hint of vermouth – critics would cry, it is just a glass of gin and has no claim to the name dry martini. But although the glass is indeed exclusively filled with gin, that is where the similarity ends.

First let us examine a glass of gin. The glass is probably of random volume and style and at room temperature. Into this an unspecified quantity of gin would be poured directly from the bottle, also room temperature. This doesn't sound particularly appetizing, especially if you are expecting a deftly mixed dry martini. I once heard a customer complain about her slightly tepid version, suggesting that 'It is so warm the olive is sweating.' You may notice that on occasions drinks with different names have the same ingredients. There may be a slight difference in the ratios or there may simply be a difference in the mixing technique. The Collins and fizz and the julep and smash come to mind; on the surface they appear to be the same drinks but the subtle differences are enough to warrant specific titles of their own. It is by these criteria that, in my opinion the naked becomes part of the martini family rather than a glass of gin. The dry martini is as much about the preparation and mixing process as it is about the ingredients. The naked martini is made by the identical method as the dry and by its own definition is the ultimate in a dry martini. I believe the naked martini will eventually become the most sought-after mixture of them all.

THE MINT JULEP

The *Concise Oxford Dictionary* defines the word 'julep' as 'a sweet drink, especially as a vehicle for medicine'. It goes on to describe it as 'iced and flavoured spirits and water'. The origin of the word is traced to the Arabic *julãb* and the Persian *gulãb*, meaning 'rose-water'. With the English translation dating back over five hundred years, and the gradual metamorphosis from sugar and water to the twentieth century version we now know, it is no wonder that the date of the first Julep remains a mystery. However, there are clues in the history of what must be the oldest cocktail of them all. In *The American Museum* of 1787 there is a mention of a *julep* made from rum, sugar and water – very different from today's cocktail but nevertheless, it illustrates that the julep was clearly a drink of universal appeal over two hundred years ago. The first mention of mint as an ingredient of the *julep* came in a book by John Davis, whose work, *Travels of four years and a half in the United States of America* was published in London in 1803. However, it was not he but Captain Frederick Marryat who popularised the Mint Julep in the UK. Whilst writing in his diary about the Fourth of July celebrations of 1837 Captain Marryatt describes with impassioned interest the making of a mint julep. Marryat's julep was a brandy-based drink using both the peach and regular versions. This has subsequently become known as the Southern mint julep. It was not until the publication of the celebrated Professor Jerry Thomas's *The Bon-Vivants Companion or How to Mix Drinks*, in 1862 that the whiskey mint julep first appeared in print. Needless to say, whiskey and in particular bourbon mint juleps had been consumed for a long time, a fact borne out by the events surrounding the founding of Mint Julep Day at New College, Oxford. In 1845, William Heyward Trapier visited the college and during a social gathering of various graduates was offered a drink. Upon requesting a mint julep he was surprised to discover that his hosts were unaware of its existence. Trapier demonstrated his method for making 'liquid gold', and to those who drank it became immortal. Trapier left Oxford bestowing a Georgian silver julep cup and an endowment to provide for an annual toasting of the Julep. This has become an annual ritual at New College, and every June 1st is celebrated in his name.

Like Marryat's, Trapier's recipe was based upon brandy but also included bourbon. In Kentucky, the home of bourbon, the mint julep is part of the heritage and the Mint Julep Season starts on May 28th.

After Prohibition, with bourbon establishing itself as the national drink of America, it was inevitable that the preferred julep of the Kentuckians should eventually become the national and international favourite. There is an infinite variety of exquisite recipes for the mint julep, some involving crushing the mint, some stirring and some simply employing the intoxicating fragrance of fresh leaves. I like the following way of making it.

1 dozen fresh Mint Leaves
1 tsp. Castor or Granulated Sugar
3–4oz. Bourbon
lots of crushed ice
2 short straws

In ideal circumstances, one would use a silver julep mug of approximately 6–8oz. capacity. An old-fashioned or highball glass will suffice. Place 8 of the mint leaves into the julep mug with the sugar and a dash of the bourbon (enough to wet the whole mixture). Muddle together with a pestle or the back of a spoon until the mint is nicely bruised. Fill the mug with crushed ice, add 1oz. of bourbon and stir until the mug has frosted. Top up with the bourbon, stir, and plant the remaining mint leaves into the top of the ice. Insert the short straws and serve. Not only do you experience the unique essence of the drink, but the short straws mean that your nose is permanently amongst the mint leaves, increasing the peppermint bouquet.

THE NEGRONI

Unlike the previous drinks in this chapter, the negroni is a bitter cocktail, based on the highly popular Campari aperitif. The negroni evolved from another Campari favourite, the Americano, which is equal measures of Campari and sweet vermouth. During the 1920s, the americano was *à la mode* for fashionable Italians. The story goes that a member of the nobility, a frequent patron of the Jacosa Bar in Florence, found himself in a dilemma. Not wishing to appear out of touch with fashion, he frequently ordered Americanos. However, the americanos did not satisfy him for long. In a moment of inspiration he fortifyied his Americano with a measure of gin, equal to that of the sweet vermouth and Campari. This invigorated americano delighted the clientele of the Jacosa and enhanced its reputation for mixing drinks. The management dedicated the cocktail to the man who conceived it.

His name…Count Camillo Negroni.

There are two accepted methods for mixing the negroni, although the ingredients remain identical.

1oz. Campari
1oz. Sweet Vermouth
1oz. Gin

Either: Shake with a scoop of ice and strain into a martini glass. Garnish with a twist of orange.
Or: Build into an ice-filled highball glass, stir and add a slice of orange.

THE OLD-FASHIONED

This is arguably the most sublime of all bourbon cocktails, the fusion of technique and recipe resulting in a drink of majestic character. In addition, so great now is its popularity that the glass from which it is drunk has become synonymous with drink itself. Its origin is unclear. The Pendennis club in Louisville, Kentucky, is reputed to be its birthplace. Apparently, a distillery representative was endeavouring to create a bourbon cocktail that would appeal to a retired general who ordinarily avoided whiskey. Henry McNulty stated that it was 'one of the best cocktails as far as I am concerned', whilst David Embury declared it a 'truly magnificent cocktail'. This cocktail combines the sweetness of sugar, the bitterness of Angostura and lavish quantities of your chosen bourbon.

3oz. Bourbon
1 Sugar-Cube
3 dashes Angostura Bitters
slice of Orange and a Maraschino Cherry

Take a 10oz. old-fashioned glass and add the sugar, bitters and a dash of bourbon. Muddle together, then add two ice-cubes, 1oz. bourbon and stir. Add two more ice-cubes, 1oz. bourbon and the orange slice (having squeezed in some of the juice) and stir again. Finally, add two more ice-cubes, the remaining bourbon and the maraschino cherry. Stir and serve.

PIMM'S No1

In 1823 a London restaurateur by the name of James Pimm opened Pimm's Oyster Bar in Lombard Street. Oysters were in plentiful supply and provided an inexpensive dish for City gentlemen. The patrons would wash down their shellfish with a tankard of ale or the speciality 'house cup'. By the 1840s, Pimm's Oyster Bar had established itself as a London landmark, and featured on contemporary street maps. It was during this period that James Pimm invented his No.1 Cup. He based it on the single most popular spirit of the day, gin. By the time he sold his business to Frederick Sawyer in 1865, his recipe had been perfected to such a degree that the Pimm's name was maintained as an endorsement of quality. Originally served by the tankard across the bar, the first bottle of Pimm's was sold in 1859. After Frederick Sawyer, the business changed hands twice in rapid succession, finally being acquired by Horatio Davies in 1880. In 1897, Horatio Davies became Sir Horatio Davies, Lord Mayor of London. The year 1906 saw the formation of Pimm's Limited, a company set up to control all of Sir Horatio's expanding empire which included hotels and restaurants. This combination of interests undoubtedly helped establish Pimm's as the most fashionable drink in London's prestigious clubs and hotels. In 1912, a separate company was formed to concentrate on the wine and spirit business, especially the production and promotion of Pimm's. Sadly Sir Horatio died in that year, too soon to witness the registering of Pimm's No.1 Cup as a trademark in 1913. After the Second World War, the market for Pimm's expanded significantly in Europe and the United States, resulting in over half the current production of Pimm's heading overseas.

Pimm's is a blend of locally produced gin with fine liqueurs and fruit extracts from around the world. The precise recipe remains a closely guarded secret known only to six of the Pimm's hierarchy, 'The Secret Six', and it is identical to the formula established over 150 years ago by James Pimm.

Known as the original gin sling, Pimm's No.1 Cup is far removed from a true sling and is more accurately described in modern terms as a punch. The range previously boasted six varieties No.1 gin,

No.2 whisky, No.3 brandy, No.4 rum, No.5 rye whiskey and No.6 vodka. Numbers 2 to 5 were generally produced for the Channel Island market and ceased to be financially viable over twenty years ago. No.1's popularity meant that for some time it was the only available Pimm's. However, with the recent boost in the western vodka trade, Pimm's decided to re-launch the vodka variety under the title Pimm's Vodka Cup.

The Pimm's cocktail is somewhat more intoxicating than the basic Pimm's and lemonade, and it's this cocktail that has become so popular at events such as the Henley Regatta and Wimbledon.

For 6 people.
12oz. Pimm's No.1
6oz. Gin
Lemonade
Cucumber, Lemon, Lime, Strawberries, Mint and any other fruit you may wish to include

Into a large jug put 20 ice-cubes and add the Pimm's No.1, gin and the various garnishes all sliced or chopped. Top up with the lemonade, stir and serve by dispensing into highball glasses or goblets.

THE SIDECAR

This cocktail dates back to 1931 and is attributed to the great Harry MacElhone, founder of the world famous Harry's New York Bar at 5 rue Daunou (known as Sank Roo Doe Noo), Paris. Unlike the many bars that adopt the 'Harry's' title, and with it the implication that they are responsible for many cocktail innovations, the Paris bar is the undisputed original. Harry and subsequently his son Andrew have been responsible for creating a number of the most popular cocktail recipes, though none are more significant than Harry's sidecar. This was the first cocktail to combine successfully the unique qualities of cognac with the popular style of the sour drink. It has stood the test of time, as is illustrated by a resurgence in its popularity among many of London's top cocktail bars. A mixture of equal measures of cointreau, cognac and freshly squeezed lemon juice, this tart and refreshing cocktail is the finest of Harry's catalogue of concoctions. The mixing of this cocktail has been the subject of ardent competition. In 1989 I officiated at a contest between two competitors to create the worlds greatest sidecar. This involved the purchase of a £500 bottle of Cognac, the acquisition of a 1920s cocktail glass and a flight to Spain to source the freshest lemon yielding the most succulent juice. Needless to say, the only thing equal to the combatants' abundance of leisure-time was the amount of money in their personal accounts. The outcome was a draw and the only lesson gleaned was that it was a heroic effort just to get smashed. Although other versions of the sidecar do appear in earlier cocktail volumes (for example the 1930 edition of *The Savoy Cocktail Book*), the recipe and ratio of Harry's 1931 blend is the one that we still recognize today.

1oz. Brandy (Cognac)
1oz. Cointreau (Triple Sec)
1oz. freshly squeezed Lemon Juice

Shake all the ingredients together with a scoop of ice and strain into a 5oz. martini glass.

THE WHITE LADY

This is another Harry MacElhone creation. Closely related to the sidecar, it could well have been its forerunner. It is widely accepted that the white lady is second only to the dry martini in the league of great gin-based cocktails, but the original creation went through a profound physical transformation before it became so. Harry first launched the white lady while at Ciro Club in London in 1919. The recipe was lemon juice, Cointreau and crème de menthe, a most enticing combination at the time. However, in 1929 ensconced within his Paris bar, Harry decided the time had come to alter dramatically the components of this drink. The new recipe of lemon juice, Cointreau and gin was a brave departure from the minty cocktail that had survived for ten years, but Harry recognized the diminishing allure of its peppermint predecessor and changed the recipe to suit the tastes of the era. Its popularity has survived to this day.

A common ingredient for the modern white lady is a dash of egg white. Many accomplished bartenders say that the use of egg white binds the cocktail, but while there is no doubt that egg white adds a delightfully smooth texture to the consistency of the drink, the idea that it possesses any adhesive qualities fails to stand up to scrutiny. If you allow the drink to stand it will separate, like many others do. The popularity of the white lady has led to some colourful variants, such as the Blue Lady, Pink Lady, Perfect Lady, etc.

1oz. Cointreau (triple sec)
1oz Gin
1oz. freshly squeezed Lemon Juice
1 dash of Egg White (optional)

Shake all the ingredients together with a scoop of ice and strain into a 5oz. martini glass.

CHAPTER FOUR

Recipes

TRADITIONAL STYLE COCKTAILS

▼

I call these drinks 'traditional-style', because many of the recipes are of such long standing. These cocktails are fashioned almost exclusively from spirits and liqueurs and are most commonly drunk as aperitifs. When non-alcoholic ingredients are used, they are in minuscule proportions: juices may be added, but only a dash or two, likewise bitters and syrups. Egg white is a frequent ingredient, though this is solely for texture, whereas the occasional inclusion of egg yolk influences the flavour as well. The purpose of all these ingredients is to delicately enhance the cocktail rather than dominate it. Naturally, this category of cocktail is the most potent of all as in many cases an entire 3–4oz cocktail will be made from wholly alcoholic ingredients.

Throughout the recipe section there are instances where cocktails are numbered (e.g. Rose 2 or Pick-me-up 4). In each case this means that other cocktails with the same name can be found elsewhere in the book.

A1

2oz. Gin, 1oz. Grand Marnier, 1 dash Lemon Juice.

Shake and strain into a martini glass. Serve with a twist of lemon.

Aberfoyle

3oz. Vodka, 2oz. Drambuie.

Build in an old-fashioned glass.

Absinthe Drip

2oz. Pernod, 1 Sugar-Cube.

In the likely event that you do not possess a drip glass, half fill a 5oz. martini glass with crushed ice and place the sugar-cube in the centre. Now, slowly drip the absinthe, one drop at a time, on to the sugar-cube until it has all been added.

Serve with a twist of lemon and a short straw.

Absinthe Special

2oz. Pernod, 2oz. Gin, 1 dash Grenadine, 1 dash Angostura Bitters.

Shake and strain into a martini glass.

Adam & Eve

1oz. Cognac, 1oz. Gin, 1oz. Forbidden Fruit Liqueur.

Shake and strain into a martini glass.

Adam & Eve 2

2oz. Gin, 1oz. Drambuie, 1oz. Amaretto, 1 dash Grenadine.

Shake and strain into a martini glass.

Addison

2oz. Gin, 3oz. Sweet Vermouth.

Stir and pour into an old-fashioned glass and serve with a twist of orange.

Adelle Special

2oz. Scotch Whisky, 2oz. Orange Curaçao.

Build into an old-fashioned glass.

Adulterer

3oz. Bourbon, 1oz. Crème de Cassis, 1 dash Orange Curaçao.

Shake and pour into an old-fashioned glass.

Affinity

2oz. Scotch Whisky, 1/2oz. Dry Vermouth, 1/2oz. Sweet Vermouth, 2 dashes Angostura Bitters.

Stir and strain into a martini glass, serve with a twist of lemon.

After Eight

1oz. Kahlúa, 1oz. Crème de Menthe, 1oz. Brown Crème de Cacao, 1 dash Cognac.

Shake and strain into a martini glass.

Alaska

3oz. Gin, 1oz. Yellow Chartreuse, 2 dashes Orange Bitters.

Stir and strain into a martini glass and serve with a twist of lemon.

Albertine

1oz. Kirschwasser, 1oz. Green Chartreuse, 1oz. Cointreau, 1 dash Maraschino Liqueur.

Shake and strain into a martini glass.

Alcazar

2oz. Canadian Club Whiskey, 1oz. Benedictine, 1 dash Orange Bitters.

Stir and strain into a martini glass. Serve with a twist of orange.

Alfie

3oz. Absolut Citron Vodka, 1/2oz. Cointreau, 1 dash Pineapple Juice.

Shake and strain into a martini glass.

Alfonso

2oz. Grand Marnier, 1oz. Gin, 1oz. Dry Vermouth, 1/4oz. Sweet Vermouth, 1 dash Angostura Bitters.

Shake and strain into a martini glass.

Alice Mine

2oz. Kümmel, 2oz. Sweet Vermouth, 1/2oz. Bourbon.

Shake and strain into a martini glass.

Allegheny

2oz. Bourbon, 1oz. Dry Vermouth, 1/2oz. Crème de Cassis, 1 dash Lemon Juice.

Shake and strain into a martini glass.

Allies
1oz. Dry Vermouth, 1oz. Gin, 1oz. Kümmel.
Stir and strain into a martini glass.

All White Frappé
1oz. White Crème de Menthe, 1oz. White Crème de Cacao, 1oz. Gin, 1oz. Anisette, 1 dash Lemon Juice.
Stir and strain into an old-fashioned glass filled with crushed ice.

Amaretto Mist
2oz. Amaretto.
Three-quarters fill an old-fashioned glass with crushed ice. Pour the amaretto over the ice and serve with a twist of lemon.

Amaretto Stinger
2oz. Amaretto, 1oz. White Crème de Menthe.
Build in a brandy balloon, stir and serve.

Amber Dream
2oz. Gin, 1oz. Sweet Vermouth, 1 tsp Green Chartreuse, 1 dash Orange Bitters.
Shake and strain into a martini glass.

American Beauty Special
1oz. Cognac, 1oz. Gold Rum, 1oz. Cointreau.
Shake and strain into a coupette.

American Whiskey Bomb
2oz. Bourbon or Rye Whiskey, 1/4oz. Gomme Syrup, 2 dashes Angostura Bitters.
Stir and strain into a martini glass.

American Whiskey Cobbler
3oz. Bourbon or Rye Whiskey, 1/4oz. Orange Curaçao, 1/4oz. Gomme Syrup.
Pour the bourbon or rye whiskey into an ice-filled wineglass. Stir in the sugar and curaçao and garnish with seasonal fruits and a sprig of mint.

American Whiskey Mist

2oz. Bourbon or Rye Whiskey.

Pour into an old-fashioned glass filled with crushed ice.
Stir until the glass is frosted.

American Whiskey Sangaree

2oz. Bourbon or Rye Whiskey, 3/4oz. Gomme Syrup.

Stir into an old-fashioned glass filled with crushed ice.
Sprinkle grated nutmeg on top and garnish with a slice of lemon.

American Whiskey Smash

2oz. Bourbon or Rye Whiskey, 1 tsp. granulated Sugar, 6 Mint Leaves, 1 tsp Water.

Muddle the mint, sugar and water in an old-fashioned glass.
Fill with crushed ice and stir in the bourbon or rye whiskey.

American Whiskey Squirt

2oz. Bourbon or Rye Whiskey, 1/4oz. Grenadine.

Shake and strain into an ice-filled old-fashioned glass.
Garnish with pineapple chunks and a cherry.

Angel Face

1oz. Gin, 1oz. Apricot Brandy, 1oz. Calvados.

Shake and strain into a martini glass.

Anisette

2oz. Anisette, 1/4oz. Benedictine, 2 dashes Angostura Bitters.

Shake and strain into a frosted martini glass, then top up with water poured through crushed ice. You can use a sieve for this.

Anisette 2

1oz. Anisette, 1oz. Bourbon, 1oz. Sweet Vermouth.

Shake and strain into a martini glass.
Serve with a twist of orange but discard the peel.

Ante

1oz. Calvados, 1oz. Cointreau, 1oz. Pernod or Dubonnet.
Shake and strain into a martini glass.

Anti-establishment

1½oz. Campari, 1oz. Grand Marnier, ½oz. Punt e Mes, 2 dashes Angostura Bitters.
Stir and strain into a martini glass.

Ants In The Pants

1oz. Grand Marnier, 2oz. Gin, 1oz. Sweet Vermouth, 2 dashes Lemon Juice.
Shake and strain into a martini glass.

Appetizer

2oz. Gin, 2oz. Dubonnet.
Stir and strain into a martini glass.

Apple Blossom

2oz. Calvados, 2oz. Sweet Vermouth.
Shake and strain into a martini glass.

Apple Pie

1oz. White Rum, 1oz. Sweet Vermouth, 1oz. Calvados, 1 dash Grenadine, 1 dash Lemon Juice.
Shake and strain into a martini glass.

Approve

3oz. Bourbon, ½oz. Triple Sec, 2 dashes Angostura Bitters.
Build into an old-fashioned glass and serve with a twist of lemon.

Aqueduct

3oz. Vodka, ½oz. Triple Sec, ½oz. Apricot Brandy, ¼oz. Lime Juice.
Shake and strain into a martini glass. Serve with a twist of orange.

Aromatherapist

3oz. Gin, 1oz. Sake, 3 dashes Angostura Bitters.
Stir and strain into a martini glass.

Artillery

3oz. Gin, 3 tsp Sweet Vermouth, 4 dashes Angostura Bitters.
Stir and strain into a martini glass.

Astor

3oz. Gin, 1 dash Orange Juice, 1 dash Lemon Juice.
Stir and pour into an old-fashioned glass.

Athos

2oz. Armagnac, 1oz. Sweet Vermouth, 1 dash Angostura Bitters.
Stir and strain into a martini glass.

Atlas

2oz. Calvados, 1oz. Overproof Dark Rum, 1oz. Cointreau, 1 dash Angostura Bitters.
Shake and strain into a martini glass.

Atta Boy

3oz. Gin, 1½oz. Dry Vermouth, 3 dashes Grenadine.
Shake and strain into a martini glass.

Aunt Jemima

1oz. Cognac, 1oz. Benedictine, 1oz. White Crème de Cacao.
Pour into a brandy balloon, stir and serve.
This recipe does not use ice.

Aurum Cocktail

2oz. Sweet Vermouth, 1oz. Aurum, 1oz. Gin.
Stir and strain into a martini glass.

B. & B.

1oz. Cognac, 1oz. Benedictine.
Build into a brandy balloon without ice.

Baby Fingers

2oz. Sloe Gin, 1oz. Gin, 1 dash Angostura Bitters.
Shake and strain into a martini glass.

Bacardi Dry

2oz. Bacardi White Rum, 2oz. Dry Vermouth.

Stir and strain into an ice-filled old-fashioned glass.

Bacardi Sweet

2oz. Bacardi White Rum, 2oz. Sweet Vermouth.

Stir and strain into a martini glass.

Bachelor's Bait

2oz. Gin, 1/2oz. Amer Picon, 1/2oz. Grenadine, 1 Egg White.

Shake and strain into a martini glass.

Bald Head

1oz. Gin, 1oz. Dubonnet, 1/2oz. Sweet Vermouth, 1/2oz. Dry Vermouth.

Shake and strain into a martini glass. Serve with a twist of lemon.

Ballantine's

2oz. Ballantine's Scotch, 1oz. Sweet Vermouth, 1 dash Crème de Cassis, 1 dash Angostura Bitters.

Shake and strain into a martini glass.

Baltimore Bracer

1 1/2oz. Anisette, 1 1/2oz. Cognac, 1 Egg White.

Shake and strain into a martini glass.

Banana Bliss

2oz. Crème de Banane, 2oz. Cognac.

Stir and strain into a martini glass.

Barking Dog

1oz. Gin, 1oz. Dry Vermouth, 1oz. Sweet Vermouth, 1 dash Pernod.

Shake and strain into a martini glass. Serve with a twist of lemon.

Barnacle Bill

1oz. Pernod, 1oz. Parfait Amour, 1oz. Benedictine.

Shake and strain into a martini glass.

Baron

2oz. Gin, 3/4oz. Dry Vermouth, 1/4oz. Triple Sec, 1 dash Sweet Vermouth.

Stir and strain into an ice-filled old-fashioned glass.

Barry

2oz. Gin, 2oz. Sweet Vermouth, 1 dash Angostura bitters, 1 tsp. White Crème de Menthe.

Stir and strain the first three ingredients into a martini glass. Float the menthe and serve.

Barton Special

2oz. Gin, 1oz. Scotch, 1oz. Calvados.

Shake and strain into a martini glass.

Beadlestone

2oz. Scotch, 2oz. Dry Vermouth.

Stir and strain into an ice-filled old-fashioned glass.

Beauty Spot

2oz. Gin, 1oz. Grenadine, 1 dash Dry Vermouth, 1 dash Orange Juice, 1 Egg White.

Shake and strain into a martini glass.

Bee Stinger

2oz. White Crème de Menthe, 1oz. Crème de Cassis.

Build into a brandy balloon without ice.

Benedictine Scaffa

1oz. Benedictine, 1oz. Gin, 3/4oz. Dark Rum, 1/2oz. Scotch, 1 dash Angostura Bitters.

Stir and strain into an ice-filled old-fashioned glass.

Bentley

2 1/2oz. Calvados, 1 1/2oz. Dubonnet.

Stir and strain into a martini glass.

Bermuda Rose

3oz. Gin, 1/2oz. Apricot Brandy, 1/2oz. Grenadine.
Shake and strain into a martini glass.

Berry Wall

2oz. Gin, 1oz. Sweet Vermouth, 3/4oz. Triple Sec.
Shake and strain into a martini glass. Serve with a twist of lemon.

Betty

1oz. Gin, 1oz. White Rum, 1oz. Cointreau.
Shake and strain into a martini glass.

Beverly Hills

3oz. Calvados, 3 dashes Angostura Bitters.
Stir and strain into a martini glass.

Bianco

2oz. Bourbon, 1oz. Dry Vermouth, 1 dash Angostura Bitters.
Shake and strain into a martini glass. Serve with a twist of lemon.

Bidou

2oz. Gin, 1oz. Peach Brandy, 1oz. Dry Vermouth.
Shake and strain into a martini glass.

Bijou

1 1/2oz. Gin, 1oz. Dry Vermouth, 1/2oz. Green Chartreuse, 1 dash Orange Bitters.
Stir and strain into a martini glass.

Billy Hamilton

1oz. Cognac, 1oz. Brown Crème de Cacao, 1oz. Orange Curaçao, 1 Egg White.
Shake and strain into a martini glass.

Biltong

1oz. Gin, 1oz. Dubonnet, 1oz. Campari, 1 dash Orange Bitters.
Shake and strain into a martini glass.

Bitter-Sweet

1oz. Campari, 1oz. Sweet Vermouth, 3 dashes Angostura Bitters.
Build into an old-fashioned glass.

Black and Tan

2oz. Sweet Vermouth, 1oz. Pernod, 1oz. Crème de Cassis.
Shake and strain into a martini glass.

Black Devil

2oz. Dark Rum, 1/2oz. Sweet Vermouth.
Shake and pour into an old-fashioned glass. Garnish with a black olive.

Black Eye Martini

See chapter three, The Classics, (pp 57–62).
Substitute a black olive for the usual olive in a dry martini.

Black Hawk

2oz. Scotch, 2oz. Sloe Gin.
Stir and strain into a martini glass.

Black Magic

2oz. Vodka, 1oz. Kahlúa, 1 dash Lemon Juice.
Stir and strain into an ice-filled old-fashioned glass.
Serve with a twist of lemon.

Black Maria

1oz. Tia Maria, 1oz. Dark Rum, 4oz. Coffee.
Shake and strain into an ice-filled old-fashioned glass.

Black Russian

2oz. Vodka, 2oz. Kahlúa.
Build into an old-fashioned glass.

Black Sombrero

2oz. Kahlúa, 1oz. Tequila, 1oz. Vodka.
Stir and strain into a martini glass.

Blackthorn

1oz. Gin, 1 1/2oz. Sloe Gin, 1oz. Sweet Vermouth.

Stir and strain into a martini glass.

Blanche

2oz. Cointreau, 1oz. Anisette.

Shake and strain into a martini glass.

Blarney

2oz. Irish Whiskey, 1oz. Sweet Vermouth.

Build into an old-fashioned glass and garnish with a slice of orange.

Blarney Stone

2oz. Irish Whiskey, 1 dash Anisette, 1 dash Cointreau, 1 dash Maraschino Liqueur, 1 dash Angostura Bitters.

Shake and strain into a martini glass.

Blended Comfort

2oz. Southern Comfort, 1oz. Wild Turkey 101 Bourbon.

Stir and strain into a martini glass.

Bloodhound

2oz. Gin, 1oz. Sweet Vermouth, 1oz. Dry Vermouth, 3 Strawberries.

Add the strawberries to the mixture, then shake and strain into a deep dish champagne saucer.

Blue Blazer

See chapter three, The Classics, (pp 51–2).

Blue Boy

3oz. Dark Rum, 1oz. Sweet Vermouth, 1 dash Orange Juice, 1 dash Orange Bitters.

Shake and pour into an old-fashioned glass.

Blue Jacket

2oz. Gin, 1oz. Blue Curaçao, 1/2oz. Orange Bitters.

Shake and strain into a martini glass.

Blue Monday

2oz. Vodka, 1oz. Triple Sec, 1 dash Blue Food Colouring.

Shake and strain into a martini glass.

Blushing Monarch

(SALIM KHOURY)

2oz. Campari, 1oz. Gin, 1oz. Cointreau, 1 dash Passion Juice.

Shake and strain into a martini glass.

Bobby Burns

2oz. Scotch, 2oz. Sweet Vermouth, 1/2oz. Benedictine.

Stir and strain into a martini glass.

Bogey

2oz. Gin, 2oz. Dry Vermouth, 1/2oz. Scotch, 1 dash Pernod.

Shake and strain into a martini glass.

Bolero

2oz. White Rum, 1oz. Calvados, 1 dash Sweet Vermouth.

Stir and strain into a martini glass.

Bombay

2oz. Cognac, 1oz. Dry Vermouth, 1oz. Sweet Vermouth, 1 dash Anisette, 1 dash Triple Sec.

Stir and strain into a martini glass.

Boston Bullet

See chapter three, The Classics, (pp 57–62).

Substitute an olive stuffed with an almond for the usual olive in a dry martini.

Bourbon Mist

2oz. Bourbon.

Stir the bourbon into an old-fashioned glass three-quarters filled with crushed ice. Garnish with a lemon peel spiral.

Bracer

2oz. Pernod, 2oz. Sweet Vermouth, 2 dashes Angostura Bitters.
Shake and strain into a martini glass.

Brain Storm

2oz. Irish Whiskey, 1/2oz. Benedictine, 1/2oz. Sweet Vermouth, 1 dash Orange Curaçao.
Build into an old-fashioned glass.

Brandy Blazer

3oz. Cognac, 1 Sugar Cube, 1 piece Orange Peel.
Combine the ingredients in a heat-proof mug. Ignite the mixture and stir until the sugar has dissolved (approx. 5–10 seconds). Strain the mixture into a brandy balloon and serve.

Brandy Cobbler

2oz. Cognac, 1 tsp. Sugar, 1/2oz. Triple Sec.
Dissolve the sugar with the triple sec in a large goblet. Fill with crushed ice, pour in the cognac and stir. Garnish with seasonal fruits and a sprig of mint.

Brandy Cocktail

2oz. Cognac, 1oz. Sweet Vermouth, 2 dashes Angostura Bitters.
Stir and strain into a martini glass.

Brandy Cocktail 2

2oz. Cognac, 1oz. Sweet Vermouth, 1oz. Grand Marnier, 1 dash Orange Bitters.
Stir and strain into an ice-filled old-fashioned glass.

Brandy Crusta

2oz. Cognac, 3/4oz. Orange Curaçao, 1 dash Maraschino Liqueur, 1 dash Lemon Juice.
Sugar-rim a large goblet, drop a lemon spiral into it and fill with ice. Shake and strain into the goblet and garnish with a slice of orange.

Brandy Julep

See chapter three, The Classics, (pp 62–4).
Substitute cognac for the bourbon in the mint julep recipe.

Brandy Mac

2oz. Cognac, 2oz. Ginger Wine.
Build into an old-fashioned glass.

Brandy Mist

2oz. Cognac.
Stir into an old-fashioned glass filled with crushed ice.

Brandy Sangaree

2oz. Cognac, 2oz. Iced Water, 1 tsp. powdered Sugar.
Stir together in an old-fashioned glass filled with crushed ice.
Sprinkle grated nutmeg over drink.

Brandy Smash

2oz. Cognac, 1 tsp. granulated Sugar, 6–8 fresh Mint Leaves.
Dissolve the sugar with a dash of the cognac in the bottom of an old-fashioned glass. Add the mint and muddle together.
Fill with ice and stir in the cognac until the glass has become frosted.
Serve with a short straw.

Brandy Vermouth

2oz. Cognac, 1/2oz. Sweet Vermouth.
Build into an old-fashioned glass.

Brave Bull

2oz. Tequila, 1 1/4oz. Kahlúa.
Build into an old-fashioned glass and serve with a twist of lemon.

Brett's Own

2oz. Pernod, 2oz. Sweet Vermouth.
Shake and strain into a martini glass.

Broadway

2oz. Gin, 1oz. Sweet Vermouth, 1 dash Grenadine, 1 dash Pineapple Juice, 1 Egg White.

Shake and strain into a martini glass.
Sprinkle grated nutmeg over the drink.

Bumper

3oz. White Rum, 1/2oz. Gin, 1 dash Lemon Juice.

Shake and strain into a martini glass. Serve with a twist of lemon.

Buster

3oz. Dark Puerto Rican Rum, 1oz. Pernod, Pineapple Chunks.

Shake and pour into an old-fashioned glass.
Garnish with the pineapple chunks.

Butterfly

2oz. Gin, 1oz. Blue Curaçao, 1oz. Dry Vermouth, 1oz. Poire Williams.

Shake and strain into a deep-dish champagne saucer.

B.V.D.

1oz. Bacardi White Rum, 1oz. Dry Vermouth, 1oz. Dubonnet.

Stir and strain into a martini glass.

Byrrh Cocktail

1oz. Byrrh, 1oz. Gin, 1oz. Dry Vermouth.

Shake and strain into a martini glass.

Cabaret

2oz. Gin, 1 dash Angostura Bitters, 1 dash Benedictine, 1/2oz. Dry Vermouth.

Stir and strain into a martini glass.

Cajun Martini

See chapter three, The Classics, (pp 57–62).
Substitute a Jalepeno chilli for the olive in the dry martini.

Cajun Vodkatini

3oz. Absolut Pepper Vodka, 1 dash Dry Vermouth, 1 Jalepeno Chilli.

Stir and strain into a frosted martini glass.
Garnish with the chilli pepper.

Campari Shakerato

2oz. Campari.

Shake with the zest of an orange and strain into a frosted martini glass.

Canada Cocktail

2oz. Canadian Club Whisky, 1/4oz. Cointreau, 2 dashes Angostura Bitters, 1 dash Gomme Syrup.

Shake and strain into a martini glass.

Canadian Cherry

2oz. Canadian Club Whisky, 1oz. Cherry Brandy, 1 dash Angostura Bitters.

Build into an old-fashioned glass.

Canadian Mist

2oz. Canadian Club Whisky.

Stir into an old-fashioned glass three-quarters filled with crushed ice.

Cappuccino

2oz. Tia Maria, 1oz. Vodka, 1oz. Bailey's.

Shake and strain into a martini glass.

Cargo

1oz. White Crème de Menthe, 2oz. Vodka, 2 Mint Leaves.

Rub the rim of an old-fashioned glass with one of the mint leaves.
Build the ingredients into the glass and garnish with the other leaf.

Carnival

1oz. Kina Lillet, 1oz. Apricot Brandy, 1oz. Cognac, 1 dash Kirschwasser.

Shake and strain into a martini glass.

Carrol

2oz. Cognac, 1oz. Sweet Vermouth.
Stir and strain into a martini glass.

Caruso

1½oz. Gin, 1oz. Dry Vermouth, ½oz. Green Crème de Menthe.
Stir and strain into a martini glass.

Cascade

2oz. Sweet Vermouth, 2oz. Crème de Cassis.
Build into an old-fashioned glass and stir.

Casino

2oz. Gin, 4 dashes Orange Bitters, 1 dash Lemon Juice.
Shake and strain into a martini glass.

Castle Dip

1½oz. Calvados, 1½oz. White Crème de Menthe, 2 dashes Pastis.
Shake and strain into a martini glass.

Centrifuge

2oz. Gin, 1oz. Chinese Rice Wine, 5 dashes Angostura Bitters.
Stir and strain into a martini glass.

Cha-Cha-Cha

2oz. Calvados, 1oz. Crème de Framboise.
Shake and strain into a martini glass.

Chapel Hill

3oz. Bourbon, 1oz. Triple sec, 1 dash Lemon Juice.
Shake and strain into a martini glass. Garnish with a twist of orange.

Charles

2oz. Cognac, 2oz. Sweet Vermouth, 2 dashes Angostura Bitters.
Build into an old-fashioned glass.

Cherry Stinger

2oz. Cherry Brandy, 1oz. White Crème de Menthe.

Build into an old-fashioned glass.

Chicago

2oz. Cognac, 1/2oz. Triple Sec, 1 dash Angostura Bitters.

Shake and pour into a sugar-rimmed old-fashioned glass.

Chinese

2oz. Dark Rum, 1/2oz. Grenadine, 1 dash Angostura Bitters, 1 dash Cointreau.

Shake and strain into a martini glass.

Chocolate Soldier

1oz. Cognac, 1oz. Brown Crème de Cacao, 1/2oz. Dry Vermouth, 1 dash Orange Bitters, 1 dash Angostura Bitters.

Shake and strain into a martini glass.

Churchill

2oz. Scotch, 3/4oz. Cointreau, 3/4oz. Sweet Vermouth.

Shake and strain into a martini glass.

Claridge

1 1/2oz. Gin, 1 1/2oz. Dry Vermouth, 1/2oz. Apricot Brandy, 1 dash Triple Sec.

Shake and strain into a martini glass.

Coffee Cocktail

1oz. Kahlúa, 1oz. Cognac, 1 Egg.

Shake and strain into a martini glass.

Cold Deck

2oz. Cognac, 1oz. Sweet Vermouth, 2 dashes White Crème de Menthe.

Stir and strain into a martini glass.

Comfortable Fashioned

See chapter three, The Classics, (p. 65).

Substitute Southern Comfort for the bourbon in the old-fashioned.

Comfortable Manhattan

2oz. Southern Comfort, 1oz. Sweet Vermouth, 1 dash Angostura Bitters.
Stir and strain into a martini glass. Garnish with a maraschino cherry.

Comfortable Mist

2oz. Southern Comfort.
Stir into an old-fashioned glass three-quarters filled with crushed ice.

Continental

2oz. White Rum, 1/4oz. Green Crème de Menthe, 1 dash Lime Juice.
Build into an old-fashioned glass. Serve with a twist of lemon.

Cooperstown

3oz. Gin, 1 dash Dry Vermouth, 1 Mint Leaf.
Rub the rim of a martini glass with the mint leaf. Add the leaf to the other ingredients, then shake and strain into the prepared glass.

Copper Illusion

(MICHAEL VEZZONI)

4oz. Gin, 1/2oz. Campari, 1/2oz. Cointreau.
Stir and strain into a martini glass. Serve with a twist of orange.

Corkscrew

2oz. White Rum, 3/4oz. Crème de Pêche, 3/4oz. Dry Vermouth.
Stir and strain into a martini glass.

Coronation

1oz. Gin, 1oz. Dubonnet, 1oz. Dry Vermouth,
Stir and strain into a martini glass.

Crillon

2oz. Noilly Prat Dry Vermouth, 1oz. Campari, 1oz. Poire Williams.
Shake and strain into a martini glass.

Cross Bow

1oz. Gin, 1oz. White Crème de Cacao, 1oz. Cointreau.
Shake and strain into a martini glass.

Czarina

2oz. Vodka, 1oz. Apricot Brandy, $\frac{1}{2}$oz. Dry Vermouth, 1 dash Angostura Bitters.

Stir and strain into a martini glass.

D&G

2oz. Benedictine, 2oz. Grand Marnier.

Build into an old-fashioned glass.

Daiquiri Liberal

2oz. White Rum, 1oz. Sweet Vermouth, 1 dash Amer Picon.

Shake and strain into a martini glass.

Dandy

2oz. Dubonnet, $1\frac{1}{2}$oz. Bourbon, $\frac{1}{2}$oz. Cointreau, 1 dash Angostura bitters.

Shake and strain into a martini glass.

Danelli

3oz. Vodka, $1\frac{1}{2}$oz. Dry Vermouth, $\frac{1}{2}$oz. Campari.

Build into a highball glass. Garnish with a slice of orange.

Darb

1oz. Gin, 1oz. Dry Vermouth, 1oz. Apricot Brandy, 1 dash Lemon Juice.

Shake and strain into a martini glass.

Daydream

2oz. Cognac, 1 dash Angostura Bitters, 1 dash Brown Crème de Cacao.

Stir and strain into a martini glass and add a splash of champagne. Serve with a twist of lemon.

Deceiver

2oz. Gin, 1oz. Green Chartreuse, 1 dash Green Crème de Menthe.

Shake and strain into a martini glass.

Deep Sea

$1\frac{1}{2}$oz. Gin, 1oz. Dry Vermouth, 1 dash Anisette, 1 dash Orange Bitters.

Shake and strain into a martini glass.

Delmonico

1oz. Gin, 1oz. Cognac, 3/4oz. Dry Vermouth, 3/4oz. Sweet Vermouth.
Stir and strain into a Delmonico or a martini glass.

Demeanour

1oz. Old Tom Gin, 1oz. Sweet Vermouth, 1/2oz. Parfait Amour.
Stir and strain into a martini glass.

Dempsey

1 1/2oz. Calvados, 1oz. Gin, 1/4oz. Anisette, 1 dash Grenadine.
Stir and strain into a martini glass.

Depth Bomb

1 1/2oz. Calvados, 1 1/2oz. Cognac, 1 dash Lemon Juice, 1 dash Grenadine.
Shake and pour into an old-fashioned glass.

Depth Charge

1oz. Gin, 1oz. Kina Lillet, 1 dash Pastis.
Shake and strain into a martini glass. Serve with a twist of lemon.

Desert Dream

1oz. Gin, 1oz. Brown Crème de Cacao, 1oz. Sweet Vermouth, 1 Egg White.
Shake and strain into a martini glass.
Sprinkle grated nutmeg over drink.

Destiny

1oz. Gin, 1oz. Sweet Vermouth, 1oz. Anisette, 1/4oz. Gomme Syrup.
Shake and strain into a martini glass.

Devil's Leap

1oz. Dark Puerto Rican Rum, 1oz. Calvados, 1oz. Swedish Punsch.
Shake and strain into a martini glass.

Diabolo

2oz. Dubonnet, 1oz. Gin, 2 dashes Orgeat.
Stir and strain into a martini glass.

Diabolo 2

1 1/2oz. Cognac, 1 1/2oz. Dry Vermouth, 1/2oz. Orange Curaçao, 1 dash Angostura Bitters.

Shake and strain into a martini glass.

Diamond

1oz. Gin, 1oz. White Rum, 1oz. Cointreau.

Shake and strain into a martini glass. Serve with a twist of lemon.

Diana

3oz. White Crème de Menthe, 1oz. Cognac.

Pour the menthe into an old-fashioned glass filled with crushed ice. Float the cognac on top.

Diplomat

3oz. Dry Vermouth, 1oz. Sweet Vermouth, 2 dashes Angostura Bitters, 1 dash Maraschino Liqueur.

Shake and strain into a martini glass.

Dirty Habit

2oz. Amaretto, 2oz. Southern Comfort.

Build into an old-fashioned glass.

Dixie Julep

3oz. Bourbon, 1oz. Gomme Syrup, 3 sprigs Mint.

Put ingredients into an old-fashioned glass then fill with crushed ice and stir until the glass is frosted.

Garnish with the mint sprigs and serve with short straws.

Doctor Cook

1oz. Gin, 1 dash Lemon Juice, 1 dash Maraschino Liqueur, 1 Egg White.

Shake and strain into a wineglass.

Doctor Monahan

3oz. Gin, 1 dash Pernod, 1 dash Orange Bitters.

Shake and strain into a martini glass.

Dodge

2oz. Gin, 2oz. Cointreau, 1 dash White Grape Juice.
Shake and strain into a martini glass.

D.O.M.

2oz. Gin, 1oz. Benedictine, 1 dash Orange Juice.
Shake and strain into a martini glass.

Double 'O' Seven

3oz. Gordon's Gin, 1oz. Vodka, 1/2oz. Kina Lillet.
Shake and strain into a deep-dish champagne saucer.
Serve with a twist of lemon.

Douglas Cocktail

2oz. Plymouth Gin, 1oz. Dry Vermouth.
Stir and strain into a martini glass and serve with a twist of lemon.

Drambo

2oz. Drambuie, 1oz. Scotch, 1 dash Crème de Cassis.
Shake and strain into a martini glass.

Dream

2oz. Cognac, 1oz. Triple sec, 1/4oz. Anisette.
Shake and strain into a martini glass.

Dry Americano

2oz. Campari, 2oz. Dry Vermouth.
Shake and strain into a martini glass. Serve with a twist of orange.

Dry Martini

See chapter three, The Classics, (pp 57–62).

Dry Presidente

2oz. White Rum, 1oz. Dry Vermouth, 1 dash Angostura Bitters.
Shake and strain into a martini glass. Garnish with an olive.

Dry Rain

1oz. Blue Curaçao, 1oz. Noilly Prat Dry Vermouth, 2 dashes Lemon Juice.

Stir into an ice-filled old-fashioned glass.

Du Barry

2oz. Gin, 1oz. Dry Vermouth, 1 dash Anisette, 1 dash Angostura Bitters.

Shake and strain into a martini glass.

Dubonnet

2oz. Dubonnet, 1oz. Gin, 1 dash Orange Bitters.

Shake and strain into a martini glass. Serve with a twist of lemon.

Dubonnet Frappé

2oz. Dubonnet.

Stir into an old-fashioned glass filled with crushed ice.

Duchess

1½oz. Anisette, ½oz. Dry Vermouth, ½oz. Sweet Vermouth.

Shake and strain into a martini glass.

Dunny

1oz. Drambuie, 1oz. Islay Malt Whisky, 1 dash Lime Juice.

Build into an old-fashioned glass.

Earthquake

1oz. Bourbon, 1oz. Gin, 1oz. Pastis.

Shake and strain into a martini glass.

East and West

2oz. Stolichnaya Vodka, 2oz. Absolut Citron Vodka.

Shake and strain into a martini glass. Serve with a twist of lemon.

East India

2oz. Cognac, ½oz. Dark Rum, 1 dash Triple Sec, 1 dash Pineapple Juice, 1 dash Angostura Bitters.

Shake and strain into a martini glass.

Eclipse

1½oz. Sloe Gin, 1½oz. Gin, 1 dash Lemon Juice, Grenadine, Olive.

Place the olive in a martini glass and pour in the grenadine until the olive is submerged. Shake the remaining ingredients and strain into the glass without disturbing the grenadine.

Eddie Brown

2oz. Gin, 1oz. Kina Lillet, 2 dashes Apricot Brandy.

Stir and strain into a martini glass. Serve with a twist of lemon.

Edward VIII

3oz. Canadian Club Whisky, ¼oz. Sweet Vermouth, 1 dash Pastis.

Stir into an ice-filled old-fashioned glass with a piece of orange peel.

Elixir

1oz. Grand Marnier, 1oz. Sweet Vermouth, 1 dash Punt e Mes, 2 dashes Angostura bitters.

Build into an old-fashioned glass.

El Presidente 2

2oz. White Rum, 1oz. Dry Vermouth, 1 dash Angostura Bitters, 1 dash Orange Bitters.

Shake and strain into a martini glass.

El Salvador

2oz. Cognac, 1oz. Tia Maria, 2 Coffee Beans.

Pour the ingredients into a liqueur glass, add the coffee beans and ignite. Extinguish flame after 5–10 seconds and allow glass to cool before drinking.

Embassy Royal

2oz. Bourbon, 1oz. Drambuie, 1oz. Sweet Vermouth, 2 dashes Orange Squash.

Shake and strain into a martini glass.

Emerald Isle

2oz. Gin, ¼oz. Green Crème de Menthe, 3 dashes Angostura Bitters.

Stir and strain into a martini glass.

Emperor Julep

1½oz. Peach Schnapps, 1oz. Cognac, 6 fresh Mint Leaves, 1 tsp. granulated Sugar.

Muddle the mint and sugar together with a dash of the schnapps in an old-fashioned glass.

Fill with crushed ice and stir in the remaining schnapps and cognac.

Empire

2oz. Gin, 1oz. Calvados, 1oz. Apricot Brandy.

Shake and strain into a martini glass.

English Rose

2oz. Gin, 1oz. Dry Vermouth, 1oz. Apricot Brandy, 1 dash Grenadine, 1 dash Lemon Juice.

Shake and strain into a sugar-rimmed martini glass.

Envelope

1oz. White Rum, 1oz. Blue Curaçao, 1oz. Sambuca.

Shake and strain into a martini glass.

Eros

1oz. Sweet Vermouth, 1oz. Calvados, 1oz. Cointreau, 1 dash Lemon Juice, 1 dash Grenadine.

Shake and strain into a martini glass.

Eskie

2oz. Bourbon, ¼oz. Sweet Vermouth, ¼oz. Benedictine, 2 dashes Angostura Bitters.

Build into an old-fashioned glass.

Esprit

1¼oz. Armagnac, 1oz. Crème de Noyau, 2 dashes White Crème de Cacao.

Build into an old-fashioned glass.

Ethel Duffy

1oz. White Crème de Menthe, 1oz. Triple Sec, 1oz. Apricot Brandy.

Shake and strain into a martini glass.

Evans

2oz. Bourbon, 1/4oz. Cointreau, 1/4oz. Apricot Brandy.
Stir and strain into an ice-filled old-fashioned glass.

Everybody's Irish

2oz. Irish Whiskey, 1 dash Green Crème de Menthe, 1 dash Green Chartreuse.
Stir and strain into a martini glass. Garnish with a green olive.

Express

2oz. Scotch, 1oz. Sweet Vermouth, 2 dashes Orange Bitters.
Stir and strain into a martini glass.

Eye-Opener

2oz. White Rum, 1 dash White Crème de Cacao, 1 dash Anisette, 1 dash Cointreau, 1 Egg Yolk.
Shake and strain into a martini glass.

Fabuloso

2oz. Spanish Fabuloso Brandy, 1/2oz. Dubonnet, 1/2oz. Sweet Vermouth.
Build into an old-fashioned glass.

Fair and Warmer

1 1/2oz. White Rum, 3/4oz. Sweet Vermouth, 1 dash Triple Sec.
Stir and strain into a martini glass.

Fairbanks

1oz. Gin, 1oz. Apricot Brandy, 1oz. Dry Vermouth, 1 dash Lemon Juice, 1 dash Grenadine.
Shake and strain into a martini glass.

Fair Weather

2oz. Calvados, 1oz. Sweet Vermouth, 2 dashes Angostura Bitters, 1 dash Gomme syrup.
Build into an old-fashioned glass.

Fairy Belle

$1^{1}/_{2}$oz. Gin, $^{3}/_{4}$oz. Apricot Brandy, 1 dash Grenadine, 1 Egg White.
Shake and strain into a martini glass.

Fancy Brandy

2oz. Cognac, $^{1}/_{4}$oz. Triple Sec, 1 dash Gomme Syrup, 1 dash Angostura Bitters.
Shake and strain into a martini glass. Serve with a twist of lemon.

Fancy Free

2oz. Bourbon, $^{1}/_{4}$oz. Maraschino Liqueur, 1 dash Angostura Bitters, 1 dash orange Bitters.
Shake and strain into a sugar-rimmed martini glass.

Fancy Gin

2oz. Gin, $^{1}/_{4}$oz. Triple Sec, 1 dash Gomme Syrup, 1 dash Angostura Bitters.
Shake and strain into a martini glass. Serve with a twist of lemon.

Fancy Rum

2oz. Dark Rum, $^{1}/_{4}$oz. Triple Sec, 1 dash Gomme Syrup, 1 dash Angostura Bitters.
Shake and strain into a martini glass. Serve with a twist of lemon.

Fancy Whiskey

2oz. Bourbon, $^{1}/_{4}$oz. Triple Sec, 1 dash Gomme Syrup, 1 dash Angostura Bitters.
Shake and strain into a martini glass. Serve with a twist of lemon.

Fan Tan

2oz. Ginger Wine, 1 dash Tabasco, 1 dash Lemon Juice, 1 Egg White.
Shake and strain into a martini glass.

Fantasio

2oz. Cognac, $1^{1}/_{2}$oz. Gin, 1 dash Maraschino Liqueur, 1 dash White Crème de Menthe.
Stir and strain into a martini glass.

Fare Thee Well

2oz. Gin, $^{3}/_{4}$oz. Dry Vermouth, 1 dash Triple Sec, 1 dash Sweet Vermouth.
Shake and strain into a martini glass.

Favourite

1oz. Apricot Brandy, 1oz. Gin, 1oz. Dry Vermouth, 1 dash Lemon Juice.
Shake and strain into a martini glass.

Feather

1oz. Pernod, $1^{1}/_{2}$oz. Sweet Vermouth, $^{1}/_{2}$oz. Dry Vermouth.
Shake and strain into a martini glass.

Fergusson's Frolic

1oz. Gin, 1oz. Peach Schnapps, 1oz. Blue Curaçao.
Stir and strain into a martini glass.

Ferrari

2oz. Dry Vermouth, 1oz. Amaretto.
Build into an old-fashioned glass.

Fiesta

2oz. White Rum, 1oz. Calvados, 1oz. Dry Vermouth.
Shake and strain into a martini glass.

Fifty-Fifty

$1^{1}/_{2}$oz. Gin, $1^{1}/_{2}$oz. Dry Vermouth.
Stir and strain into a martini glass.

Filby

$1^{1}/_{2}$oz. Gin, $^{3}/_{4}$oz. Campari, $^{3}/_{4}$oz. Dry Vermouth, $^{3}/_{4}$oz. Amaretto.
Stir and strain into a martini glass.

Fioupe

1oz. Cognac, 1oz. Sweet Vermouth, 1 dash Benedictine.
Stir and strain into a martini glass. Serve with a twist of lemon.

Fire Devil

$1^{1}/_{2}$oz. Sloe Gin, $1^{1}/_{2}$oz. Sweet Vermouth, $1^{1}/_{2}$oz. Dry Vermouth, 2 dashes Angostura Bitters.

Stir and strain into a martini glass.

Fitchett

2oz. Gin, $1^{1}/_{2}$oz. Sweet Vermouth, $^{3}/_{4}$oz. Benedictine, 1 dash Orange Bitters.

Stir and strain into a martini glass.

Flash

1oz. Cointreau, 1oz. Kirschwasser, 1oz. Benedictine, 1oz. Maraschino Liqueur.

Shake and strain into a martini glass. Sprinkle grated nutmeg over drink.

Flying Dutchman

3oz. Dutch Gin (Genever), 1 dash Triple Sec.

Shake and strain into an ice-filled old-fashioned glass.

Flying Grasshopper

1oz. Green Crème de Menthe, 1oz. White Crème de Cacao, 1oz. Vodka.

Shake and strain into a martini glass.

Flying Scotsman

$1^{1}/_{2}$oz. Scotch, $1^{1}/_{2}$oz. Sweet Vermouth, 1 dash Gomme Syrup, 2 dashes Angostura Bitters.

Stir and strain into a martini glass.

Fontainebleau

1oz. Cognac, 1oz. Anisette, $^{1}/_{2}$oz. Dry Vermouth.

Shake and strain into a martini glass.

Forty-Eight

2oz. Gin, 1oz. Apricot Brandy, 1oz. Grand Marnier, 1 dash Dry Vermouth, 1 dash Lemon Juice.

Shake and strain into a martini glass.

Four Score

2oz. Cognac, $1\frac{1}{4}$oz. Kina Lillet, $\frac{3}{4}$oz. Yellow Chartreuse.

Stir and strain into a martini glass. Serve with a twist of lemon.

Fourth Degree

1oz. Gin, 1oz. Sweet Vermouth, 1oz. Dry Vermouth, $\frac{1}{4}$oz. Anisette.

Stir and strain into a martini glass.

Fox River

2oz. Bourbon, $\frac{1}{4}$oz. Brown Crème de Cacao, 5 dashes Angostura Bitters.

Shake and strain into a martini glass.

Francis

$1\frac{1}{2}$oz. Cognac, $1\frac{1}{2}$oz. Gin, 1oz. Dry Vermouth, 1 dash Grand Marnier.

Shake and strain into a martini glass.

Frankenjack

2oz. Gin, $1\frac{1}{2}$oz. Dry Vermouth, 1oz. Apricot Brandy, $\frac{1}{4}$oz. Triple Sec.

Stir and strain into a martini glass.

Frank Hill

1oz. Cognac, 1oz. Cherry Brandy.

Shake and strain into a martini glass. Serve with a twist of lemon.

French Connection

2oz. Cognac, 1oz. Amaretto.

Build into an old-fashioned glass.

French Emperor

2oz. Mandarine Napoléon, 1oz. Green Crème de Menthe, 1 Egg White.

Shake and strain into a martini glass.

French Rose

$1\frac{1}{2}$oz. Gin, 1oz. Cherry Brandy, $\frac{3}{4}$oz. Kirschwasser.

Stir and strain into a martini glass.

French Whore

$1^1/_2$oz. Cognac, $1^1/_2$oz. Tia Maria.

Build into an old-fashioned glass.

Froth Blower

2oz. Gin, 1 dash Grenadine, 1 Egg White.

Shake and strain into a martini glass.

Froupe

$1^1/_2$oz. Cognac, $1^1/_2$oz. Sweet Vermouth, $^1/_4$oz. Benedictine.

Stir and strain into a martini glass.

Full House

2oz. White Rum, 1oz. Swedish Punsch, 1oz. Dry Vermouth.

Shake and strain into a martini glass.

Full House 2

1oz. Calvados, 1oz. Yellow Chartreuse, 1oz. Benedictine, 1 dash Angostura Bitters.

Shake and strain into a martini glass.

Futurity

2oz. Sloe Gin, 2oz. Sweet Vermouth, 1 dash Angostura Bitters.

Build into an old-fashioned glass.

Gangadine

1oz. Gin, 1oz. Oxygénée Cusenière, 1 dash White Crème de Menthe, 2 Raspberries, 1 dash Gomme Syrup.

Shake vigorously and strain into a martini glass.

Gargoyle

1oz. Gin, 1oz. Cointreau, 1oz. Cognac.

Shake and strain into a martini glass.

Gaspar

1oz. Gin, 1oz. Apricot Brandy, 1oz. Anisette.

Shake and strain into a martini glass.

Gene Tunney

2oz. Plymouth Gin, 1oz. Dry Vermouth, 1 dash Orange Juice, 1 dash Lemon Juice.

Shake and strain into a martini glass.

Genever Cocktail

3oz. Genever (Dutch Gin), 2 dashes Angostura Bitters.

Stir and strain into a martini glass.

Genoa

1 1/4oz. Grappa, 3/4oz. Sambuca, 1/2oz. Dry Vermouth.

Shake and pour into an old-fashioned glass.

Georgia Mint Julep

See chapter three, The Classics, (p. 54). Substitute equal measures of cognac and peach brandy for the bourbon in the mint julep.

Giada

3/4oz. Campari, 3/4oz. Galliano, 1 1/2oz. Vodka, 1 dash Pineapple Juice.

Shake and strain into a martini glass. Garnish with a cherry.

Gibson

See chapter three, The Classics, (pp 57–62).

Substitute 1–3 silver-skin cocktail onions for the olive in the dry martini.

Gin and Bitters

3 dashes Angostura Bitters, 3oz. Chilled Gin.

Swill bitters around a martini glass then add the gin. (Do not add ice).

Gin Camp

2oz. Gin, 1oz. Campari.

Stir and strain into a martini glass.

Gin Cobbler

2oz. Gin, 1oz. Soda Water, 1 tsp. powdered Sugar.

In an old fashioned glass, dissolve the sugar in the water.

Fill with ice, stir in the gin and garnish with seasonal fruits.

Gin Cocktail

3oz. Gin, 2 dashes Orange Bitters.

Stir and strain into a martini glass.

Gin & French

1½oz. Gin, 1½oz. Dry Vermouth.

Stir and strain into a martini glass.

Gin & It

2oz. Gin, 1oz. Sweet Vermouth.

Build into a martini glass without ice.

Gin Julep

See chapter three, The Classics, (pp 62–4).

Substitute gin for the bourbon in the mint julep.

Gin Mist

2oz. Gin.

Stir into an old-fashioned glass, three-quarters filled with crushed ice.

Gin Smash

2oz. Gin, 1 tsp granulated Sugar, 6–8 fresh Mint Leaves, 1 tsp. Water.

Muddle the mint, sugar and water together in an old-fashioned glass. Add ice and stir in the gin. Serve with short straws.

Gin Stinger

2oz. Gin, 1oz. White Crème de Menthe.

Build into a brandy balloon without ice.

Gipsy

2oz. Vodka, 1oz. Benedictine, 2 dashes Angostura Bitters.

Shake and strain into a martini glass.

Gizmo

2oz. Kahlúa, 2oz. Crème de Noyau.

Build into an old-fashioned glass.

Glacier Mint

2oz. Vodka, 1oz. Green Crème de Menthe, 2 dashes PLJ Lemon Juice.
Stir and strain into a martini glass. Garnish with a mint leaf.

Gloom Raiser

2oz. Gin, 1oz. Dry Vermouth, 1/4oz. Anisette, 2 dashes Grenadine.
Shake and strain into a martini glass.

Goddess

1 1/2oz. Pernod, 1/2oz. Anisette.
Shake and strain into a martini glass.

Godfather

2oz. Scotch, 1oz. Amaretto.
Build into an old-fashioned glass.

Godmother

2oz. Vodka, 1oz. Amaretto.
Build into an old-fashioned glass.

Gold Ermine

2oz. Gin, 3/4oz. Dry Vermouth, 1/4oz. Sweet Vermouth.
Shake and strain into a martini glass.

Golf

2oz. Gin, 1oz. Dry Vermouth, 2 dashes Angostura Bitters.
Stir and strain into a martini glass.

Good Fellow

1 1/2oz. Cognac, 1 1/2oz. Benedictine, 2 dashes Angostura Bitters, 1/4oz. Gomme Syrup.
Shake and strain into a martini glass.

Goodnight

1oz. Vodka, 1oz. Gin, 1oz. Bourbon, 1 dash Crème de Noyau.
Stir and strain into a martini glass.

Grand Nord

1oz. Green Chartreuse, 1oz. Vodka.
Build into an old-fashioned glass.

Grand Slam

1oz. Cognac, 1oz. Apricot Brandy, 1oz. Gin, 1 dash Lime Juice.
Shake and strain into a martini glass.

Grappa Strega

1oz. Grappa, 1oz. Strega.
Stir and strain into an ice-filled old-fashioned glass.

Great Secret

2oz. Gin, 1oz. Kina Lillet, 2 dashes Angostura Bitters.
Stir and strain into a martini glass.

Greek Stinger

2oz. Metaxa Brandy, 1oz. White Crème de Menthe.
Build into a brandy balloon without ice.

Green Eye

1 1/2oz. Kina Lillet, 1/2oz. Green Crème de Menthe, 2 dashes Orange Bitters.
Shake and strain into a martini glass.

Green-Eyed Monster

1oz. Gin, 1oz. Green Chartreuse, 1oz. Sweet Vermouth.
Stir and strain into a martini glass.

Green Lady

2oz. Gin, 1/2oz. Green Chartreuse, 1/2oz. Yellow Chartreuse.
Shake and strain into a martini glass. Serve with a twist of lemon.

Green Room

2oz. Dry Vermouth, 1oz. Cognac, 1/2oz. Cointreau.
Shake and strain into a martini glass.

Green Star

2oz. Kirschwasser, 1 dash Green Crème de Menthe, 1 dash Cointreau, 1 dash Gomme Syrup.

Shake and strain into a martini glass.

Guards

2oz. Gin, 1oz. Sweet Vermouth, 4 dashes Triple Sec.

Stir and strain into a martini glass.

Gum Drop

2oz. Scotch, 1oz. Galliano.

Build into an old-fashioned glass.

Gypsy

$1^1/_2$oz. Gin, $1^1/_2$oz. Sweet Vermouth.

Stir and strain into a martini glass.

Gypsy 2

2oz. Vodka, 1oz. Benedictine, 3 dashes Angostura Bitters.

Shake and strain into a martini glass.

Hague

$1^1/_4$oz. Bourbon, $1^1/_4$oz. Green Chartreuse, $^1/_4$oz. Dry Vermouth.

Stir and strain into a martini glass.

Hair Raiser

2oz. 100 Proof Vodka, $^3/_4$oz. Rye Whiskey, 1 dash Lemon Juice.

Shake and strain into a martini glass.

Half & Half

2oz. Dry Vermouth, 2oz. Sweet Vermouth.

Build into an old-fashioned glass. Serve with a twist of lemon.

Happy Birthday

1oz. Cointreau, 1oz. Blue Curaçao, $^1/_2$oz. Galliano, $^1/_2$oz. White Rum.

Stir and strain into a martini glass.

Harley Davidson

1oz. Yukon Jack Whiskey, 1oz. Jack Daniel's Whiskey.
Build into an old-fashioned glass.

Harmony

2oz. Cognac, 1/4oz. Crème de Fraises, 2 dashes Orange Bitters, 1 dash Maraschino Liqueur.
Build into an old-fashioned glass.

Harry Lauder

1oz. Scotch, 1oz. Sweet Vermouth, 2 dashes Gomme Syrup.
Build into an old-fashioned glass.

Harry's Cocktail

2oz. Gin, 1oz. Sweet Vermouth, 1 dash Pastis, 1 sprig of Mint.
Shake all including the mint and strain into a martini glass.
Garnish with a stuffed olive.

Harvard

2oz. Cognac, 1oz. Sweet Vermouth, 1 dash Angostura Bitters, 1 dash Grenadine, 1/4oz. Lemon Juice.
Shake and strain into a martini glass.

Hasty

2oz. Gin, 1oz. Dry Vermouth, 1 dash Anisette, 1/4oz. Grenadine.
Shake and strain into a martini glass.

Havana Brandy

2oz. Apricot Brandy, 1oz. Gin, 1oz. Swedish Punsch, 1 dash Lemon Juice.
Shake and strain into a martini glass.

Hearn's Cocktail

1oz. Irish Whiskey, 1oz. Pernod, 1oz. Dry Vermouth, 1 dash Angostura Bitters.
Shake and strain into a martini glass.

Heart Stopper

2oz. Bourbon, 1/2oz. White Crème de Menthe, 2 dashes Angostura Bitters.
Shake and strain into a martini glass.

Heather

2oz. Bourbon, 1/2oz. Dry Vermouth, 3 dashes Angostura Bitters, 1/4oz. Grenadine.
Stir and strain into a martini glass.

Hell

1oz. Cognac, 1oz. White Crème de Menthe, 1 pinch Chilli Powder.
Shake and strain into a martini glass.

H.G.Wells

2oz. Bourbon, 1/2oz. Dry Vermouth, 1/2oz. Pernod, 1 dash Angostura Bitters.
Stir and strain into an ice-filled old-fashioned glass.

H&H

2oz. Gin, 1oz. Kina Lillet, 2 dashes Orange Curaçao.
Stir and strain into a martini glass.

Highland Fling

2oz. Scotch, 1oz. Sweet Vermouth, 2 dashes Orange Bitters.
Shake and strain into a martini glass.

Hill-Billy

2oz. Corn Whiskey, 2 dashes Angostura Bitters.
Stir and strain into an ice-filled old-fashioned glass.

Hobby

1oz. Bourbon, 1oz. Gin, 1/2oz. Orange Curaçao, 1 dash Orange Bitters.
Stir and strain into a martini glass.

Hoffman House

1 1/2oz. Gin, 3/4oz. Dry Vermouth, 2 dashes Orange Bitters.
Stir and strain into a martini glass. Garnish with a green olive.

Hokkaido

1½oz. Gin, 1oz. Sake, ½oz. Triple Sec.
Shake and strain into a martini glass.

Hole in One

2oz. Scotch, 1oz. Sweet Vermouth, 1 dash Lemon Juice, 1 dash Angostura Bitters.
Shake and strain into a martini glass.

Holland

1oz. Genever (Dutch Gin), 1oz. Triple Sec, 6 dashes Orange Bitters.
Shake and strain into a martini glass.

Homestead

1½oz. Gin, ¾oz. Sweet Vermouth.
Stir and strain into a martini glass. Garnish with a slice of orange.

Honolulu 2

1oz. Gin, 1oz. Maraschino Liqueur, 1oz. Benedictine.
Stir and strain into a martini glass.

Honolulu Silver

1oz. Gin, 1oz. Maraschino Liqueur, 1oz. Benedictine, 1 Egg White.
Shake and strain into a martini glass.

Hoots Mon

2oz. Scotch, 1oz. Sweet Vermouth, 1 dash Benedictine.
Stir and strain into a martini glass. Serve with a twist of lemon.

Hoover

2oz. Dark Rum, 1oz. Sweet Vermouth, ½oz. Orange Curaçao.
Shake and strain into a martini glass.

Hot Martini

See chapter three, The Classics, (pp 57–62).
Substitute an olive stuffed with a Jalepino chilli for the regular olive in the dry martini.

Hot Pants

2oz. Tequila, 3/4oz. Peppermint Schnapps, 1 dash Grapefruit Juice.

Shake and pour into a salt-rimmed old-fashioned glass.

Hot Spiced Rum

2oz. Captain Morgan's Spiced Rum, 3 dashes Tabasco Sauce, 1 dash Grenadine.

Shake and strain into a martini glass.

H.P.W.

2oz. Old Tom Gin, 1 dash Sweet Vermouth, 1 dash Dry Vermouth.

Shake and strain into a martini glass. Serve with a twist of orange.

H.R.W.

2oz. Gin, 1oz. Dry Vermouth, 4 fresh Cherries.

Crush cherries and add to shaker with remaining ingredients. Shake and strain into a martini glass.

Hudson Bay

2oz. Gin, 1oz. Cherry Brandy, 2 dashes Overproof Rum, 2 dashes Lime Juice, 1 dash Orange Juice.

Shake and strain into a martini glass.

Hunter

2oz. Bourbon or Rye Whiskey, 1oz. Cherry Brandy.

Stir and strain into a martini glass. Garnish with a cherry.

Hurricane

1 1/2oz. Dark Rum, 1 1/2oz. White Rum, 1/4oz. Grenadine, 2 dashes Lime Juice.

Shake and strain into a martini glass.

Hurricane 2

1oz. Gin, 1oz. Scotch, 1oz. White Crème de Menthe, 1 dash Lemon Juice.

Shake and strain into a martini glass.

Hurricane 3

1oz. Gin, 1oz. Bourbon, 1oz. White Crème de Menthe, 1 dash Lemon Juice.
Shake and strain into a martini glass.

Iceberg

2oz. Vodka, 1 dash Pernod.

Stir into an old-fashioned glass three-quarters filled with ice.

I Don't Care

1oz. Bourbon, 1oz. Green Crème de Menthe, 1/4oz. Crème de Framboise.
Stir and strain into a martini glass.

Ika

2oz. Gin, 1oz. Grenadine.
Stir and strain into a martini glass.

Imperial

1 1/2oz. Gin, 1 1/2oz. Dry Vermouth, 1 dash Maraschino Liqueur, 1 dash Angostura Bitters.
Shake and strain into a martini glass.

Incognito

1oz. Cognac, 1oz. Apricot Brandy, 1oz. Dry Vermouth, 1 dash Angostura Bitters.
Shake and strain into a martini glass.

Indispensable

2oz. Gin, 1/4oz. Sweet Vermouth, 1/4oz. Pernod, 1 dash Dry Vermouth.
Shake and strain into a martini glass.

Inspiration

3/4oz. Gin, 3/4oz. Grand Marnier, 3/4oz. Calvados, 3/4oz. Dry Vermouth.
Stir and strain into a martini glass.

Irish Blackthorn

1 1/2oz. Irish Whiskey, 1oz. Dry Vermouth, 1/4oz. Pernod,
3 dashes Angostura Bitters.

Stir and strain into an ice-filled old-fashioned glass.

Irish Cheer

2oz. Irish Whiskey, 1/2oz. Sweet Vermouth.

Stir and strain into a martini glass.

Irish Mist

2oz. Irish Whiskey.

Stir into an old-fashioned glass three-quarters filled with crushed ice.

Irish Nut

1oz. Irish Whiskey, 1oz. Bailey's, 1oz. Frangelico.

Build into an old-fashioned glass.

Irish Whiskey Cocktail

2oz. Irish Whiskey, 2 dashes Maraschino Liqueur, 1 dash Anisette,
1 dash Cointreau, 1 dash Angostura Bitters.

Shake and strain into a martini glass. Garnish with an olive.

Irresistible

2oz. White Rum, 1oz. Sweet Vermouth, 1 dash Benedictine,
1 dash Lemon Juice.

Stir and strain into a martini glass.

Isabella

2oz. Gin, 1oz. Sweet Vermouth, 1 dash Grenadine, 1 dash Orange Juice.

Stir and strain into a martini glass.

Italian Doctor

1oz. Amaretto, 1oz. Green Crème de Menthe.

Build into an old-fashioned glass.

Italian Stinger

2oz. Amaretto, 1oz. White Crème de Menthe.

Stir together in a brandy balloon.

Itchiban

3oz. Cognac, 1 dash White Crème de Cacao, 1 dash Benedictine, 1 Egg.

Shake and strain into an ice-filled highball glass.

Sprinkle grated nutmeg over drink.

Itza Paramount

1oz. Gin, 1oz. Drambuie, 1oz. Cointreau.

Stir and strain into a martini glass.

Jack Dempsey

2oz. Gin, 1oz. White Rum, 1 dash Lemon Juice, 1 dash Gomme Syrup.

Shake and strain into a martini glass.

Jack Rabbit

2oz. Applejack or Calvados, 1 dash Lemon Juice, 1 dash Orange Juice, 1 dash Gomme Syrup.

Shake and strain into a martini glass.

Jack Zeller

1 1/2oz. Old Tom Gin, 1 1/2oz. Dubonnet.

Stir and strain into a martini glass.

Jamaican Old-Fashioned

See chapter three, The Classics, (p. 65).

Substitute dark Jamaican rum for the bourbon in the old-fashioned.

Janet Howard

2oz. Cognac, 1/4oz. Orgeat, 1 dash Angostura Bitters.

Shake and strain into a martini glass.

Jean Lafitte

2oz. Gin, 1oz. Cointreau, 1 dash Anisette, 1 Egg Yolk.

Shake and strain into a martini glass.

Jenks

1 1/2oz. Gin, 1 1/2oz. Dry Vermouth, 2 dashes Benedictine.

Stir and strain into a martini glass.

Jewel

1oz. Gin, 1oz. Green Chartreuse, 1oz. Sweet Vermouth, 1 dash Orange Bitters.

Shake and strain into a martini glass.

Jeyplak

1 1/2oz. Gin, 3/4oz. Sweet Vermouth, 2 dashes Anisette.

Stir and strain into a martini glass.

Jimmy Blanc

2oz. Gin, 1oz. Kina Lillet, 3 dashes Dubonnet.

Stir and strain into a martini glass. serve with a twist of lemon.

Joburg

1 1/2oz. White Cuban Rum, 1 1/2oz. Caperitif, 2 dashes Orange Bitters, 2 dashes Angostura Bitters.

Shake and strain into a martini glass. Serve with a twist of lemon.

Jockey Club

1 1/2oz. Bourbon, 1 1/2oz. Sweet Vermouth, 1/4oz. Maraschino Liqueur.

Stir and strain into a martini glass.

Johnnie

2oz. Sloe Gin, 1oz. Triple Sec, 1/4oz. Anisette.

Shake and strain into a martini glass.

J.O.S.

1oz. Gin, 1oz. Dry Vermouth, 1oz. Sweet Vermouth, 1 dash Cognac, 1 dash Angostura Bitters, 1 dash Lemon Juice.

Shake and strain into a martini glass. Serve with a twist of lemon.

Josette

1oz. Cognac, 1oz. Triple Sec, 1oz. Anisette, 1 dash Egg White.

Shake and strain into a martini glass.

Jumbo

1oz. Cognac, 1oz. Dry Vermouth, 1oz. Sweet Vermouth, 1oz. Caperitif.
Stir and strain into a martini glass.

Juniper

2oz. Genever (Dutch Gin), 1/2oz. Dry Vermouth, 2 dashes Grenadine.
Stir and strain into a martini glass.

Kahlúa Cocktail

1 1/2oz. Kahlúa, 1 1/2oz. Cognac.
Build into an old-fashioned glass.

Kaiser

1oz. Gin, 1oz. Kümmel, 1/4oz. Dry Vermouth.
Stir and strain into a martini glass.

Kangaroo

2oz. Vodka, 1oz. Dry Vermouth.
Shake and strain into a martini glass. Serve with a twist of lemon.

Kentucky Colonel

2 1/4oz. Bourbon, 3/4oz. Benedictine.
Stir and strain into a martini glass. Serve with a twist of lemon.

Kentucky Sunset

2oz. Bourbon, 3/4oz. Strega, 3/4oz. Anisette.
Stir and strain into a martini glass. Serve with a twist of orange.

Kicker

2oz. Dark Rum, 3/4oz. Calvados, 2 dashes Sweet Vermouth.
Stir and strain into a martini glass.

Kiltie

1oz. Bourbon, 1oz. Dry Vermouth, 2 dashes Angostura Bitters.
Stir and strain into a martini glass. Serve with a twist of lemon.

Kina Citron

2oz. Absolut Citron Vodka, 1oz. Kina Lillet.

Stir and strain into a martini glass.

Kina Cocktail

2oz. Gin, 1oz. Kina Lillet, 1/2oz. Sweet Vermouth.

Stir and strain into a martini glass.

King George

1oz. Plymouth Gin, 1oz. Benedictine, 1oz. Sweet Vermouth, 1oz. Caperitif.

Shake and strain into a martini glass.

Kiss

1oz. Dubonnet, 1oz. Gin, 1oz. Sweet Vermouth, 1 dash Maraschino Liqueur.

Shake and strain into a martini glass.

Kiss From Heaven

1oz. Cognac, 1oz. Dry Vermouth, 1oz. Drambuie.

Stir and strain into a martini glass.

Kiss In The Dark

1oz. Gin, 1oz. Dry Vermouth, 1oz. Cherry Brandy.

Stir and strain into a martini glass.

Kiss Me Quick

2oz. Pernod, 1/4oz. Triple Sec, 3 dashes Angostura Bitters.

Shake and strain into a martini glass.

Klondike

1oz. Calvados, 1oz. Dry Vermouth, 3 dashes Orange Bitters.

Stir and strain into a martini glass.

Knee-Breaker

1oz. Cointreau, 1oz. Parfait Amour, 1/2oz. Cherry Brandy, 1/2oz. Frangelico, 1 dash Grenadine.

Shake and strain into a martini glass.

Knickerbein

1oz. Benedictine, 1oz. Kümmel, 1oz. Yellow Chartreuse, 1 Egg, 2 dashes Angostura Bitters.

Place the bitters into the bottom of a martini glass and add the egg yolk (whole). Pour in the liqueurs and top with the beaten egg white.

Knickerbocker

2oz. Gin, 1oz. Dry Vermouth, 2 dashes Sweet Vermouth.

Stir and strain into a martini glass. Serve with a twist of lemon.

Knickerbocker Special

2oz. White Rum, 1/4oz. Triple Sec, 1 dash Orange Juice, 1 dash Lemon Juice, 1 dash Raspberry Syrup.

Shake and strain into a martini glass.

Knock Out

1oz. Gin, 1oz. Dry Vermouth, 1/2oz. Anisette, 1 dash White Crème de Menthe.

Stir and strain into a martini glass.

KO

2oz. Gin, 1/2oz. Kirschwasser, 1 dash Apricot Brandy, 1 dash Lemon Juice.

Stir and strain into a martini glass.

Kriss Kross

2oz. Benedictine, 1 dash Kümmel.

Stir and strain into a martini glass.

Kup's Indispensable

1 1/2oz. Gin, 1/2oz. Sweet Vermouth, 1/2oz. Dry Vermouth, 1 dash Angostura Bitters.

Stir and strain into a martini glass.

Ladies

1 3/4oz. Bourbon, 1 dash Anisette, 1 dash Angostura Bitters.

Shake and strain into a martini glass. Garnish with a slice of pineapple.

Lady Be Good

2oz. Cognac, 1/2oz. Sweet Vermouth, 1/2oz. White Crème de Menthe.

Shake and strain into a martini glass.

Lady Finger

1oz. Gin, 1oz. Cherry brandy, 1oz. Kirschwasser.

Shake and strain into a martini glass.

Lady Lyssa

2 1/4oz. Gin, 1/2oz. Apricot Brandy, 1/2oz. Cointreau.

Shake and strain into a martini glass.

Laguna

2oz. Italian Grappa, 1oz. Bianco Vermouth, 1oz. Vodka, 1/4oz. Campari.

Shake and strain into a martini glass.

Lakeside

1 1/2oz. Brown Crème de Cacao, 1/2oz. Cognac,
1/2oz. White Crème de Menthe, 1/2oz. Cointreau.

Shake and strain into a martini glass.

Lamb's Club

1oz. Gin, 1oz. Dry Vermouth, 1oz. Sweet Vermouth,
2 dashes Angostura Bitters.

Stir and strain into a martini glass.

L'Amour

2oz. Gin, 1 dash Cherry Brandy, 1 dash Grenadine, 1 dash Lemon Juice,
2 sprigs Mint.

Shake all including the mint and strain into a martini glass.

Landlady

2oz. Gin, 1 dash Grenadine, 1 dash Egg White.

Shake and strain into a martini glass.

La Place

1oz. Bourbon, 1oz. Sweet Vermouth, 3 dashes Orange Bitters.
Shake and strain into a martini glass.

Laser Beam

1oz. Jack Daniel's Whiskey, 1oz. Tequila, 1oz. Amaretto, 1/2oz. Triple Sec.
Shake and pour into an old-fashioned glass.

Latin Quarter

2oz. Dubonnet, 1oz. Amer Picon, 1 dash Cointreau.
Shake and strain into a martini glass.

Law Hill

2oz. Bourbon, 1oz. Dry Vermouth, 1 dash Anisette, 1 dash Angostura Bitters.
Stir and strain into a martini glass.

Leave It To Me

1oz. Gin, 1oz. Apricot brandy, 1/2oz. Dry Vermouth, 1 dash Lemon Juice, 1 dash Grenadine.
Shake and strain into a martini glass.

Leeward

2oz. White Rum, 3/4oz. Calvados, 1/2oz. Sweet Vermouth.
Shake and strain into a martini glass. Serve with a twist of lemon.

Legend

1oz. Midori Melon Liqueur, 1 1/2oz. Frangelico, 1oz. Kahlúa.
Build into an old-fashioned glass.

Lena

(A. CHIRICI)

3/4oz. Bourbon, 1/2oz. Sweet Vermouth, 1/4oz. Galliano, 1/4oz. Dry Vermouth, 1/4oz. Campari.
Shake and strain into a martini glass.

Les Petit Pois

1oz. Gin, 1oz. Cognac, 1oz. Green Izarra.
Shake and strain into a martini glass.

Liars

2oz. Gin, 1oz. Dry Vermouth, 1 dash Grand Marnier, 1 dash Sweet Vermouth.
Stir and strain into a martini glass.

Liberal

2oz. Bourbon, 1oz. Amer Picon, 2 dashes Gomme Syrup.
Shake and strain into a martini glass. Serve with a twist of lemon.

Liberty

2oz. Calvados, 1oz. White Rum, 1/4oz. Gomme Syrup.
Shake and strain into a martini glass.

Liberty Bell

2oz. Bourbon, 1/2oz. Peach Schnapps, 1 dash Apricot Brandy, 1 dash Campari.
Stir and strain into a martini glass.

Lillane

1oz. Cognac, 1oz. Kirschwasser, 1oz. White Crème de Cacao, 1 dash Grenadine.
Shake and strain into a martini glass.

Lillet Citron

2oz. Kina Lillet, 1oz. Syrop de Citron.
Stir and strain into a martini glass.

Lillet Cocktail

2oz. Kina Lillet, 1oz. Gin, 1 dash Angostura Bitters.
Stir and strain into a martini glass.

Limp Dick

1oz. Southern Comfort, 1oz. Grand Marnier, 1/2oz. Amaretto, 1/2oz. White Crème de Menthe.
Stir and strain into a martini glass.

Little Princess

1½oz. White Rum, 1½oz. Sweet Vermouth.
Stir and strain into a martini glass.

Loch Lomond

2oz. Scotch, ½oz. Gomme Syrup, 3 dashes Angostura Bitters.
Shake and strain into a martini glass.

Loensky

2oz. Kümmel, 1oz. Scotch.
Stir into an ice-filled old-fashioned glass.

Loftus

1oz. Pernod, 1oz. Sweet Vermouth, 1oz. Dry Vermouth.
Shake and strain into a martini glass.

London Cocktail

2oz. Gin, 1 dash Maraschino Liqueur, 2 dashes Orange Bitters, 1 dash Gomme Syrup.
Shake and strain into a martini glass. Serve with a twist of lemon.

Lone Tree

1½oz. Gin, ¾oz. Sweet Vermouth.
Stir and strain into a martini glass.

Louis

2oz. Gin, 1oz. Dry Vermouth, 1 dash Cointreau, 1 dash Grand Marnier.
Shake and strain into a martini glass.

Lucy's

1oz. Vodka, 1oz. Green Crème de Menthe, 1oz. Brown Crème de Cacao.
Shake and pour into an old-fashioned glass.

Lugger

1½oz. Cognac, 1oz. Calvados, ½oz. Apricot Brandy.
Shake and strain into a martini glass.

Macaroni

2oz. Pernod, 1oz. Sweet Vermouth.

Shake and strain into a martini glass.

Ma Chérie

2oz. Gin, 1oz. Cherry Brandy, 1 dash Grenadine.

Stir and strain into a martini glass.

Madame Lou

1oz. Gin, 2oz. Dry Vermouth, 1/4oz. Pineapple Syrup.

Stir and strain into a martini glass.

Mad Russian

1oz. Vodka, 1oz. Kahlúa, 1oz. Bailey's.

Stir the vodka and Kahlúa into an ice-filled old-fashioned glass and float the Bailey's on top.

Mah-Jong

2oz. Gin, 1/2oz. White Rum, 1/2oz. Cointreau.

Stir and strain into a martini glass.

Mahogany

2oz. Gin, 1oz. Golden Syrup.

Stir syrup into gin until dissolved, then stir over ice and strain into a martini glass.

Maiden's Blush

2oz. Gin, 1/4oz. Triple Sec, 2 dashes Grenadine, 1 dash Lemon Juice.

Shake and strain into a martini glass.

Maiden's Wish

1oz. Gin, 1oz. Kina Lillet, 1oz. Calvados.

Stir and strain into a martini glass.

Major Bailey

2oz. Gin, 1 tsp. granulated Sugar, 1 dash Lime Juice, 1 dash Lemon Juice, 8–10 fresh Mint Leaves.

Muddle the juice, sugar and mint together in an old-fashioned glass. Fill with ice and stir in the gin until the glass frosts.

Malibu Cocktail

2oz. Gin, 1oz. Dry Vermouth, 2 dashes Angostura, 2 dashes Anisette.

Stir and strain into a martini glass. Garnish with an olive.

Mallorca

1 1/2oz. White Rum, 1/2oz. Crème de Banane, 1/2oz. Drambuie, 1/2oz. Dry Vermouth.

Stir and strain into a martini glass.

Manhattan

See chapter three, The Classics, (pp 55–6).

Manhattan (French)

2oz. Bourbon, 1oz. Dry Vermouth, 1 dash Cointreau, 1 dash Angostura Bitters.

Stir and strain into an ice-filled old-fashioned glass. Garnish with a cherry and serve with a twist of lemon.

Marconi

2oz. Calvados, 1oz. Sweet Vermouth, 2 dashes Orange Bitters.

Stir and strain into a martini glass.

Marguerite

2oz. Gin, 1oz. Dry Vermouth, 1 dash Lime Juice, 2 dashes Orange Bitters.

Stir and strain into a martini glass.

Marney

2oz. Gin, 1oz. Grand Marnier.

Stir and strain into a martini glass.

Martinez

(ORIGINAL RECIPE: JERRY THOMAS)

1 pony Old Tom Gin, 1 Wineglass Vermouth (Dry), 1 dash Bitters (unspecified), 2 dashes Maraschino Liqueur.

Stir with 2 lumps of ice and strain into a martini glass.

Martinez

(Post 1900 Version)

1½oz. Gin, 1½oz. Dry Vermouth, ¼oz. Triple sec or Maraschino Liqueur, 1 dash Orange Bitters.

Stir and strain into a martini glass.

Martini

See chapter three, The Classics, (pp 57–62).

Mary Garden

2oz. Dubonnet, 1oz. Dry Vermouth.

Stir and strain into a martini glass.

Maxim

1½oz. Gin, 1oz. Dry Vermouth, 1 dash White Crème de Cacao.

Shake and strain into a martini glass.

Mayflower

2oz. Dubonnet, 1oz. Cognac.

Shake and strain into a martini glass.

McClelland

2oz. Sloe Gin, 1oz. Cointreau, 1 dash Orange Bitters.

Shake and strain into a martini glass.

Mediterranean Stinger

2oz. Ouzo, 1oz. White Crème de Menthe.

Stir and strain into a martini glass.

Melba

1oz. White Rum, 1oz. Swedish Punsch, 1/4oz. Anisette, 2 dashes Grenadine.

Shake and strain into a martini glass.

Melon Stinger

1oz. Midori Melon Liqueur, 1oz. Cognac, 1oz. White Crème de Menthe.

Stir and strain into a martini glass.

Merry-Go-Round

2oz. Gin, 1/2oz. Dry Vermouth, 1/2oz. Sweet Vermouth.

Stir and strain into a martini glass.

Garnish with an olive and serve with a twist of lemon.

Merry Widow

1 1/2oz. Gin, 1 1/2oz. Dry Vermouth, 1 dash Benedictine, 1 dash Anisette, 1 dash Orange Bitters.

Stir and strain into a martini glass. Serve with a twist of lemon.

Merry Widow 2

1 1/2oz. Cherry Brandy, 1 1/2oz. Maraschino Liqueur, 1 dash Grenadine.

Shake and strain into a martini glass.

Metropole

1oz. Cognac, 1oz. Dry Vermouth, 1 dash Angostura Bitters, 1 dash Orange Bitters.

Stir and strain into a martini glass.

Metropolitan

1 1/2oz. Cognac, 1 1/2oz. Sweet Vermouth, 1 dash Gomme Syrup, 1 dash Angostura Bitters.

Stir and strain into a martini glass.

Mickey

1oz. Dark Rum, 1/2oz. Cointreau, 1/2oz. Bourbon, 1 dash Grenadine.

Shake and strain into a martini glass.

Midori Cocktail

(CAIZZO FRANCESCO)

2oz. Gin, 1oz. Dry Vermouth, 1/2oz. Midori Melon Liqueur, 1 dash Green Chartreuse.

Shake and strain into a martini glass.

Mikado

11/2oz. Cognac, 1/2oz. Cointreau, 1/4oz. Crème de Noyaux, 1 dash Grenadine, 1 dash Angostura Bitters.

Stir and strain into an ice-filled old-fashioned glass.

Miles of Smiles

1oz. Canadian Club Whiskey, 1oz. Amaretto, 1oz. White Crème de Menthe.

Stir and strain into a martini glass.

Millionaire

21/2oz. Bourbon, 3/4oz. Cointreau, 2 dashes Grenadine, 1 Egg White.

Shake and strain into a martini glass.

Mint Julep

See chapter three, The Classics, (pp 62–4).

Mint Mist

2oz. Green Crème de Menthe.

Stir into an old-fashioned glass, three-quarters filled with crushed ice.

Misty

1oz. Vodka, 1oz. Cointreau, 1oz. Apricot Brandy, 1 dash Crème de Banane.

Stir and strain into a martini glass.

Mocha Mint

2oz. Kahlúa, 1oz. White Crème de Menthe.

Build into an old-fashioned glass.

Modern River

2oz. Gin, 1/2oz. Caperitif, 1/2oz. Dry Vermouth.

Stir and strain into a martini glass. Serve with a twist of lemon.

Mofuco

2oz. White Rum, 1/4oz. Gomme Syrup, 1 Egg, 1 dash Angostura Bitters, 1 slice Lemon Peel.

Shake all including the peel and strain into a martini glass.

Molly Picon

1 1/2oz. Amer Picon, 1oz. Gin, 1/2oz. Sweet Vermouth.

Stir and strain into a martini glass.

Montmartre

2 1/2oz. Gin, 1oz. Sweet Vermouth, 1oz. Cointreau.

Build into an old-fashioned glass.

Moody Blues

1oz. Gin, 1oz. Blue Curaçao, 1oz. Parfait Amour, 1 Egg White, 1 dash Lime Juice.

Shake and strain into a martini glass.

Moonraker

1oz. Cognac, 1oz. Dubonnet, 1oz. Crème de Pêche, 1 dash Pastis.

Shake and strain into a martini glass.

Moose

2 1/4oz. Bourbon, 3/4oz. Apricot Brandy, 1 dash Angostura Bitters.

Shake and strain into a martini glass.

Morning

1oz. Cognac, 1oz. Dry Vermouth, 1/2oz. Cointreau, 1 dash Maraschino, 1 dash Angostura Bitters.

Stir and strain into a martini glass.

Morro

2oz. Gin, 1oz. Dark Rum, 1 dash Lemon Juice, 1 dash Pineapple Juice.

Shake and strain into an ice-filled, sugar-rimmed old-fashioned glass.

Moscow Moose

2oz. Peppermint Schnapps, 1 1/4oz. Vodka.
Build into an old-fashioned glass.

Moulin Rouge

2oz. Sloe Gin, 1oz. Sweet Vermouth, 2 dashes Angostura Bitters.
Stir and strain into a martini glass.

Mountie

2oz. Canadian Club Whiskey, 1oz. Campari.
Stir and strain into a martini glass.

Naked Manhattan

See chapter three, The Classics, (pp 55–6).
Omit vermouth from the manhattan.

Naked Martini

See chapter three, The Classics, (pp 61–2).
Omit vermouth from the dry martini.

Napoléon

2oz. Gin, 2 dashes Orange Curaçao, 2 dashes Dubonnet.
Stir and strain into a martini glass.

Napoléon 2

2oz. Gin, 2 dashes Orange Curaçao, 2 dashes Dubonnet, 1 dash Fernet Branca.
Stir and strain into a martini glass.

Napoléon 3

2oz. Armagnac, 1oz. Dry Vermouth, 1 dash Cointreau.
Stir and strain into a martini glass.

Narragansett

2oz. Bourbon, 1 1/4oz. Sweet Vermouth, 1/4oz. Anisette.
Stir and strain into a martini glass. Serve with a twist of lemon.

Naturally Naked

2oz. Cognac, 2 dashes Angostura Bitters.

Stir and strain into a martini glass.

Naval

1½oz. Gin, 1½oz. Sweet Vermouth, 3 Silver-Skin Cocktail Onions.

Stir and strain into a martini glass.

Garnish with the onions on a cocktail stick.

Neapolitan

2oz. Cointreau, 1oz. Grand Marnier, 1oz. White Rum.

Shake and strain into a martini glass.

Negroni

See chapter three, The Classics, (pp 64–5).

Netherlands

1½oz. Cognac, 1½oz. Triple Sec, 1 dash Orange Bitters.

Build into an old-fashioned glass.

Newbury

1oz. Gin, 1oz. Sweet Vermouth, ¼oz. Orange Curaçao, 1 strip Lemon Peel, 1 strip Orange Peel.

Shake all including the peel and strain into a martini glass.

Newton's Special

2¼oz. Cognac, 1½oz. Cointreau, 1 dash Angostura Bitters.

Stir and strain into a martini glass.

Nick's Own

1oz. Cognac, 1oz. Sweet Vermouth, ¼oz. Pernod, 2 dashes Angostura Bitters.

Stir and strain into a martini glass.

Night Cap 2

1oz. Cognac, 1oz. Orange Curaçao, ½oz. Anisette, 1 Egg Yolk.

Shake and strain into a martini glass. Sprinkle grated nutmeg over drink.

Night Cap 3

1oz. Cognac, 1oz. Grand Marnier, 1oz. Anisette, 1 Egg Yolk.
Shake and strain into a martini glass.

Night-Light

2oz. Dark Rum, 1oz. Grand Marnier, 1 Egg Yolk.
Shake and strain into a martini glass.

Nineteen

2oz. Dry Vermouth, 1/2oz. Kirschwasser, 1/4oz. Gin, 2 dashes Angostura Bitters, 1/4oz. Gomme Syrup.
Shake and strain into a martini glass.

Nixon's Blues

2oz. Bourbon, 1oz. Blue Curaçao, 2 dashes Angostura Bitters, 1 dash Lemon Juice, 1 dash Egg White.
Shake and strain into a martini glass.

Nude Eel

1oz. Cognac, 1oz. Dubonnet, 1/2oz. Gin, 1/2oz. Green Chartreuse.
Shake and strain into a martini glass.

Nuptial

2oz. Gin, 1oz. Kirschwasser, 1 dash Cointreau, 1 dash Lemon Juice.
Shake and strain into a martini glass.

Nutcracker

1oz. Kahlúa, 1oz. Amaretto, 1/2oz. Grand Marnier, 1/2oz. Bailey's.
Build into an old-fashioned glass.

Nutty Irishman

1oz. Irish Whiskey, 1oz. Bailey's, 1oz. Frangelico.
Build into an old-fashioned glass.

Oast House

2oz. Bourbon, 1oz. Drambuie, 2 dashes Amaretto, 2 dashes Angostura Bitters.
Shake and strain into a martini glass.

Odd One Out

2oz. Gold Tequila, 1oz. Goldwasser, 1/2oz. Peach Schnapps, 1/2oz. Amaretto.
Stir and strain into a martini glass.

Oh Henry

1oz. Bourbon, 1oz. Benedictine, 1oz. Ginger Wine.
Stir and strain into a martini glass.

Old Etonian

1oz. Gin, 1oz. Kina Lillet, 1/4oz. Crème de Noyaux, 1 dash Orange Bitters.
Shake and strain into a martini glass.

Old Faithful

2 1/2oz. Bourbon, 1/2oz. Apricot Brandy.
Stir and strain into a martini glass.

Old-Fashioned

See chapter three, The Classics, (p. 65).

Old Pal

2 3/4oz. Bourbon, 3/4oz. Sweet Vermouth, 3/4oz. Grenadine.
Shake and strain into a martini glass.

Old Pepper

1oz. Bourbon, 1oz. Absolut Pepper Vodka, 2 dashes Tabasco Sauce.
Stir and strain into a martini glass.

Old Puss

1oz. Gin, 1oz. Calvados, 1oz. Grenadine.
Shake and strain into a martini glass.

Old Vermouth

1oz. Old Tom Gin, 1oz. Dry Vermouth, 1/2oz. Sweet Vermouth,
2 dashes Angostura Bitters.
Build into an old-fashioned glass and garnish with a slice of lemon.

Onion Breath

2oz. Vodka, 1/2oz. Vinegar from a jar of Cocktail Onions, 1 dash Worcestershire Sauce, 1/4oz. Lemon Juice.

Shake and strain into a martini glass.
Garnish with 2 silver-skin cocktail onions.

Opening

2 1/4oz. Bourbon, 1oz. Sweet Vermouth, 1oz. Grenadine.

Shake and strain into a martini glass.

Opera

2 1/4oz. Gin, 3/4oz. Dubonnet, 1/4oz. Maraschino Liqueur.

Stir and strain into a martini glass.

Orbit

1oz. Vodka, 1/2oz. Gin, 1/2oz. Kümmel, 1oz. Silverwasser.

Stir and strain into a martini glass.

Orchid

2oz. Gin, 1oz. Parfait Amour, 1 Egg White.

Shake and strain into a martini glass.

Order Of Merit Cocktail

1oz. Order of Merit Whiskey, 1oz. Kina Lillet, 1/2oz. Grand Marnier, 2 dashes Orange Bitters.

Build into an old-fashioned glass.

Pacific Gold

1 1/2oz. Crème de Banane, 1oz. Cointreau, 1/2oz. Grand Marnier, 2 dashes Kümmel.

Stir and strain into a martini glass.

Paddy

1 1/2oz. Irish Whiskey, 1 1/2oz. Sweet Vermouth, 2 dashes Angostura Bitters.

Stir and strain into a martini glass.

Paisley Martini

See chapter three, The Classics, (pp 57–62).
Substitute 1 tsp. Scotch for the dry vermouth in the dry martini.

Pall Mall

1oz. Gin, 1oz. White Crème de Menthe, $\frac{1}{2}$oz. Dry Vermouth, $\frac{1}{2}$oz. Sweet Vermouth.
Shake and strain into a martini glass.

Panache

$1\frac{1}{2}$oz. Vodka, $1\frac{1}{2}$oz. Dry Vermouth, 2 dashes Cherry Brandy.
Stir and strain into a martini glass.

Pan-Am

$1\frac{1}{2}$oz. Bourbon, $1\frac{1}{2}$oz. Mezcal, 1 dash Angostura Bitters, 1 dash Gomme Syrup.
Build into an old-fashioned glass.

Panty Burner

1oz. Kahlúa, 1oz. Frangelico, 1oz. Absolut Pepper Vodka.
Stir and strain into a martini glass.

Paradise 2

$2\frac{1}{4}$oz. White Rum, $\frac{3}{4}$oz. Apricot Brandy.
Shake and strain into a martini glass.

Paris

1oz. Gin, 1oz. Dry Vermouth, 1oz. Crème de Cassis.
Shake and strain into a martini glass.

Parisian

$1\frac{1}{2}$oz. Gin, $1\frac{1}{2}$oz. Dry Vermouth, $\frac{1}{4}$oz. Crème de Cassis.
Shake and strain into a martini glass.

Parked Car

1oz. Campari, 1oz. Tequila, $\frac{1}{2}$oz. Cointreau, 1 Egg White.
Shake and strain into a martini glass.

Parson's Nose

2oz. Vodka, 1/2oz. Amaretto, 1/4oz. Crème de Pêche, 2 dashes Angostura Bitters.
Stir and strain into a martini glass.

Passenger List '95

1oz. Gin, 1oz. Cognac, 1oz. Parfait Amour, 2 dashes Pernod.
Shake and strain into a martini glass.

Pat Bra

2oz. Gin, 1oz. Sweet Vermouth, 1/4oz. Maraschino Liqueur, 1 dash Rose's Lime Cordial.
Shake and strain into a martini glass.

Patricia

1oz. Vodka, 1oz. Sweet Vermouth, 1oz. Grand Marnier.
Shake and strain into a martini glass.

Peach Cocktail

2oz. Crème de Pêche, 1oz. Dry Vermouth, 1 dash Grenadine.
Shake and strain into a martini glass.

Peacock

2 1/2oz. Cognac, 1/4oz. Amer Picon, 1 dash Pernod.
Shake and strain into a martini glass.

Pear-Drop

2oz. Poire Williams, 1oz. Vodka, 1 dash Grenadine.
Stir and strain into a martini glass.

Pearl Diver

1oz. Gin, 1oz. Vodka, 3/4oz. Dry Vermouth, 1 dash Angostura Bitters.
Stir and strain into a martini glass.
Garnish with 1 silver skin cocktail onion for the pearl.

Peggy

2oz. Gin, 1oz. Dubonnet, 1 dash Anisette, 2 dashes Cherry Brandy.
Shake and strain into a martini glass.

Peppermint Patty

2oz. White Crème de Menthe, 1oz. White Crème de Cacao.

Build into an old-fashioned glass.

Perfect

2oz. Gin, 1/4oz. Dry Vermouth, 1/4oz. Sweet Vermouth, 1 dash Angostura Bitters.

Stir and strain into a martini glass. Garnish with an olive.

Perfect Manhattan

See chapter three, The Classics, (pp 55–6).

Use 1/2oz. each of dry and sweet vermouth in the Manhattan.

Perfect Martini

See Perfect Manhattan, above.

Perfect Rob Roy

2oz. Scotch, 1/2oz. Sweet Vermouth, 1/2oz. Dry Vermouth.

Stir and strain into a martini glass. Serve with a twist of lemon.

Perfect Royal

2oz. Gin, 1/4oz. dry Vermouth, 1/4oz. Sweet Vermouth, 1 dash Angostura Bitters, 1 dash Pernod.

Shake and strain into a martini glass. Garnish with a cherry.

Pernod Cocktail

2oz. Pernod, 2oz. Iced Water, 2 dashes Angostura Bitters.

Build into an old-fashioned glass.

Phoebe

1 1/2oz. Cognac, 1 1/2oz. Dubonnet, 2 dashes Pastis.

Shake and strain into a martini glass.

Phyllis

1 1/2oz. Cognac, 3/4oz. Cointreau, 1/2oz. Maraschino Liqueur, 1 dash Lemon Juice.

Shake and strain into a martini glass.

Piccad

1oz. Gin, 1oz. Caperitif, 1/4oz. Angostura Bitters, 3 strips Lemon Peel.

Stir all ingredients, including the peel, and strain into a martini glass.

Piccadilly

2oz. Gin, 1/2oz. Dry Vermouth, 1/2oz. Anisette, 2 dashes Grenadine.

Shake and strain into a martini glass.

Picon Cocktail

1oz. Amer Picon, 1oz. Bourbon, 1/4oz. Gomme Syrup, 2 dashes Angostura Bitters.

Shake and strain into a martini glass.

Pink Gin

1oz. Plymouth Gin, 3 dashes Angostura Bitters, Iced Water.

Swill the bitters around a small wineglass until surface is coated. Add the gin and top with the iced water.

Pink Gin 2

1oz. Plymouth Gin, 3 dashes Angostura Bitters.

Swill the bitters around a small wineglass until surface is coated. Add the gin and serve.

Plush Horse

2oz. Gin, 1oz. Grand Marnier, 2 dashes Angostura Bitters.

Shake and strain into a martini glass.

Plymouth

1oz. Plymouth Gin, 3 dashes Orange Bitters, Iced Water.

Swill the bitters around a small wineglass until surface is coated. Add the gin and top with the iced water.

Plymouth 2

1oz. Plymouth Gin, 3 dashes Orange Bitters.

Swill the bitters around a small wineglass until surface is coated. Add the gin and serve.

Poet

1oz. Gin, 1oz. Benedictine, 1oz. Dry Vermouth.

Stir and strain into a martini glass.

Poker

2oz. White Rum, 1oz. Sweet Vermouth.

Stir and strain into a martini glass.

Polly

2oz. Gin, 1oz. White Crème de Cacao.

Stir and strain into a martini glass.

Prima

1oz. White Rum, 1oz. Gin, 1/2oz. Anisette, 3 dashes Angostura Bitters.

Stir and strain into a martini glass.

Primos

1oz. Cognac, 1oz. Bourbon, 1/4oz. Cointreau.

Stir and strain into an ice-filled old-fashioned glass.

Prince Cocktail

1oz. Gin, 1oz. White Crème de Menthe, 1oz. Sweet Vermouth.

Shake and strain into a martini glass.

Princess Pride

2oz. Calvados, 1oz. Sweet Vermouth, 1oz. Dubonnet.

Shake and strain into a martini glass.

Prohibition

1oz. Gin, 1oz. Kina Lillet, 1/4oz. Apricot Brandy, 2 dashes Lemon Juice.

Shake and strain into a martini glass. Serve with a twist of orange.

Quebec

2oz. Canadian Club Whiskey, 1/2oz. Dry Vermouth,
1/4oz. Maraschino Liqueur, 1/4oz. Amer Picon.

Shake and strain into a martini glass.

Queen Elizabeth

2oz. Gin, $^{3}/_{4}$oz. Dry Vermouth, $^{1}/_{4}$oz. Benedictine.

Stir and strain into a martini glass.

Queen Victoria

1oz. Cognac, 1oz. Sweet Vermouth, $^{1}/_{4}$oz. Orange Curaçao.

Stir and strain into a martini glass.

Quick

1oz. Cognac, 1oz. Anisette, $^{1}/_{4}$oz. Triple Sec, 2 dashes Angostura Bitters.

Shake and strain into a martini glass.

Quinquina Cocktail

1oz. Quinquina, 1oz. Cognac, 2 dashes Grenadine, 1 dash Angostura Bitters.

Shake and strain into a martini glass.

RAC

1oz. Gin, $^{1}/_{2}$oz. Dry Vermouth, $^{1}/_{2}$oz. Sweet Vermouth,
2 dashes Orange Bitters, 1 dash Grenadine.

Shake and strain into a martini glass. Serve with a twist of orange.

Racer

2oz. Vodka, 1oz. Pisang Ambon, 2 dashes Amaretto.

Stir and strain into a martini glass.

Racquet Club

1$^{1}/_{2}$oz. Gin, $^{3}/_{4}$oz. Dry Vermouth, 2 dashes Orange Bitters.

Stir and strain into a martini glass.

Raidime

2oz. Gin, 1oz. Pernod, $^{1}/_{2}$oz. Campari.

Shake and strain into a martini glass.

Raspberry Cocktail

1oz. Gin, 1oz. Dry Vermouth, 1oz. Sweet Vermouth, 4 fresh Raspberries.

Crush the raspberries and combine with the remaining ingredients in the shaker. Shake and strain into a martini glass.

Ray Long

2oz. Cognac, 1oz. Sweet Vermouth, 1/4oz. Pernod.
Stir and strain into a martini glass.

Ready To Wear

1oz. White Rum, 1oz. Orange Curaçao, 1oz. Poire Williams.
Shake and strain into a martini glass.

Rebel Yell Cocktail

2oz. Rebel Yell Bourbon, 1oz. Cointreau, 1 dash Grenadine.
Stir and strain into a martini glass.

Red Azure

2oz. Cointreau, 1oz. Kirschwasser, 1/2oz. Dry Vermouth, 1 dash Grenadine.
Shake and strain into a martini glass.

Red Jack

(GUIDO AGNELINI)

1 1/2oz. Vodka, 1/2oz. Dry Vermouth, 1/4oz. Campari, 1/4oz. Cointreau.
Stir and strain into a martini glass. Serve with a twist of orange.

Red Russian

1 1/2oz. Vodka, 1 1/2oz. White Crème de Cacao, 2 dashes Grenadine.
Shake and strain into an ice-filled old-fashioned glass.

Red Skin

2oz. Bourbon, 1oz. Dry Vermouth, 2 dashes Angostura, 2 dashes Grenadine.
Build into an old-fashioned glass.

Red Sky

2oz. Cointreau, 1/2oz. Kümmel, 1/2oz. Grenadine.
Shake and strain into a martini glass.

Richmond

2oz. Gin, 1oz. Kina Lillet.
Shake and strain into a martini glass. Serve with a twist of lemon.

Robert Burns

2oz. Scotch, 1oz. Sweet Vermouth, 1 dash Angostura Bitters, 1 dash Pastis.
Stir and strain into a martini glass.

Rob Roy

2oz. Scotch, 1oz. Sweet Vermouth, 1 dash Angostura Bitters.
Stir and strain into a martini glass.

Rolls-Royce

1 1/2oz. Gin, 1/2oz. Dry Vermouth, 1/4oz. Sweet Vermouth, 1/4oz. Benedictine.
Stir and strain into a martini glass.

Ron-Cacao

1oz. Dark Rum, 1oz. Dry Vermouth, 1oz. Brown Crème de Cacao.
Shake and strain into a martini glass.

Rosa

1oz. Gin, 1oz. Kirschwasser, 1oz. Cherry Brandy.
Stir and strain into a martini glass.

Rosa 2

1oz. Gin, 1oz. Kirschwasser, 1oz. Apricot Brandy.
Stir and strain into a martini glass.

Rose 2

1 1/2oz. Gin, 3/4oz. Dry Vermouth, 1/2oz. Dubonnet, 1/4oz. Grenadine.
Shake and strain into a martini glass.

Rose 3

1oz. Gin, 1oz. Cherry Brandy, 1oz. Kirschwasser, 2 dashes Grenadine.
Shake and strain into a martini glass.

Roselyn

2oz. Gin, 3/4oz. Dry Vermouth, 1 dash Grenadine.
Stir and strain into a martini glass.

Rosita

1oz. Campari, 1oz. Tequila, 1 dash Dry Vermouth, 1 dash Sweet Vermouth.
Build into an old-fashioned glass. Serve with a twist of orange.

Roulette

1oz. Calvados, 1oz. Swedish Punsch, 1oz. White Rum.
Shake and strain into a martini glass.

Royal Male

1oz. Benedictine, 1oz. Scotch, 1/2oz. Peach Schnapps, 1/2oz. Dry Vermouth.
Shake and strain into a martini glass.

Royal Scandinavian

1oz. Aquavit, 1oz. Cointreau, 1/2oz. Silverwasser.
Stir and strain into a sugar-rimmed martini glass.

Royal Smile

2oz. Calvados, 1oz. Gin, 1oz. Grenadine, 1 dash Lemon Juice.
Shake and strain into a martini glass.

Royal Smile 2

1 1/2oz. Gin, 1 1/2oz. Grenadine, 2 dashes Lemon Juice.
Shake and strain into a martini glass.

Rum Julep

See chapter three, The Classics, (pp 62–4).
Substitute dark rum for the bourbon in the mint julep.

Rum Manhattan

See chapter three, The Classics, (pp 55–6).
Substitute dark rum for the bourbon in the manhattan.

Rum Old-Fashioned

See chapter three, The Classics, (p. 65).
Substitute dark rum for the bourbon in the old-fashioned.

Rum Stinger

2oz. Dark Rum, 1oz. White Crème de Menthe.
Build into an old-fashioned glass.

Russian Cocktail

1oz. Vodka, 1oz. Gin, 1oz. White Crème de Cacao.
Shake and strain into a martini glass.

Russian Mist

2oz. Stolichnaya Russian Vodka.
Stir into an old-fashioned glass filled with crushed ice until glass is frosted.
Serve with a twist of lime.

Russian Stinger

2oz. Vodka, 1oz. White Crème de Menthe.
Pour together in a brandy balloon.

Rusty Nail

2oz. Scotch, 1oz. Drambuie.
Build into an old-fashioned glass. Alternatively, layer into a martini glass.

Rye Cocktail

2oz. Rye Whiskey, 1/4oz. Gomme Syrup, 2 dashes Angostura.
Build into an old-fashioned glass.

Sakini

2 1/2oz. Gin, 1/2oz. Sake.
Stir and strain into a martini glass. Garnish with an olive.

Salome

1oz. Gin, 1oz. Dubonnet, 1oz. Dry Vermouth.
Stir and strain into a martini glass.

Sandro

2 1/4oz. Sweet Vermouth, 3/4oz. Campari, 3/4 White Rum.
Stir into an ice-filled highball glass.
Serve with a twist of orange (discard the peel).

San Francisco

1oz. Sloe Gin, 1oz. Dry Vermouth, 1oz. Sweet Vermouth,
1 dash Orange Bitters, 1 dash Angostura Bitters.

Shake and strain into a martini glass. Garnish with a cherry.

Saratoga

2oz. Cognac, 1/4oz. Maraschino Liqueur, 1 dash Angostura Bitters,
1 dash Pineapple Juice, 1 dash Lemon Juice.

Shake and strain into a martini glass.

Savoy

2oz. Gin, 1oz. Dry Vermouth, 1/4oz. Dubonnet.

Stir and strain into a martini glass. Serve with a twist of orange.

Scotch Mist

2oz. Scotch.

Stir into an old-fashioned glass three-quarters filled with crushed ice. Serve with a twist of lemon.

Scotch Old-Fashioned

See chapter three, The Classics, (p. 65).
Substitute Scotch for the bourbon in the old-fashioned.

Scotch Stinger

2oz. Scotch, 1oz. White Crème de Menthe.

Build into an old-fashioned glass.

Seventh Heaven

2oz. Gin, 1oz. Maraschino Liqueur, 2 dashes Grapefruit Juice.

Shake and strain into a martini glass.

Shamrock

2oz. Irish Whiskey, 1oz. Dry Vermouth, 2 dashes green Crème de Menthe.

Stir and strain into a martini glass.

Silver Bullet

2oz. Vodka, 1oz. Kümmel.

Build into an old-fashioned glass.

Silver Cocktail

1oz. Gin, 1oz. Dry Vermouth, 1/2oz. Maraschino Liqueur, 1/2oz. Gomme Syrup, 1 dash Angostura Bitters.

Stir and strain into a martini glass.

Silver Streak

2oz. Gin, 1oz. Kümmel.

Build into an old-fashioned glass.

Sir Knight

1oz. Cognac, 1oz. Yellow Chartreuse, 1oz. Cointreau, 1 dash Angostura Bitters.

Shake and strain into a martini glass. Serve with a twist of lemon.

Six Cylinder

1/2oz. Gin, 1/2oz. Campari, 1/2oz. Dubonnet, 1/2oz. Dry Vermouth, 1/2oz. Sweet Vermouth, 1/2oz. Cherry Brandy.

Shake and strain into a martini glass.

Six Feet Under

1oz. White Rum, 1oz. Swedish Punsch, 1oz. Calvados.

Shake and strain into a martini glass. Serve with a twist of orange.

Sloe Comfortable Mist

1oz. Sloe Gin, 1oz. Southern Comfort.

Stir into an old-fashioned glass three-quarters filled with crushed ice. Serve with a twist of lemon.

Sloe Turkey

1 1/2oz. Wild Turkey 101 Bourbon, 1oz. Sloe Gin, 1/4oz. Gomme Syrup.

Stir and strain into a martini glass.

Snoopy

(PIERO REGGIOLI)

2oz. Bourbon, 1oz. Campari, 1oz. Galliano, 1 dash Grand Marnier, 2 dashes Lemon Juice.

Shake and strain into a champagne flute. Serve with a twist of lemon.

Snow-Shoe

1oz. Wild Turkey 101 Bourbon, 1oz. White Crème de Menthe.

Build into an old-fashioned glass.

Society

2oz. Gin, 3/4oz. Dry Vermouth, 1/4oz. Grenadine.

Shake and strain into a martini glass.

Sol Y Sombra

1 1/2oz. Gin, 1 1/2oz. Spanish Brandy.

Stir and strain into a martini glass.

Some Moth

2oz. Gin, 1oz. Dry Vermouth.

Stir and strain into a martini glass. Garnish with a silver skin cocktail onion.

Soul Kiss 2

1oz. Dubonnet, 1oz. Bourbon, 1/2oz. Dry Vermouth, 1 dash Orange Juice.

Shake and strain into a martini glass.

Southern Bull

1oz. Kahlúa, 1oz. Southern Comfort, 1/2oz. Tequila.

Build into an old-fashioned glass.

Southern Manhattan

See chapter three, The Classics, (pp 55–6).
Substitute Southern Comfort for the bourbon in the manhattan.

Southern Mint Julep

See chapter three, The Classics, (pp 62–4). Substitute equal measures of apricot brandy and cognac for the bourbon in the mint julep.

Spanish Fly

2oz. Mezcal, 1oz. Grand Marnier, 1 tsp. Instant Coffee.
Build into an old-fashioned glass and sprinkle coffee over drink.

Special Rough

1oz. Cognac, 1oz. Calvados, 1/4oz. Pastis.
Shake and strain into a martini glass.

Sphinx

2oz. Gin, 1/4oz. Sweet Vermouth, 1 dash Dry Vermouth.
Stir and strain into a martini glass. Garnish with a slice of lemon.

Star

1 1/2oz. Calvados, 1 1/2oz. Sweet Vermouth, 2 dashes Angostura Bitters.
Stir and strain into a martini glass. Serve with a twist of lemon.

Starlight

2oz. Gin, 1oz. Orange Curaçao, 4 dashes Angostura Bitters.
Shake and strain into a martini glass.

Stinger

2oz. Cognac, 1oz. White Crème de Menthe.
Either shake and strain into a martini glass or build into an old-fashioned glass or pour into a brandy balloon.

Stinger Royal

2oz. Cognac, 1oz. White Crème de Menthe, 2 dashes Pernod.
Stir and strain into a martini glass.

Strawberry Cocktail

1oz. Gin, 1oz. Dry Vermouth, 1oz. Sweet Vermouth, 4 fresh Strawberries.
Crush the strawberries and combine with the remaining ingredients in the shaker. Shake and strain into a martini glass.

Strawberry Cocktail 2

2oz. Cognac, 6 fresh Strawberries.

Crush the strawberries and combine them with the cognac in a shaker. Shake and strain into a martini glass.

Suissesse

2oz. Anisette, 1 Egg White, 1/4oz. Gomme Syrup.

Shake and strain into a martini glass.

Swamp Water

1oz. Green Crème de Menthe, 1oz. Cherry Brandy, 1oz. Bailey's.

Stir into an ice-filled brandy balloon.

The mixture will congeal to give the swamp effect.

Swan Song

1oz. Midori Melon Liqueur, 3/4oz. Cointreau, 1/2oz. Frangelico.

Shake and strain into a martini glass filled with crushed ice. Sprinkle grated chocolate over the drink.

Tailspin Cocktail

1oz. Gin, 1oz. Sweet Vermouth, 1oz. Green Chartreuse, 1 dash Angostura Bitters.

Shake and strain into a martini glass.

Tango

1oz. Gin, 1/2oz. Sweet Vermouth, 1/2oz. Dry Vermouth, 1/4oz. Cointreau, 1 dash Orange Juice.

Shake and strain into a martini glass.

Tapestry

1oz. Green Crème de Menthe, 1oz. Cherry Brandy, 1oz. Grenadine.

Stir and strain into a martini glass.

Television

1oz. Gin, 1oz. Crème de Noyaux, 1/2oz. Sweet Vermouth, 1/2oz. Dry Vermouth.

Stir and strain into a martini glass.

Temptation

2oz. Bourbon, 1/4oz. Cointreau, 1/4oz. Dubonnet, 1/4oz. Anisette.
Shake and strain into a martini glass. Serve with a twist of orange.

Ten Strike

1 1/2oz. Pernod, 3/4oz. Gin, 2 dashes Orange Bitters, 2 dashes Angostura Bitters.
Shake and strain into a martini glass.

Ten Ton

1 1/2oz. Gin, 1 1/2oz. Kümmel, 1/4oz. Dry Vermouth.
Shake and strain into a martini glass.

Tequila Manhattan

See chapter three, The Classics, (pp 55–6).
Substitute tequila for bourbon in the manhattan.

Tequila Martini

2oz. Tequila, 1/2oz. Gin, 1/2oz. Dry Vermouth.
Stir and strain into a martini glass. Garnish with a green olive.

Tequila Mist

2oz. Tequila.
Stir into an old-fashioned glass three-quarters filled with crushed ice. Serve with a twist of lemon.

Tequila Old-Fashioned

See chapter three, The Classics, (p. 65).
Substitute tequila for bourbon in the old-fashioned.

Tequila Pink

2oz. Tequila, 1oz. Dry Vermouth, 3 dashes Grenadine.
Shake and strain into a martini glass.

Tequini

2 1/2oz. Tequila, 1/2oz. Dry Vermouth, 1 dash Orange Bitters.
Stir and strain into a martini glass. Serve with a twist of lemon.

Thanksgiving

1oz. Gin, 1oz. Dry Vermouth, 1oz. Apricot Brandy, 1 Egg Yolk.

Shake and strain into a martini glass.

Thick Mick

2oz. Irish Whiskey, 1oz. Bailey's.

Build into an old-fashioned glass.

Third Degree

2oz. Gin, 1oz. Dry Vermouth, 1/4oz. Anisette.

Stir and strain into a martini glass.

Third Rail

1oz. Cognac, 1oz. White Rum, 1oz. Calvados, 1 dash Pernod.

Shake and strain into a martini glass.

Thistle

1 1/2oz. Scotch, 1 1/2oz. Sweet Vermouth, 2 dashes Angostura Bitters.

Stir and strain into a martini glass.

Three C's

1oz. Calvados, 1oz. Cointreau, 1oz. Brown Crème de Cacao.

Shake and strain into a martini glass.

Three D's

1oz. Dubonnet, 1oz. Drambuie, 1oz. Dry Vermouth,
3 dashes Angostura Bitters.

Stir and strain into a martini glass. Serve with a twist of orange.

Three Faces

1oz. Golden Rum, 1oz. Galliano, 1/2oz. Campari, Soda Water.

Build into an old-fashioned glass, topping with the soda.

Three Feathers

2oz. Three Feathers Canadian Whiskey, 1/2oz. Benedictine,
1 dash Maraschino Liqueur, 2 dashes Angostura Bitters.

Build into an old-fashioned glass.

Three Kings

1oz. Beefeater Gin, 1oz. Absolut Citron Vodka,
1oz. Noilly Prat Dry Vermouth.

Stir and strain into a martini glass. Serve with a twist of lemon.

Three Millers

2oz. White Rum, 1oz. Cognac, 2 dashes Grenadine, 1 dash Lemon Juice.

Shake and strain into a martini glass.

Thunder

2oz. Cognac, 1/4oz. Gomme Syrup, 1 Egg Yolk, 4 dashes Tabasco Sauce.

Shake and strain into a martini glass.

Thunder & Lightning

2oz. Cognac, 1oz. Cointreau, 1 Egg Yolk, 4 dashes Tabasco Sauce.

Shake and strain into a martini glass.
Sprinkle cayenne pepper on top of drink.

Thunderclap

1oz. Bourbon, 1oz. Cognac, 1oz. Gin.

Shake and strain into a martini glass.

Tiger's Milk

1 1/2oz. Cognac, 1 1/2oz. Sloe Gin.

Shake and strain into a martini glass. Serve with a twist of lemon.

Tipperary

1oz. Irish Whiskey, 1oz. Sweet Vermouth, 1oz. Green Chartreuse.

Shake and strain into a martini glass.

Tiptoes

1oz. Bourbon, 1oz. Gin, 1/2oz. Kirschwasser, 1/2oz. Sweet Vermouth.

Shake and strain into a martini glass.

TNT

1 1/2oz. Scotch, 1 1/2oz. Anisette.

Shake and strain into a martini glass.

Tokyo Traffic Light

(MICHAEL ROYSTON-YORKE)

1oz. Suntory Strawberry Liqueur, 1oz. Suntory Mango Liqueur, 1oz. Midori Melon Liqueur.

Layer into a chilled martini glass.

Top Notch

1½oz. Sloe Gin, 1½oz. Dry Vermouth, ¼oz. Crème de Framboise.

Build into an old-fashioned glass. Garnish with a cherry.

Torpedo

2oz. Calvados, 1oz. Cognac, ¼oz. Gin.

Shake and strain into a martini glass.

Transvaal

1½oz. Gin, 1½oz. Caperitif, 4 dashes Orange Bitters.

Stir and strain into a martini glass.

Trilby

2oz. Bourbon, 1oz. Sweet Vermouth, 2 dashes Orange Bitters.

Shake and strain into a martini glass.

Trinity

1oz. Gin, 1oz. Sweet Vermouth, 1oz. Dry Vermouth.

Shake and strain into a martini glass.

Trois Rivières

2oz. Canadian Club Whiskey, ½oz. Dubonnet, ½oz. Cointreau.

Stir and strain into a martini glass. Serve with a twist of orange.

Tropical

2oz. Cognac, 1oz. Galliano, 2 dashes Pimento Dram.

Shake and strain into a martini glass.

Tsarina

1 1/2oz. Vodka, 3/4oz. Dry Vermouth, 3/4oz. Apricot Brandy, 1 dash Angostura Bitters.

Shake and strain into a martini glass.

Tulip

1oz. Calvados, 1oz. Sweet Vermouth, 1/4oz. Apricot Brandy, 2 dashes Lemon Juice, 1/4oz. Gomme Syrup.

Shake and strain into a martini glass.

Turf

1oz. Gin, 1oz. Dry Vermouth, 1/4oz. Pernod, 1/4oz. Maraschino Liqueur.

Shake and strain into a martini glass. Serve with a twist of lemon.

Ulanda

2oz. Gin, 1oz. Triple Sec, 1 dash Anisette.

Stir and strain into a martini glass.

Une Idée

1oz. Gin, 1oz. Sweet Vermouth, 1oz. Cognac, 1/4oz. Apricot Brandy.

Shake and strain into a martini glass.

Union Jack

2oz. Gin, 1oz. Sloe Gin, 2 dashes Grenadine.

Shake and strain into a martini glass.

Union Jack 2

2oz. Gin, 1oz. Crème Yvette.

Shake and strain into a martini glass.

Vail

1 1/2oz. Rye Whiskey, 3/4oz. Benedictine, 3/4oz. Dry Vermouth.

Stir and strain into a martini glass.

Vampire

1oz. Gin, 1oz. Dry Vermouth, 2 dashes Lime Juice.

Shake and strain into a martini glass.

Van

2oz. Gin, 1oz. Dry Vermouth, 1/4oz. Grand Marnier.

Shake and strain into a martini glass.

Vanderbilt

2oz. Cognac, 1oz. Cherry Brandy, 1 dash Gomme Syrup, 2 dashes Angostura Bitters.

Shake and strain into a martini glass.

Varsity Blue

1oz. Vodka, 1oz. Blue Curaçao, 1/2oz. Parfait Amour, 1/2oz. Gin.

Shake and strain into a martini glass.

Velocity

2oz. Gin, 1oz. Sweet Vermouth, 1 slice Orange.

Crush the orange in a shaker and add remaining ingredients. Shake and strain into a martini glass. Serve with a twist of orange.

Velvet

1oz. Gin, 1oz. Dubonnet, 1/2oz. Mandarine Napoléon.

Stir and strain into a martini glass.

Vendôme

1oz. Gin, 1oz. Dubonnet, 1/2oz. Dry Vermouth.

Shake and strain into a martini glass. Serve with a twist of lemon.

Verboten

2oz. Gin, 1/2oz. Forbidden Fruit Liqueur, 1 dash Lemon Juice, 1 dash Orange Juice.

Shake and strain into a martini glass.

Vermont

1/2oz. Gin, 1/2oz. Benedictine, 1/2oz. Calvados, 1/2oz. Apricot Brandy, 1/2oz. Maple Syrup.

Shake and strain into a martini glass.

Vermouth Cassis

2oz. Dry Vermouth, 1oz. Crème de Cassis.

Build into an old-fashioned glass.

Vermouth Cocktail

1oz. Dry Vermouth, 1oz. Sweet Vermouth, 2 dashes Angostura Bitters.

Stir and strain into a martini glass. Garnish with a cherry.

Vermouth Cocktail 2

2oz. Dry Vermouth, 1 dash Anisette.

Stir and strain into a martini glass.

Vesper

(JAMES BOND'S VODKA MARTINI)

3oz. Gordon's Gin, 1oz. Vodka, 1/2oz. Kina Lillet.

Shake and strain into a deep-dish champagne saucer.
Serve with a twist of lemon.

Victor

1 1/2oz. Gin, 3/4oz. Cognac, 3/4oz. Sweet Vermouth.

Shake and strain into a martini glass.

VIP

1oz. Cointreau, 1oz. Bourbon, 1oz. Dry Vermouth.

Build into an old-fashioned glass. Garnish with a slice of orange.

Virgin Cocktail

2oz. Gin, 1oz. Forbidden Fruit Liqueur, 1oz. White Crème de Menthe.

Shake and strain into a martini glass.

Vodka Cobbler

3oz. Vodka, 1/4oz. Orange Curaçao, 1/4oz. Gomme Syrup.

Pour the vodka into an ice-filled wineglass.
Stir in the syrup and curaçao and garnish with seasonal fruits
and a sprig of mint.

Vodka Gibson

3oz. Vodka, 1 dash Dry Vermouth.

Stir and strain into a chilled martini glass.
Garnish with a silver skin cocktail onion.

Vodka Grasshopper

1oz. Green Crème de Menthe, 1oz. White Crème de Cacao, 1oz. Vodka.

Shake and strain into a martini glass.

Vodka Martini

3oz. Vodka, 1/4oz. Dry Vermouth.

Stir and strain into a frosted martini glass. Serve with a twist of lemon.

Vodka Mist

2oz. Vodka.

Pour into an old-fashioned glass filled with crushed ice.
Stir until glass is frosted.

Vodka Old-Fashioned

See chapter three, The Classics, (p. 65).
Substitute vodka for the bourbon in the old-fashioned.

Vodka Sangaree

2oz. Vodka, 3/4oz. Gomme Syrup.

Stir into an old-fashioned glass filled with crushed ice.
Sprinkle grated nutmeg on top and garnish with a slice of lemon.

Vodka Smash

2oz. Vodka, 1 tsp. granulated Sugar, 6 Mint Leaves, 1 tsp. Water.

Muddle the mint, sugar and water in an old-fashioned glass.
Fill with crushed ice and stir in the vodka.

Vodka Stinger

2oz. Vodka, 1oz. White Crème de Menthe.

Build into an old-fashioned glass.

Walters

2oz. Scotch, 1 dash Lemon Juice, 1 dash Orange Juice.
Shake and strain into a martini glass.

Wanda

2oz. Cognac, 1oz. Kümmel.
Stir and strain into a martini glass.

War Days

1oz. Gin, 1oz. Calvados, 1oz. Sweet Vermouth, 1 dash Green Chartreuse.
Shake and strain into a martini glass.

Ward Eight Cocktail

See chapter three, The Classics, (pp 57–62).
Substitute 2 pieces of orange peel for the olive in the dry martini.

Ward's Cocktail

1oz. Green Chartreuse, 1oz. Cognac, 1 long piece of Orange Peel.
Place the peel in a circle in the bottom of an old-fashioned glass.
Fill with crushed ice, pour in the spirits and garnish with a sprig of mint.

Warsaw

1 1/2oz. Vodka, 1oz. Crème de Mûre, 1/4oz. Dry Vermouth, 1 dash Lemon Juice.
Shake and strain into a martini glass.

Washington

2oz. Dry Vermouth, 1oz. Cognac, 1 dash Angostura Bitters,
1 dash Orange Bitters, 1 dash Gomme Syrup.
Stir and strain into a martini glass.

Wax

2oz. Gin, 4 dashes Orange Bitters.
Stir and strain into a martini glass. Garnish with a twist of orange.

Wembley

2oz. Gin, 1oz. Dry Vermouth, 2 dashes Calvados, 1 dash Apricot Brandy.
Stir and strain into a martini glass.

What The Hell

1oz. Gin, 1oz. Apricot Brandy, 1oz. Dry Vermouth, 1 dash Lemon Juice.
Shake and strain into a martini glass.

Which Way

1oz. Cognac, 1oz. Anisette, 1oz. Pastis.
Stir and strain into a martini glass.

Whip

2oz. Cognac, 1/2oz. Sweet Vermouth, 1/2oz. Dry Vermouth, 1/4oz. Cointreau, 1 dash Anisette.
Stir and strain into a martini glass.

Whip 2

3/4oz. Cognac, 3/4oz. Dry Vermouth, 3/4oz. Cointreau, 3/4oz. Pernod.
Shake and strain into a martini glass.

Whisky Bomb

2oz. Scotch, 1/4oz. Gomme Syrup, 2 dashes Angostura Bitters.
Stir and strain into a martini glass.

Whisky Cobbler

3oz. Scotch, 1/4oz. Orange Curaçao, 1/4oz. Gomme Syrup.
Pour the Scotch whisky into an ice-filled wineglass.
Stir in the sugar and curaçao and garnish with seasonal fruits and a sprig of mint.

Whisky Cocktail

3oz. Scotch, 3 dashes Angostura Bitters, 1/4oz. Gomme Syrup.
Stir and strain into a martini glass. Garnish with a cherry.

Whisky Mac

1 1/2oz. Scotch, 1oz. Stone's Ginger Wine.
Build into an old-fashioned glass.

Whisky Mist

2oz. Scotch.

Pour into an old-fashioned glass filled with crushed ice.
Stir until glass is frosted.

Whisky Old-Fashioned

See chapter three, The Classics, (p. 65).
Substitute Scotch whisky for the bourbon in the old-fashioned.

Whisky Sangaree

2oz. Scotch, 3/4oz. Gomme Syrup.

Stir into an old-fashioned glass filled with crushed ice.
Sprinkle grated nutmeg on top and garnish with a slice of lemon.

Whisky Smash

2oz. Scotch, 1 tsp. granulated Sugar, 6 Mint Leaves, 1 tsp. Water.

Muddle the mint, sugar and water in an old-fashioned glass.
Fill with crushed ice and stir in the Scotch whisky.

Whisky Squirt

2oz. Scotch, 1/4oz. Grenadine.

Shake and strain into an ice-filled old-fashioned glass.
Garnish with pineapple chunks and a cherry.

Whisky Stinger

2oz. Scotch, 1oz. White Crème de Menthe.

Build into an old-fashioned glass.

White Cocktail

2 1/4oz. Gin, 3/4oz. Anisette, 3 dashes Orange Bitters.

Stir and strain into a martini glass.

White Lady

See chapter three, The Classics, (pp 68–9).

White Lily

1oz. Cointreau, 1oz. Gin, 1oz. White Rum, 1 dash Anisette.

Stir and strain into a martini glass.

White Way

2oz. Gin, 1oz. White Crème de Menthe.

Shake and strain into a martini glass.

Widow's Kiss

$1\frac{1}{2}$oz. Cognac, $\frac{3}{4}$oz. Benedictine, $\frac{3}{4}$oz. Yellow Chartreuse, 2 dashes Angostura Bitters.

Shake and strain into a martini glass.

Widow's Kiss 2

$1\frac{1}{2}$oz. Calvados, $\frac{3}{4}$oz. Benedictine, $\frac{3}{4}$oz. Yellow Chartreuse, 2 dashes Angostura Bitters.

Shake and strain into a martini glass.

Wimbledon

1oz. Campari, 1oz. Dry Vermouth, $1\frac{1}{4}$oz. Tequila, $\frac{1}{4}$oz. Galliano, $\frac{1}{4}$oz. Peach Syrup.

Stir and strain into a champagne flute.
Garnish with a spiral of orange peel.

Windsor

2oz. Gin, 1oz. Green Crème de Menthe.

Stir and strain into a martini glass.

Windy Corner

2oz. Crème de Mûre, Nutmeg.

Stir into an old-fashioned glass filled with crushed ice.
Sprinkle grated nutmeg over drink.

Xanthia

1oz. Gin, 1oz. Cherry Brandy, 1oz. Yellow Chartreuse.

Stir and strain into a martini glass.

Yale

2oz. Gin, $\frac{3}{4}$oz. Dry Vermouth, 1 dash Angostura Bitters, 1 dash Blue Curaçao.
Stir and strain into a martini glass.

Yellow Daisy

$1\frac{1}{2}$oz. Gin, $1\frac{1}{2}$oz. Dry Vermouth, $\frac{3}{4}$oz. Grand Marnier, 1 dash Pernod.
Shake and strain into a martini glass.

Yellow Glow

1oz. Gin, 1oz. Sweet Vermouth, 1oz. Yellow Chartreuse.
Shake and strain into a martini glass.

Yellow Parrot

1oz. Apricot Brandy, 1oz. Anisette, 1oz. Yellow Chartreuse.
Shake and strain into a martini glass.

Yellow Sea 2

$1\frac{1}{2}$oz. Vodka, 1oz. White Rum, 1oz. Galliano, $\frac{1}{2}$oz. Maraschino Liqueur, 1 dash Lime Juice, 1 dash Gomme Syrup.
Shake and strain into a martini glass.

Yolanda

1oz. Sweet Vermouth, 1oz. Cognac, $\frac{1}{2}$oz. Gin, $\frac{1}{2}$oz. Anisette, 2 dashes Grenadine.
Shake and strain into a martini glass. Serve with a twist of orange.

Young Man

1oz. Cognac, 1oz. Dry Vermouth, $\frac{1}{4}$oz. Triple Sec, 2 dashes Angostura Bitters.
Stir and strain into a martini glass.

Yvette

2oz. Gin, 1oz. Crème Yvette, $\frac{1}{4}$oz. Gomme Syrup, 1 dash Angostura Bitters.
Shake and strain into a martini glass.

Zaza

2oz. Gin, 1oz. Dubonnet, 1 dash Angostura (optional).

Stir and strain into a martini glass. Serve with a twist of orange.

Zaza 2

2oz. Dubonnet, 1oz. Gin, 1 dash Orange Bitters (optional).

Stir and strain into a martini glass. Serve with a twist of orange.

Zazerac

1oz. Rye Whiskey, 1/2oz. White Rum, 1/2oz. Anisette, 1/4oz. Pastis, 1/2oz. Gomme Syrup, 1 dash Orange Bitters, 1 dash Angostura Bitters.

Shake and strain into a martini glass.

Zephyr

2oz. Cognac, 1/4oz. Maraschino Liqueur, 2 dashes Pineapple Syrup, 2 dashes Triple Sec, 2 dashes Angostura Bitters.

Shake and strain into a martini glass that has been wiped with lemon peel.

LONG MIXED DRINKS

▼

The drinks featured in this section do not fall into any of the specific categories of the following chapters. These are drinks that exploit the full range of spirits and liqueurs, combining them with a variety of juices and sodas, syrups, bitters and other natural ingredients. The taste sensations range from sweet to sharp, fruity to sour and dry to bitter. In general, the long drink has a greater proportion of non-alcoholic constituent (juice, etc.) than the short drink.

Adios Amigos

1½oz. White Rum, 1oz. Gin, ½oz. Dry Vermouth, 1 dash of Cognac, 1½oz. Lemon Juice.

Shake and pour into a highball glass.

Affair

2oz. Crème de Fraises, 3oz. Orange Juice, 3oz. Cranberry Juice.

Shake and pour into a highball glass.

Alcudia

2oz. Gin, 1oz. Crème de Banane, 1oz. Galliano, 1oz. Grapefruit Juice.

Shake and pour into a highball glass.

Alleluia

3oz. Tequila, 1oz. Blue Curaçao, 1oz. Lemon Juice, ½oz. Maraschino, Tonic Water or Bitter Lemon.

Shake and pour into a highball glass, top with the tonic or bitter lemon and serve with a slice of orange.

Alma

2oz. Mandarine Napoléon, 1oz. Vodka, 1/2oz. Campari, 2oz. Grapefruit Juice.

Shake and pour into a large goblet.

Almond Blossom

1 1/2oz. Crème de Noyaux, 1oz. Amaretto, 3oz. Orange Juice.

Shake and strain into an ice-filled highball glass.

American Whiskey Cooler

2oz. Bourbon or Rye Whiskey, 1oz. Lime Juice, 1/2oz. Gomme Syrup, Ginger Beer.

Shake all but the ginger beer and pour into a highball glass. Top with the ginger beer and garnish with an orange peel spiral.

Amigo

2oz. Vodka, 1oz. Apricot Brandy, 5oz. Lemon Juice, 1/2oz. Grenadine, 3 dashes Angostura Bitters, 1 dash Pineapple Juice.

Shake and pour into a highball glass.

Animaniac

1oz. Dark Rum, 1/2oz. Captain Morgan's Spiced Rum, 1oz. Crème de Fraises, 4oz. Orange Juice, 1 dash Grenadine.

Shake and pour into a highball glass. Garnish with two melon balls.

Apricot Cooler

2oz. Apricot Brandy, 1/2oz. Grenadine, 1oz. Orange Juice, 1 dash Lemon Juice.

Shake and pour into a highball glass and top with lemonade.

Arcadia

2oz. Gin, 1oz. Galliano, 1oz. Crème de Banane, 3oz. Grapefruit Juice.

Shake and pour into a highball glass.

Astronaut

1oz. Vodka, 1oz. White Rum, 1oz. Lemon Juice, 3oz. Passion Fruit Juice.

Shake and pour into a highball glass.

Atlantic

2oz. Vodka, 1½oz. Strega, 3oz. Orange Juice, 1 Egg Yolk.
Shake and strain into a deep-dish champagne saucer.

Bahama Mama

1oz. Dark Rum, ½oz. Kahlúa, ½oz. Overproof Rum, 1oz. Coconut Liqueur, 1oz. Lemon Juice, 4oz. Pineapple Juice.
Build into a highball glass.

Bahama Sunrise

2oz. Mount Gay Gold Rum, 1½oz. Galliano, 4oz. Grapefruit Juice.
Shake and strain into an ice-filled highball glass.
Garnish with a sprig of mint.

Bartender

1oz. Dubonnet, 1oz. Dry Vermouth, 1oz. Sweet Vermouth, 3oz. Orange Juice, 2 dashes Angostura Bitters.
Shake and pour into a highball glass.

Bay Breeze

2oz. Vodka, 2oz. Cranberry Juice, 2oz. Pineapple Juice.
Shake and pour into a large goblet.

Beachcomber Belle

2oz. Dark Rum, 4oz. Grapefruit Juice, Ginger Beer.
Build into a highball glass and top with the ginger beer.

Beer Buster

2oz. 100 Proof Vodka, 5 dashes Tabasco Sauce, Bottled Lager.
Pour the vodka into a highball glass and top up with the lager.
Add the tabasco, stir and serve.

Big Chill

1oz. Midori Melon Liqueur, 1oz. White Rum, ½oz. Crème de Banane, 3oz. Pineapple
Build into a highball glass.

Bitter Melon

2oz. Midori Melon Liqueur, 6oz. Bitter Lemon.

Build into a highball glass.

Blondie

1oz. Vodka, 1oz. Peach Brandy, 1oz. Apricot Brandy, 2oz. Orange Juice, 1oz. Lemon Juice.

Shake and pour into a highball glass.

Blue Lagoon

1oz. Vodka, 1½oz. Blue Curaçao, Lemonade.

Build into a highball glass, topping with the lemonade.

Blue Mountain

1oz. Tia Maria, 1oz. Dark Rum, 1oz. Gomme Syrup, 5oz. Blue Mountain Coffee.

Shake and strain into a highball glass.

Blushing Barmaid

1oz. Campari, 1oz. Amaretto, 1 Egg White, Bitter Lemon.

Shake and strain into an ice-filled highball glass and top with the bitter lemon.

Boomerang

1oz. Gin, 1oz. Cognac, 1oz. Peach Brandy, 3oz. Orange Juice.

Shake and pour into a highball glass.

Bora Bora

2oz. Vodka, 3oz. Cranberry Juice, 2oz. Peach Juice.

Shake and pour into a highball glass.

Boston Blue Tea

1oz. Vodka, 1oz. Blue Curaçao, 1oz. Gin, ½oz. Tequila, ½oz. White Rum, Juice of 1 Lemon, Lemonade.

Shake all but the lemonade and pour into a napoli grande glass. Top with lemonade and serve.

Boston Gold

2oz. Vodka, 1oz. Crème de Banane, Orange Juice.
Build into a highball glass and top with the orange juice.

Brooklyn Bomber

1oz. Tequila, 1oz. Cherry Brandy, 1/2oz. Galliano, 1/2oz. Orange Curaçao, 1oz. Lemon Juice, 1 dash Grenadine.
Shake and pour into a large goblet.

Buckaroo

2oz. Bourbon, 2 dashes Angostura Bitters, Cola.
Build into a highball glass and top with the cola.

Bullfrog

2oz. Vodka, 6oz. Lemonade.
Build into a highball glass.

Cadillac Iced Tea

1oz. Tequila, 1oz. Vodka, 1oz. Grand Marnier, 1/2oz. Gin, 1/2oz. White Rum, 1oz. Lemon Juice, Cola.
Shake all but the cola and pour into a napoli grande glass.
Top with the cola.

California

2oz. Vodka, 4oz. Grapefruit Juice, 2oz. Orange Juice.
Build into a highball glass.

Calimero

2oz. Cognac, 1oz. Tia Maria, 1/2oz. Grand Marnier, 1oz. Orange Juice, 1/2oz. Lemon Juice, 1 Egg White.
Shake and pour into a highball glass.

Campari Citrus

(PAUL BOLLES-BEAVEN)

2oz. Campari, 6oz. Orangina, 1 dash Lime Juice.
Stir the campari and lime in an ice-filled highball and top with the orangina. Garnish with a slice of orange.

Campari Clipper

2oz. Campari, 2oz. Orange Juice, 2oz. Cranberry Juice, 1 dash Amaretto.
Shake and strain into an ice-filled highball glass.
Garnish with a slice of lime.

Campari Nobile

(SALVATORE CALABRESE)

2oz. Campari, 2oz. Vodka, 1oz. Lemoncello, 2oz. Raspberry Juice, 1oz. Bitter Lemon, 1 dash Grenadine.
Shake and strain into a sugar-rimmed old-fashioned glass.
Garnish with a sprig of mint.

Cape Cod Cooler

2oz. Vodka, 4oz. Cranberry Juice, 2oz. Lemonade.
Build into a highball glass.

Cape Codder

2oz. Vodka, 4oz. Cranberry Juice.
Shake and pour into a highball glass.

Car Crash

1oz. Southern Comfort, 1oz. White Crème de Cacao, 1oz. Cointreau, 1oz. Lime Juice, 2oz. Lemonade.
Build into a highball glass.

Cherry Blossom

2oz. Cherry Brandy, 1/2oz. Gin, 1/2oz. Grenadine, 3oz. Orange Juice, 1oz. Lemon Juice.
Shake and pour into a highball glass.

Cider Cocktail

4oz. Chilled Cider, 1oz. Calvados, 3 dashes Angostura Bitters.
Stir together in an ice-filled highball glass.

Cider Cup

2 pints Chilled Cider, 3oz. Cognac, 3oz. Calvados, 2oz. Maraschino Liqueur.
Stir together with 10–15 ice-cubes in a large jug. Garnish with sliced apple soaked in lemon juice. Serve in a highball glass.

Clansman

1oz. White Rum, 1oz. Apricot Brandy, 2oz. Orange Juice, 1oz. Lemon Juice, 1 Egg White.
Shake and pour into a highball glass.

Clark Bar

1oz. Amaretto, 1oz. Brown Crème de Cacao, 4oz. Orange Juice.
Build into a highball glass.

Cool Dude

1 1/2oz. Cachaça, 3/4oz. Blue Curaçao, 1oz. Lime Juice, 3oz. Lemonade.
Build into a highball glass.

Cooler Than You Think

1oz. Gin, 1/2oz. Vodka, 2oz. Grapefruit Juice, 3oz. Cranberry Juice.
Shake and pour into a highball glass.

Coral Reef

2oz. Advocaat, 4oz. Pineapple Juice, 1oz. Lime Juice.
Shake and pour into a highball glass.

Cranapple

1oz. Calvados, 1oz. Apfel Korn (Apple Schnapps), 4oz. Cranberry Juice.
Shake and pour into a highball glass.

Cranberry Cooler

1oz. Vodka, 1oz. Amaretto, 2oz. Orange Juice, 2oz. Cranberry Juice.
Shake and pour into a highball glass.

Creamy Screwdriver

2oz. Vodka, 5oz. Orange Juice, 1 Egg Yolk, 1/2oz. Gomme Syrup.
Shake and pour into a highball glass.

Danish Dynamite

(FREDDIE TOFTE HANSEN)

1oz. Cointreau, 1oz. Gin, $^{1}/_{2}$oz. Campari, $2^{1}/_{2}$oz. Orange Juice.

Shake and strain into an ice-filled highball glass.

Add a splash of soda and garnish with a slice of orange.

Danish Mary

See chapter three, The Classics, (pp 50–1).

Substitute aquavit for the vodka in the Bloody Mary.

Deadly Mary

1oz. Vodka, 1oz. Tequila, 4oz. Tomato Juice, 1 dash Tabasco Sauce, 2 dashes Worcestershire Sauce, 2 dashes Lemon Juice.

Shake and pour into a highball glass.

Dizzy Blonde

2oz. Advocaat, 1oz. Pernod, 5oz. Lemonade.

Build into a highball glass.

Dracula's Bite

(CHRIS YORK)

$1^{1}/_{2}$oz. Gin, $1^{1}/_{2}$oz. Campari, $1^{1}/_{2}$oz. Orange Juice, 1 dash Crème de Cassis.

Build into a highball glass and stir.

Garnish with a slice of orange peel wrapped around a cherry.

Dubonnet Cassis

2oz. Dubonnet, 1oz. Crème de Cassis, Perrier.

Build into a highball glass, topping with the Perrier.

El Cerro

1oz. Dark Rum, 1oz. White Rum, $^{1}/_{2}$oz. Galliano, $^{1}/_{2}$oz. Orange Curaçao, 2oz. Pineapple Juice, 1 dash Grenadine.

Shake and pour into a highball glass. Garnish with strawberries.

Electric Lemonade

1oz. Vodka, 1oz. Triple sec, 3/4oz. Gin, 3/4oz. White Rum, 1oz. Lemon Juice, Lemonade.

Shake all but the lemonade and pour into a highball glass. Top with the lemonade.

Elm Creek

1oz. Vodka, 1oz. Gold Tequila, 3/4oz. Gin, 3/4oz. White Rum, 1oz. Rose's Lime Cordial, Orange Juice.

Build into a highball glass, topping with the orange.

Elmer Fudpucker

2oz. Apricot Brandy, 1oz. Vodka, 1oz. Gin, 3oz. Orange Juice.

Shake and pour into a highball glass.

Evergreen

1oz. Tequila, 1oz. Green Crème de Menthe, 1/2oz. Midori Melon Liqueur, 2oz. Grapefruit Juice, 2oz. Pineapple Juice.

Shake and pour into a highball glass.

Firecracker 500

1oz. Wild Turkey 101 Bourbon, 1oz. Absolut 100 Vodka, 1oz. Green Chartreuse, 1oz. Southern Comfort, 1oz. Bacardi 151 Rum, 1 dash Orange Juice, 1 dash Lemon Juice, 1 dash Grenadine.

Shake and pour into a highball glass. (Warning: This is the most potent cocktail in the entire volume. It is equivalent to consuming over 12 units of alcohol. If you decide to try this cocktail, use 1/4oz. of each spirit instead of the full 1oz.)

Fireman's Sour

2oz. White Rum, 1 dash Grenadine, 1 dash Gomme Syrup, Juice of 2 Limes.

Shake and pour into a highball glass. Fill with soda if desired.

First Noel

1oz. Campari, 1oz. Peach Schnapps, 4oz. Orange Juice, 1 dash Egg White.

Shake and strain into a wineglass and garnish with a slice of orange and three cherries.

Flamboyant

1oz. White Rum, 1oz. Dark Rum, $^1/_2$oz. Apricot Brandy, $^1/_2$oz. Orange Curaçao, 2oz. Orange Juice, 1oz. Lemon Juice, 1 dash Grenadine, 1 dash Orgeat, 1oz. Wood's 100 Dark Rum.

Shake all but the Wood's and pour into a large goblet. Float the Wood's on top.

Floor Polish

2oz. Gin, $^1/_2$oz. Dry Vermouth, $^1/_2$oz. Sweet Vermouth, 2oz. Pineapple Juice.

Shake and pour into a highball glass.

Floridian

1oz. Gin, 1oz. Dark Rum, 4oz. Orange Juice.

Shake and pour into an old-fashioned glass. Serve with a twist of orange.

Fluffy Duck

1oz. Advocaat, 1oz. Gin, 1oz. Cointreau, $^1/_2$oz. Orange Juice, Soda.

Build into a highball glass, topping with the soda.

Flying Fish

2oz. Gin, 1oz. Peach Schnapps, 1oz. Grand Marnier, 2oz. Lemon Juice, Lemonade.

Shake and pour into a highball glass, topping with the lemonade.

Formula 1

1$^1/_4$oz. Bell's Scotch, $^3/_4$oz. Galliano, 2oz. Orange Juice, $^1/_4$oz. Lime Juice, Soda.

Build into a highball glass, topping with the soda.

Freddy Fudpucker

1oz. Gold Tequila, 1oz. Galliano, 4oz. Orange Juice.

Shake and pour into a highball glass.

Free Breeze

2oz. Vodka, 1oz. Cointreau, 1oz. Grapefruit Juice, 3oz. Cranberry Juice.

Shake and pour into a highball glass.

Frog
2oz. Midori Melon Liqueur, Lemonade.
Build into a highball glass, topping with the lemonade.

Frosty Amour
1oz. Vodka, 1oz. Southern Comfort, 1oz. Parfait Amour, 1 dash Crème de Banane, 1 dash Apricot Brandy, Lemonade.
Build into a highball glass, topping with the lemonade.

Funky Monkey
1oz. Crème de Banane, 1oz. White Rum, 4oz. Orange Juice.
Shake and pour into a highball glass.

Fuzzy Navel
2oz. Peach Schnapps, 4oz. Orange Juice.
Shake and pour into a highball glass.

Fuzzy Prick
2oz. Peach Schnapps, 4oz. Pineapple Juice.
Shake and pour into a highball glass.

Galley Slave
2oz. Galliano, 1 dash Angostura Bitters, 4oz. Orange Juice.
Shake and strain into a highball glass.

Gentle Ben
1oz. Vodka, 1oz. Tequila, 1oz. Gin, 3oz. Orange Juice.
Shake and pour into a highball glass.

Geronimo
1oz. White Rum, 1 dash Angostura Bitters, 1 dash Grenadine, 1oz. Orange Juice, 1oz. Pineapple Juice, 1/2oz. Lime Juice.
Shake and strain into an ice-filled highball glass.

Ghost Buster

1½oz. Vodka, 1½oz. Midori Melon Liqueur, 2oz. Pineapple Juice, 2oz. Orange Juice.

Shake and pour into a highball glass.

Gin Squirt

2oz. Gin, 1oz. Gomme Syrup, 1 dash Grenadine, Soda.

Build into a highball glass, topping with the soda. Stir and garnish with strawberries.

Gold Driver

2oz. Gold Tequila, 4oz. Orange Juice.

Shake and pour into a highball glass.

Golden Bull

2oz. Amaretto, 1oz. Southern Comfort, 4oz. Orange Juice, Lemonade.

Shake all but the lemonade and pour into a highball glass. Top with the lemonade.

Golden Friendship

1oz. White Rum, 1oz. Sweet Vermouth, 1oz. Amaretto, Ginger Ale.

Build into a highball glass, topping with the ginger ale.

Goldie

1½oz. White Rum, 1oz. Cherry Brandy, 1oz. Cointreau, 1½oz. Orange Juice, Lemonade.

Shake and pour into a highball glass. Top with the lemonade.

Granada

1oz. Campari, 1oz. Mandarine Napoléon, 1oz. Gin, Juice of 1 Lemon.

Shake and pour into a highball glass.

Green Demon

1oz. Midori Melon Liqueur, 1oz. Vodka, 1oz. White Rum, Lemonade.

Build into a large goblet, topping with the lemonade.

Green Gilbert

1oz. Amaretto, 1oz. Blue Curaçao, 1oz. Lemon Juice, 2oz. Orange Juice.
Shake and pour into a medium goblet.

Green Goddess

2oz. Scotch, 1oz. Midori Melon Liqueur, 1/4oz. Dry Vermouth, Lemonade.
Build into a highball glass, topping with the lemonade.

Greenland

1 1/2oz. Midori Melon Liqueur, 1 1/2oz. White Wine, Tonic Water.
Build into a highball glass, topping with the tonic.

Green Meanie

1oz. Midori Melon Liqueur, 1/2oz. Vodka, 1/2oz. Blue Curaçao, 2oz. Pineapple Juice.
Shake and pour into a highball glass.

Green Star 2

1oz. Midori Melon Liqueur, 1oz. Vodka, 1/2oz. Apricot Brandy, 1oz. Pineapple Juice, 1oz. Orange Juice.
Shake and pour into a highball glass.

Greyhound

2oz. Gin, 6oz. Grapefruit Juice.
Build into a highball glass.

Grizzly Bear

2oz. Southern Comfort, 1/2oz. Grenadine, 4oz. Grapefruit Juice.
Shake and pour into a highball glass.

Guglia

(DAVIDE CAMPARI MILANO)

1oz. Campari, 1oz. Vodka, 1/2oz. Papaya Syrup, 2 1/2oz. Orangina.
Build into a highball glass. Garnish with a slice of orange.

Hadrian's Wall

2oz. Scotch, 1oz. Galliano, 4oz. Orange Juice.

Build into a highball glass, floating the Galliano on top.

Hairless Duck

1 1/2oz. Vodka, 1 1/2oz. Advocaat, 3/4oz. White Rum, 3oz. Orange Juice.

Shake and pour into a highball glass.

Hairy Navel

1oz. Peach Schnapps, 1oz. Vodka, 4oz. Orange Juice.

Shake and pour into a highball glass.

Hanky-Panky

1oz. Vodka, 1oz. White Rum, 1oz. Galliano, 1oz. Pineapple Juice, 1/2oz. Grenadine.

Shake and pour into a large goblet.

Happy Hour

1oz. White Rum, 1/2oz. Crème de Fraises, 1/2oz. Peach Schnapps, 1/2oz. Grenadine, 4oz. Orange Juice.

Shake and pour into a highball glass.

Harvey Wallbanger

2oz. Vodka, 1oz. Galliano, 5oz. Orange Juice.

Build into a highball glass and float the Galliano on top.

High Diver

1oz. Montezuma Silver Tequila, Lemonade.

Build into a highball glass, topping with the lemonade.

Hope

1oz. Midori Melon Liqueur, 1oz. White Rum, 1oz. Triple Sec, 1oz. Lychee Syrup, 1oz. Lime Juice.

Shake and pour into a highball glass.

Hula Koola

2oz. Crème de Fraises, 4oz. Pineapple Juice.
Shake and pour into a highball glass.

Ice-Pick

2oz. Gold Tequila, 5oz. Lipton Ice (Chilled Lemon Tea).
Build into a highball glass.

Illusion 2

1½oz. Cointreau, 1oz. Midori Melon Liqueur, 1oz. Vodka, 1oz. Orange Juice, ½oz. Lime Juice.
Shake and pour into a highball glass.

In-cider

2oz. Scotch, 6oz. Apple Cider.
Build into a highball glass.

Indian Summer 2

1oz. Scotch, ½oz. Campari, 2 dashes Angostura Bitters, 6oz. Indian Tonic Water.
Build into a napoli grande glass.

Ipanema Sunset

1oz. Grand Marnier, 1oz. Orange Curaçao, 2oz. Lemon Juice, 1oz. Orange Juice, 1 dash Grenadine.
Shake and pour into a large goblet.

Irish Cola

1oz. Irish Whiskey, 1oz. Bailey's, 4oz. Cola.
Shake all but the cola and strain into an ice-filled old-fashioned glass. Top with the cola.

Jack's Apple

1oz. Scotch, 1 dash Campari, 6oz. Appletize.
Build into a highball glass.

Jamaica Granito

1½oz. Cognac, 1oz. Cointreau, 1 scoop Lemon Water Ice, 3oz. Soda Water.
Build into a highball glass.

Jamaican Dust

1oz. Dark Rum, 1oz. Tia Maria, 1 dash Rose's Lime Cordial, 4oz. Pineapple Juice.
Shake and pour into a highball glass.

Japanese Slipper

1oz. Tequila, 1oz. Midori Melon Liqueur, 1oz. Lemon Juice, 1oz. Lime Juice, 1 Egg White.
Shake and strain into a sugar-rimmed salude grande glass.

Japanese Slipper 2

1oz. Cognac, 1oz. Midori Melon Liqueur, 1oz. Orange Juice, 1oz. Pineapple Juice, ½oz. Lemon Juice.
Shake and pour into a highball glass.

Jealous June

1oz. Cointreau, 1oz. Midori Melon Liqueur, ½oz. White Rum, 4oz. Pineapple Juice.
Shake and pour into a highball glass.

J.J.'s Best

1oz. Midori Melon Liqueur, 1oz. White Rum, ½oz. White Crème de Cacao, 2oz. Pineapple Juice.
Shake and pour into a highball glass. Garnish with a cherry.

Key West

(MARK JONES)

1oz. Midori Melon Liqueur, 1oz. Vodka, 1oz. Peach Schnapps, ¼oz. Malibu, 1oz. Orange Juice, 1oz. Cranberry Juice.
Shake and pour into a highball glass.

Killer Zombie

1oz. Dark Rum, 1oz. White Rum, 1oz. Apricot Brandy, 1oz. Orange Juice, 1oz. Pineapple Juice, 1/2oz. Lemon Juice.

Shake and pour into a large goblet.

King's Cross

(RICHARD ASPINALL)

1oz. Campari, 1oz. Amaretto, 1 dash Angostura Bitters, 6oz. Bitter Lemon.

Build into a highball glass. Garnish with a slice of orange.

Kriss

1oz. Cognac, 3/4oz. Amaretto, 1/2oz. Dry Vermouth, 1/4oz. Gomme Syrup, Tonic Water.

Build into a highball glass, topping with the tonic.

LA Iced Tea

1oz. Vodka, 1oz. Midori Melon Liqueur, 1oz. Gin, 1/2oz. White Rum, 1/2oz. Triple Sec, 1oz. Lemon Juice, Lemonade.

Shake all but the lemonade and pour into a napoli grande glass. Top with the lemonade.

Light Of Havana

(MERCEDES GAMBOA)

1oz. Midori Melon Liqueur, 1oz. Malibu, 1oz. Orange Juice, 1oz. Pineapple Juice, 1 dash Soda.

Shake and pour into a highball glass.

Li'l Devil

1 1/2oz. 100 Proof Gin, 1oz. Lemon Juice, 3oz. Lemonade.

Build into a highball glass.

Limbo

2oz. Crème de Pêche, 4oz. Pineapple Juice.

Build into a highball glass.

Liquid Valium

1oz. Cognac, 1oz. Golden Rum, 1oz. Galliano, 4oz. Lemonade.

Build into a highball glass.

Long Beach Iced Tea

1oz. Vodka, 1oz. Tequila, 1oz. Gin, 1/2oz. White Rum, 1/2oz. Triple Sec, 1oz. Lemon Juice, Cranberry Juice.

Shake all but the cranberry juice and pour into a napoli grande glass. Top with the cranberry juice.

Long Black Russian

1oz. Kahlúa, 1oz. Vodka, 4oz. Cola.

Build into an old-fashioned glass.

Long Hot Summer

1 1/2oz. Scotch, 1/2oz. Campari, 6oz. Lemonade.

Build into a highball glass. Garnish with three slices orange.

Long Island Iced Tea

1oz. Vodka, 1oz. Tequila, 1oz. Gin, 1/2oz. White Rum, 1/2oz. Triple Sec, 1oz. Lemon Juice, Cola.

Shake all but the cola and pour into a napoli grande glass. Top with the cola.

Long Island Lemonade

1oz. Vodka, 1oz. Tequila, 1oz. Gin, 1/2oz. White Rum, 1/2oz. Triple Sec, 1oz. Lemon Juice, Lemonade.

Shake all but the lemonade and pour into a napoli grande glass. Top with the lemonade.

Lucky Summer

1oz. Scotch, 1oz. Grand Marnier, 1/2oz. Cointreau, 1 1/2oz. Orange Juice, 1/2oz. Lemon Juice, 1 dash Grenadine.

Shake and pour into a highball glass.

Lynchburg Lemonade

1 1/2oz. Jack Daniel's, 1oz. Triple Sec, 1oz. Lemon Juice, Lemonade.

Shake and pour into a highball glass, topping with the lemonade.

Madness Becomes You

2oz. Apricot Brandy, 1oz. Grand Marnier, 2 dashes Punt e Mes, 3oz. Orange Juice, 1oz. Tonic Water.

Build into a highball glass.

Madras

2oz. Vodka, 2oz. Orange Juice, 4oz. Cranberry Juice.

Build into a highball glass.

Mai Tai

2oz. White Rum, 1/2oz. Cointreau, 2oz. Lime Juice, 1/2oz. Orgeat Syrup.

Shake and pour into a highball glass.

Mai Tai 2

1oz. White Rum, 1oz. Orange Curaçao, 1/2oz. Apricot Brandy, 1oz. Dark Overproof Rum, 1 dash Orgeat Syrup, 1 dash Grenadine, 1oz. Lime Juice, 1oz. Orange Juice.

Shake all but the dark rum and pour into a large goblet. Float the rum on top.

Maître D'

1 1/2oz. Crème de Banane, 1oz. Tequila, 1 dash Grenadine, 1oz. Lemon Juice, 2oz. Orange Juice, 1 Egg Yolk.

Shake and strain into an ice-filled highball glass.

Malibu Driver

2oz. Malibu, 4oz. Orange Juice.

Build into a highball glass.

Manila Fizz

2oz. Gin, 1/2oz. Gomme Syrup, 2oz. Root Beer, 1oz. Lime Juice, 1 Egg.

Shake and strain into an ice-filled highball glass.

Man Overboard

1oz. White Rum, 1oz. Bourbon, 1oz. Apricot Brandy, 1oz. Lemon Juice, 1 dash Lime Cordial.

Build into a highball glass.

Marmalade

2oz. Orange Curaçao, 6oz. Tonic Water.
Build into a highball glass.

Matador

2oz. Gold Tequila, 4oz. Pineapple Juice.
Build into a highball glass.

Maul Midori

1oz. Midori Melon Liqueur, 1/2oz. Malibu, 1/2oz. White Rum, 4oz. Apple Juice.
Build into a highball glass.

Ma Ziegel

1oz. Dark Rum, 1oz. Mount Gay Golden Rum, 4oz. Pineapple Juice.
Build into a highball glass.

Melon Ball

1oz. Midori Melon Liqueur, 1oz. Vodka, 3oz. Pineapple Juice.
Shake and pour into an old-fashioned glass.
Garnish with honeydew melon balls.

Melon Collins

See chapter three, The Classics, (p. 52).
Substitute Midori Melon Liqueur for the gin in the Collins.

Melon Driver

2oz. Midori Melon Liqueur, 4oz. Orange Juice.
Shake and pour into a highball glass.

Melon Pearl Diver

2oz. Midori Melon Liqueur, 2oz. Noix de Coco, 2oz. Pineapple Juice.
Shake and pour into a highball glass.

Menage à Trois

1oz. Vodka, 1oz. White Crème de Cacao, 4oz. Cranberry Juice.
Shake and pour into a highball glass.

Mexicano

1oz. Puerto Rican Rum, 1oz. Tequila, 2oz. Pineapple Juice, 1oz. Orange Juice, 1 dash Grenadine.
Shake and pour into a highball glass.

Mexicola

2oz. Tequila, 1oz. Lime Juice, 6oz. Cola.
Build into a highball glass.

Midori Beachcomber

2oz. Midori Melon Liqueur, 1/2oz. Gomme Syrup, 4oz. Grapefruit Juice.
Shake and pour into a highball glass.

Midori Dawn

1oz. Midori Melon Liqueur, 1oz. Vodka, 4oz. Tonic Water.
Build into a highball glass.

Midori On The Beach

(PHILIPPE GENTAL)

1oz. Midori Melon Liqueur, 1oz. Vodka, 4oz. Pineapple Juice.
Shake and pour into a highball glass.

Midori Sharp

1 1/2oz. Midori Melon Liqueur, 7oz. Grapefruit Juice.
Build into a highball glass.

Mint Cocktail

3oz. White Crème de Menthe, 1oz. Gin, 2oz. Lime Juice, 1 dash Angostura Bitters, 2oz. Soda Water.
Build into a highball glass.

Missouri Mule

2oz. Southern Comfort, 6oz. Ginger Beer.
Build into a highball glass.

Mockingbird

2oz. Tequila, 4oz. Grapefruit Juice, 1oz. Lime Juice.
Shake and pour into a highball glass.

Monopoly

2oz. Crème de Fraises, 1oz. Crème de Cassis, 1/2oz. Grenadine, 4oz. Cranberry Juice.
Shake and pour into a highball glass.

Moscow Mule

2oz. Vodka, 1oz. Lime Juice, 6oz. Ginger Beer.
Build into a highball glass. Garnish with a wedge of lime.

Mother's Day-Dream

(NATALIE MISON)

1oz. Midori Melon Liqueur, 1oz. Gin, 1oz. Lemon Juice, 4oz. Lemonade, 4 drops Blue Curaçao.
Build into a highball glass and drop the curaçao over the top.

National

2oz. White Rum, 1oz. Apricot Brandy, 2oz. Pineapple Juice, 1oz. Lime Juice.
Shake and pour into a highball glass.

Night Time

2oz. Kahlúa, 1oz. Crème de Mûre, 5oz. Cola.
Build into a highball glass.

Novo

2oz. Strega, 1oz. Lime Juice, 1 Egg Yolk, 5oz. Lemonade.
Shake all but the lemonade and strain into a highball glass. Top with the lemonade.

Nutty Wallbanger

2oz. Vodka, 1oz. Frangelico, 1oz. Galliano, 4oz. Orange Juice.
Build into a highball glass.

Old Bag

1oz. Tequila, 1oz. Apple Schnapps, 4oz. Cranberry Juice.
Build into a highball glass.

Old Bill

2oz. Blue Curaçao, 1oz. Crème de Cassis, 4oz. Cranberry Juice, 4oz. Apple Juice.
Shake and pour into a napoli grande glass.

Old Gold

2oz. Golden Rum, 1/2oz. Grand Marnier, 2 dashes Angostura Bitters, 3oz. Apple Juice.
Shake and pour into a highball glass.

Omega

2oz. Crème de Fraises, 1oz. Gomme Syrup, 4oz. Cranberry Juice.
Shake and pour into a highball glass.

One Fine Day

1oz. Vodka, 1oz. Crème de Pêche, 1oz. Lemon Juice, 1oz. Orange Juice, 1 tsp. Honey.
Shake and pour into a highball glass.

Orange Blossom

2oz. Gin, 4oz. Orange Juice, 1/4oz. Gomme Syrup.
Build into a highball glass.

Orange Oasis

2 1/4oz. Gin, 3/4oz. Cherry Brandy, 6oz. Orange Juice, Ginger Ale.
Build into a highball glass, topping with the ginger ale.

Pacific Coast

1oz. Cointreau, 1oz. Vodka, 2 dashes Angostura Bitters, Juice of 1/2 Orange.
Shake and pour into a highball glass.

Pain In The Neck

$1\frac{1}{2}$oz. Vodka, 1oz. Spiced Rum, $\frac{1}{2}$oz. Crème de Fraises, 4oz. Cranberry Juice, 1oz. Lemonade.

Build into a highball glass.

Palm Tree

1oz. Dark Rum, 1oz. Crème de Banane, 4oz. Banana Juice, 1oz. Cranberry Juice.

Shake and pour into a highball glass.

Peach Blossom

1oz. Gin, 1oz. Crème de Pêche, 4oz. Orange Juice.

Shake and pour into a highball glass.

Pearl Harbour

2oz. Vodka, 1oz. Crème de Fraises, $\frac{1}{2}$oz. Midori Melon Liqueur, 2oz. Pineapple Juice.

Shake and pour into a highball glass.

Percolator

1oz. Tia Maria, 1oz. Cognac, $\frac{1}{2}$oz. Bailey's, $\frac{1}{2}$oz. Gomme Syrup, 3oz. Cold Black Coffee.

Shake and pour into a highball glass. Sprinkle grated chocolate over drink.

Pimm's Cocktail

See chapter three, The Classics, (p. 66).

Plantation

3oz. Dark Rum, 3 dashes Grenadine, 6oz. Lemonade, 4 Sprigs Mint.

Place the mint in a napoli grande glass and fill with ice. Stir in the remaining ingredients.

Planter's Punch

2oz. White Rum, 2oz. Lime Juice, 1oz. Gomme Syrup, 1 dash Grenadine, 2 dashes Angostura Bitters.

Build into a highball glass and stir until glass is frosted. Garnish with slices of orange, lemon and pineapple.

Planter's Punch 2

2oz. White rum, 1oz. Dark Rum, 1 dash Grenadine, 2oz. Lime Juice, 1oz. Orange Juice, 1oz. Pineapple Juice.

Shake all but the dark rum and pour into a highball glass.
Float the dark rum on top.
Garnish with slices of orange, lemon and pineapple.

Portofino

1oz. Campari, 1oz. Galliano, 1oz. Sweet Vermouth, 2oz. Pineapple Juice.

Shake and pour into a highball glass. Serve with a twist of orange.

Private Lesson

2oz. Benedictine, 1 dash Crème de Fraises, 1 dash Angostura Bitters, Juice of Ruby Orange.

Shake and pour into a highball glass.

Prizewinner

1oz. Midori Melon Liqueur, 1/2oz. Vodka, 1/2oz. Blue Curaçao, 2 dashes Grenadine, 5oz. Lemonade.

Build into a highball glass.

Purple Passion

2oz. Vodka, 2oz. Grapefruit Juice, 2oz. Cranberry Juice, 1 dash Grenadine.

Shake and pour into a highball glass.

Pussy Crusher

1oz. Vodka, 1oz. Gin, 1oz. White Rum, 1/2oz. Triple Sec, 1/2oz. Galliano, 1 dash Grenadine, 4oz. Orange Juice.

Shake and pour into a napoli grande glass.

Queen Mary

2oz. Gin, Ginger Beer, 1/2 Lime.

Squeeze the juice of the lime into an ice-filled highball glass and add the gin. Drop in the spent lime shell and top with the ginger beer.

Raffles Singapore Sling

2oz. Gin, 1oz. Cherry Brandy, 1/4oz. Benedictine, 1oz. Lime Juice, 1 dash Angostura Bitters, 1 dash Grenadine, Ginger Beer.

Shake all but the ginger beer and pour into a sling glass. Top with the ginger beer.

Ragamuffin

1oz. Crème de Framboise, 1oz. Crème de Banane, 1/2oz. Amaretto, 3oz. Orange Juice.

Shake and pour into a highball glass.

Rainbow Punch

11/2oz. White Rum, 1oz. Midori Melon Liqueur, 1/2oz. Sloe Gin, 2oz. Orange Juice, 1oz. Pineapple Juice.

Shake and pour into a highball glass. Garnish with a wedge of pineapple.

Rainstorm

11/2oz. Gin, 1oz. Grand Marnier, 2oz. Pineapple Juice, 1/2oz. Lemon Juice, 1 dash Grenadine.

Shake and pour into a highball glass.

Red Baron

2oz. Bourbon, 4oz. Orange Juice, 1/4oz. Grenadine.

Shake and pour into a highball glass.

Red In Bed

(ANTHONY RATCLIFFE)

1oz. Campari, 1oz. Gin, 2oz. Grapefruit Juice, 1 tbsp. Grapefruit Sorbet.

Shake all but the sorbet and strain into a wineglass. stir in the sorbet and garnish with a slice of orange.

Riviera

1oz. White Rum, 1oz. Blue Curaçao, 1/2oz. Midori Melon Liqueur, 3oz. 7Up.

Build into a highball glass. Garnish with a mint leaf.

Robin's Nest

2oz. Vodka, 1oz. White Crème de Menthe, 2oz. Cranberry Juice.
Shake and pour into a highball glass.

Rock & Roll Root Beer

1oz. Strega, 1oz. Frangelico, 6oz. Cola.
Build into a highball glass.

Roman Candle

1oz. White Rum, 1/2oz. Orange Curaçao, 1/2oz. Crème de Pêche, 3oz. Orange Juice, 1/2oz. Polish Pure Spirit.
Stir all but the Polish spirit and strain into a champagne flute.
Float the Polish spirit on top and ignite.
Extinguish flame, allow glass to cool, then drink.

Root Beer Cocktail

1oz. Galliano, 1/2oz. Vodka, 1/2oz. Kahlúa, 5oz. Cola.
Build into a highball glass.

Ruby Red

2oz. Vodka, 1oz. Campari, 4oz. Grapefruit Juice.
Build into a highball glass.

Rum Driver

2oz. Dark Rum, 4oz. Orange Juice.
Build into a highball glass.

Salty Dog

2oz. Gin, 5oz. Grapefruit Juice.
Shake and pour into a salt-rimmed highball glass.

Salty Dog 2

2oz. Vodka, 5oz. Grapefruit Juice.
Shake and pour into a salt-rimmed highball glass.

Scorpion

2oz. Golden Rum, 1oz. Cognac, 1/2oz. Dark Rum, 1oz. Pineapple Juice, 1oz. Orange Juice, 1/2oz. Lime Juice, 1 dash Grenadine.

Shake all but the dark rum and pour into a highball glass. Float the dark rum on top.

Screwdriver

2oz. Vodka, 5oz. Orange Juice.

Build into a highball glass.

Sea Breeze

2oz. Vodka, 2oz. Cranberry Juice, 2oz. Grapefruit Juice.

Build into a highball glass.

Sex On The Beach 2

(DELLA FEMINA)

1oz. Midori Melon Liqueur, 1/2oz. Vodka, 1/2oz. Crème de Framboise, 1oz. Pineapple Juice, 1oz. Cranberry Juice.

Shake and pour into a highball glass.

Shady Grove

2oz. Gin, 1oz. Lemon Juice, 1/2oz. Gomme Syrup, Ginger Beer.

Shake all but the ginger beer and strain into an ice-filled highball glass. Top with the ginger beer.

Shady Lady

1oz. Tequila, 1oz. Midori Melon Liqueur, 4oz. Grapefruit Juice.

Build into a highball glass.

Singapore Sling

2oz. Gin, 1oz. Cherry Brandy, 1oz. Lemon Juice, 1/4oz. Grenadine, Soda Water.

Shake all but the soda and pour into a large goblet. Top with the soda.

Sloe Comfortable Screw

1oz. Sloe Gin, 1oz. Southern Comfort, 4oz. Orange Juice.

Shake and pour into a highball glass.

Sloe Comfortable Screw 2

1oz. Sloe Gin, 1oz. Southern Comfort, 3/4oz. Vodka, 3oz. Orange Juice.
Shake and pour into a highball glass.

Sloe Comfortable Screw Against The Wall

1oz. Sloe Gin, 1oz. Southern Comfort, 1oz. Galliano, 3oz. Orange Juice.
Shake all but the Galliano and pour into a highball glass.
Pour the Galliano over the top.

Sloe Comfortable Screw Against The Wall 2

1oz. Sloe Gin, 1/2oz. Southern Comfort, 1/2oz. Vodka, 1oz. Galliano, 3oz. Orange Juice.
Shake all but the Galliano and pour into a highball glass.
Pour the Galliano over the top.

Sloe Comfortable Screw Against The Wall With A Kiss

1oz. Sloe Gin, 1oz. Southern Comfort, 1oz. Galliano, 1 dash Amaretto, 3oz. Orange Juice.
Shake all but the amaretto and pour into a highball glass.
Dash the amaretto over the top.

Sloe Comfortable Screw Against The Wall With A Kiss 2

1oz. Sloe Gin, 1/2oz. Southern Comfort, 1/2oz. Vodka, 1oz. Galliano, 1 dash Amaretto, 3oz. Orange Juice.
Shake all but the amaretto and pour into a highball glass.
Dash the amaretto over the top.

Sloe Dog

2oz. Sloe Gin, 5oz. Grapefruit Juice.
Build into a highball glass.

Sloe Driver

2oz. Sloe Gin, 1oz. Vodka, 4oz. Orange Juice.
Shake and pour into a highball glass.

Sloe Screw

2oz. Sloe Gin, 4oz. Orange Juice.

Shake and pour into an old-fashioned glass.

Sloe Screw Mildly Comfortable Slightly Wild

1 1/2oz. Sloe Gin, 1/2oz. Southern Comfort, 1/2oz. Wild Turkey 101 Bourbon, 3oz. Orange Juice.

Shake and pour into a highball glass.

Sloe Screw Mildly Comfortable Slightly Wild 2

1oz. Sloe Gin, 1/2oz. Vodka, 1/2oz. Southern Comfort, 1/2oz. Wild Turkey 101 Bourbon, 3oz. Orange Juice.

Shake and pour into a highball glass.

Snowball

2oz. Advocaat, 1/2oz. Lime Juice, 6oz. Lemonade.

Build into a highball glass.

South Beach

1oz. Campari, 1oz. Amaretto, 5oz. Orange Juice, 1 dash Gomme Syrup.

Build into a highball glass. Garnish with a slice of orange.

Southern Bride

2oz. Gin, 1/2oz. Maraschino Liqueur, 3oz. Grapefruit Juice.

Shake and pour into a highball glass.

Strawberry Sunrise

2oz. Crème de Fraises, 4oz. Orange Juice, 1/2oz. Grenadine.

Build into a highball glass.

Drop the grenadine to the bottom of the drink to create the sunrise.

Strip And Go Naked

2oz. Vodka, 1 dash Lime Juice, Chilled Beer.

Pour into a highball glass, topping with the beer.

Sweetest Taboo

1oz. Gin, 1/2oz. Campari, 1/2oz. Cointreau, 4oz. Orange Juice.

Stir all but the orange and pour into a highball glass.
Stir in the orange juice and garnish with a slice of fresh orange.

Sweet Tart

1oz. Amaretto, 1oz. Crème de Mûre, 1oz. Peach Schnapps, 1oz. Lime Juice, 1oz. Orange Juice.

Shake and pour into a highball glass.

Tahiti Club

2oz. White Rum, 1/4oz. Maraschino Liqueur, 1 dash Lime Juice, 1 dash Lemon Juice, 1 dash Pineapple Juice.

Shake and pour into a highball glass.

Tall Boy

1oz. Crème de Fraises, 1oz. Crème de Framboise, 1oz. Lime Juice, 4oz. Lemonade.

Build into a highball glass.

Tampico

2oz. Campari, 1 1/2oz. Cointreau, 1 1/2oz. Lemon Juice.

Build into a highball glass and garnish with a sprig of mint.

Tap Water

2oz. Gin, 1oz. Cointreau, 5oz. Iced Tap Water.

Pour into a highball glass without ice.

Tennessee Tea

2oz. Jack Daniel's Whiskey, 1/2oz. White Crème de Cacao, 6oz. Cranberry Juice.

Shake and pour into a highball glass.

Tequila Sunrise

2oz. Tequila, 4oz. Orange Juice, 1/2oz. Grenadine.

Build into a highball glass. Slowly pour the grenadine into the completed drink allowing it to settle in the bottom and create a sunrise effect.

Tequila Sunset

2oz. Tequila, 2oz. Lemon Juice, 1 tbsp. Honey.
Shake and pour into a highball glass.

T.K.O.

1oz. Gin, 1oz. White Rum, 1oz. Vodka, 1oz. Blue Curaçao, 1oz. Orange Juice, Lemonade.
Shake all but the lemonade and pour into a highball glass. Top with the lemonade.

Tomato Cocktail

1oz. Pernod, 1/4oz. Grenadine, Iced Water.
Build into a highball glass, topping with the iced water.

Tom Boy

5oz. Tomato Juice, 5oz. Bitter.
Pour into a half-pint beer glass.

Top Banana

1oz. Crème de Banane, 1oz. Vodka, 3oz. Orange Juice.
Shake and pour into an old-fashioned glass.

Tropical Sunset

1 1/2oz. Midori Melon Liqueur, 1 1/2oz. Cointreau, 4oz. Peach Nectar.
Shake and pour into a highball glass.

Tropicana

1oz. Midori Melon Liqueur, 1/2oz. White Rum, 1/4oz. White Crème de Cacao, 2oz. Orange Juice, 1oz. Pineapple Juice, Soda Water.
Shake all but the soda and pour into a highball glass. Top with the soda.

Unicorn

2oz. Vodka, 1oz. Apfel Korn (Apple Schnapps), 3oz. Cranberry Juice.
Shake and pour into a highball glass.

VAT

2oz. Vodka, 6oz. Tonic Water.

Build into a highball glass. Garnish with a slice of lemon.

Venetian Nightfall

2oz. Gin, 1oz. Campari, 1oz. Sambuca, 1oz. Dry Vermouth.

Build into a highball glass. Garnish with a cherry.

Venetian Sunset

1oz. Grand Marnier, 1oz. Campari, 4oz. Ruby Orange Juice, 2 dashes Angostura Bitters.

Shake and pour into a highball glass.

Vera Highball

2oz. Pernod, 1/2oz. Gomme Syrup, Iced Water.

Build into a highball glass, topping with the water. Serve with a slice of lemon.

Vesuvius

2oz. Tequila, 1 dash Campari, 6oz. Orange Juice.

Build into a highball glass, dash the Campari over the top. Garnish with an orange peel spiral.

Virgin's Prayer

1oz. Gin, 1oz. Orange Curaçao, 1oz. Orange Juice, 1oz. Lemon Juice.

Shake and pour into a highball glass.

Vodka '7'

2oz. Vodka, 1/2 Lime, Lemonade.

Squeeze the lime juice into an ice-filled highball glass and drop in the spent lime shell. Stir in the vodka and lemonade.

Vodka Cooler

2oz. Vodka, 1oz. Lime Juice, 1/2oz. Gomme Syrup, Ginger Beer.

Shake all but the ginger beer and pour into a highball glass. Top with the ginger beer and garnish with an orange peel spiral.

Vodka Salty Dog

2oz. Vodka, 5oz. Grapefruit Juice.

Shake and pour into a salt-rimmed highball glass.

Volcano

1oz. Dark Rum, 1oz. White Rum, 1oz. Captain Morgan's 146 Proof Dark Rum, 1/2oz. Apricot Brandy, 3oz. Orange Juice, 3oz. Pineapple Juice.

Shake and pour into a napoli grande glass.

Watermelon

1oz. Vodka, 1oz. Crème de Fraises, 1oz. Orange Juice, 1/2oz. Lemon Juice, 1/2oz. Lime Juice, 1/4oz. Gomme Syrup.

Build into a highball glass.

Watermelon 2

1oz. Crème de Fraises, 1oz. Midori Melon Liqueur, 1/2oz. Grenadine, 2oz. Orange Juice, 2oz. Cranberry Juice.

Shake and pour into a highball glass.

Watermelon Cooler

1oz. Midori Melon Liqueur, 1oz. Vodka, 1/2oz. Crème de Fraises, 1/2oz. Captain Morgan's Spiced Rum, 1/2oz. Grenadine, 4oz. Cranberry Juice.

Shake and pour into a highball glass.

Whisky Cooler

2oz. Scotch, 1oz. Lime Juice, 1/2oz. Gomme Syrup, Ginger Beer.

Shake all but the ginger beer and pour into a highball glass. Top with the ginger beer and garnish with an orange peel spiral.

White Power Ranger

1oz. Vodka, 1oz. White Rum, 1oz. Sweetened Coconut Cream, 1oz. Lime Juice, Lemonade.

Shake all but the lemonade and pour into a highball glass. Top with the lemonade.

Wild Comfortable Screw

1oz. Wild Turkey 101 Bourbon, 1oz. Southern Comfort, 4oz. Orange Juice.
Shake and pour into a highball glass.

Wild Comfortable Screw 2

1oz. Wild Turkey 101 Bourbon, $^3/_4$oz. Southern Comfort, $^1/_2$oz. Vodka, 4oz. Orange Juice.
Shake and pour into a highball glass.

Wild Comfortable Screw Against The Wall

1oz. Wild Turkey 101 Bourbon, $^3/_4$oz. Southern Comfort, $^1/_2$oz. Galliano, 3oz. Orange Juice.
Shake all but the Galliano and pour into a highball glass.
Pour the Galliano over the top.

Wild Comfortable Screw Against The Wall 2

$^3/_4$z. Wild Turkey 101 Bourbon, $^3/_4$oz. Southern Comfort, $^1/_2$oz. Vodka, $^1/_2$oz. Galliano, 3oz. Orange Juice.
Shake all but the Galliano and pour into a highball glass.
Pour the Galliano over the top.

X-Rated Cocktail

2oz. Captain Morgan's 146 Proof Dark Rum, 1oz. Apricot Brandy, 1oz. Crème de Pêche, $^1/_2$oz. Grenadine, 1oz. Lime Juice, 2oz. Pineapple Juice.
Shake and pour into a highball glass.

Yacht Club Punch

2oz. White Rum, $^1/_4$oz. Pernod, 1oz. Lemon Juice, $^1/_2$oz. Grenadine, Soda Water.
Shake all but the soda and pour into a highball glass. Top with the soda.

Yellow Bird 2

1oz. White Rum, $^3/_4$oz. Galliano, $^3/_4$oz. Crème de Banane, 2oz. Pineapple Juice, 2oz. Orange Juice.
Shake and pour into a highball glass.

Yellow Bird 3

1oz. White Rum, 1oz. Crème de Banane, 3/4oz. Kahlúa, 1oz. Sweetened Coconut Cream, 1oz. Pineapple Juice.

Shake and pour into a highball glass.

Yellow Fever

1oz. Gin, 1oz. Yellow Chartreuse, 3/4oz. Lemon Syrup, 4oz. Tonic Water.

Build into a highball glass.

Zenith

1oz. Crème de Mûre, 1oz. Crème de Cassis, 1oz. Blue Curaçao, 4oz. Cranberry Juice.

Shake and pour into a large goblet.

Zombie

1oz. Dark Rum, 1oz. White Rum, 1oz. Apricot Brandy, 1oz. Orange Juice, 1oz. Pineapple Juice, 1/2oz. Lemon Juice.

Shake and pour into a highball glass. Garnish with seasonal fruits.

Zombie 2

1oz. Dark Rum, 1oz. Golden Rum, 1/2oz. Apricot Brandy, 1/2oz. Dark Overproof Rum, 2oz. Orange Juice, 1oz. Lime Juice.

Shake all but the overproof rum and pour into a large goblet.
Float overproof rum on top.
Garnish with slices of orange and a sprig of mint.

SHORT MIXED DRINKS

▼

The drinks in this category are selected by the same method as the long mixed drink in that they use all manner of juices, syrups, bitters, liqueurs and spirits whilst not falling within the specific styles of those drinks in the following chapters (e.g. Blended or Hot drinks). The one difference between the long and short mixed drink is the proportion of non-alcoholic constituents. This is why the shorter drinks often appear to be stronger.

Abbey

2oz. Gin, 1oz. Orange Juice, 1/2oz. Sweet Vermouth, 1 dash Angostura Bitters.

Shake and strain into a martini glass, garnish with a maraschino cherry.

Abbey 2

2oz. Gin, 1oz. Orange Juice, 1oz. Kina Lillet, 1 dash Angostura Bitters.

Shake and strain into a martini glass.

Abyssinia

1oz. Brown Crème de Cacao, 1oz. Cognac, 1oz. Grapefruit Juice.

Shake and strain into a martini glass.

Acapulco

3oz. White Rum, 1/4oz. Triple Sec, 1/4oz. Lime Juice, 1 Egg White.

Shake and pour into an old-fashioned glass.

Acapulco 2

2oz. Tequila, 1oz. White Rum, 1/2oz. Gomme Syrup, Juice of 1/2 Lime.
Shake and strain into a martini glass.

Admiral

2 1/2oz. Gin, 1 3/4oz. Cherry Brandy, Juice of 1/2 Lime, 1 dash Gomme Syrup.
Shake and strain into a martini glass.

After All

1 1/2oz. Calvados, 1 1/2oz. Crème de Pêche, 1oz. Lemon Juice.
Shake and strain into a martini glass.

After Dinner

2oz. Cointreau, 2oz. Apricot Brandy, Juice of 1 Lime.
Shake and strain into a martini glass, serve with a lime wedge garnish.

After Supper

1oz. Cointreau, 1 1/2oz. Apricot Brandy, 1oz. Lemon Juice.
Shake and strain into a martini glass.

Alabama Cocktail

1 1/2oz. Cognac, 1oz. Cointreau, 1oz. Lemon Juice, 1/2oz. Gomme Syrup.
Shake and strain into a martini glass.

Alabama Slammer

1oz. Southern Comfort, 1oz. Amaretto, 1oz. Sloe Gin, 1oz. Lemon Juice.
Shake and pour into an old-fashioned glass.

Algonquin

2oz. Bourbon, 1oz. Dry Vermouth, 1oz. Pineapple Juice.
Shake and strain into a martini glass.

Almaria

2oz. Kahlúa, 2oz. Dark Rum, 1 Egg White, 1 dash Lemon Juice.
Shake and strain into a martini glass.

Amaretto (Stone) Sour

3oz. Amaretto, Juice of 1 Lemon.

Shake and pour into an old-fashioned glass and serve with a twist of lemon or a slice of orange.

American Beauty

1oz. Cognac, 1oz. Dry Vermouth, 1oz. Orange Juice, 1oz. Grenadine, 1/2oz port, 1 dash White Crème de Menthe (optional).

Shake and strain into a martini glass, float port and serve.

American Margarita

2oz. Tequila, 1oz. Cointreau, 1/2oz. Lime Juice, 1/2oz. Lemon Juice.

Shake and strain into a salt-rimmed coupette.

American Whiskey Daisy

2oz. Bourbon or Rye Whiskey, 1oz. Lemon Juice, 1/4oz. Grenadine, Soda Water.

Shake all but the soda and strain into an ice-filled tankard. Stir in the required amount of soda and garnish with seasonal fruits.

American Whiskey Fix

2oz. Bourbon or Rye Whiskey, 1oz. Lemon Juice, 1/2oz. Gomme Syrup.

Stir into an old-fashioned glass three-quarters filled with crushed ice. Garnish with a slice of lemon.

American Whiskey Sling

2oz. Bourbon or Rye Whiskey, 1oz. Lemon Juice, 1 tsp. granulated Sugar, 1oz. Water.

Stir the sugar and water together in an old-fashioned glass. Fill with ice and stir in the bourbon or rye whiskey and lemon juice.

American Whiskey Sour

2oz. Bourbon or Rye Whiskey, 1oz. Lemon Juice, 1/2oz. Gomme Syrup, 1 Egg White.

Shake and strain into a martini glass.

Amer Picon Cocktail

3oz. Amer Picon, 1oz. Lime Juice, 2 dashes Grenadine.
Shake and strain into a martini glass.

Amsterdam

2oz. Dutch Gin (Genever), 1oz. Cointreau, 1oz. Orange Juice, 4 dashes Orange Bitters.
Shake and strain into a martini glass.

Animator

1oz. Peach Schnapps, 1oz. Crème de Fraises, 3oz. Cranberry Juice.
Shake and pour into an old-fashioned glass. Garnish with a sliced strawberry.

Announcer

$1\frac{1}{2}$oz. Cognac, $1\frac{1}{2}$oz. Gin, $\frac{3}{4}$oz. Lemon Juice, $\frac{3}{4}$oz. Cointreau.
Shake and strain into a martini glass.

Anvil

1oz. Midori Melon Liqueur, $\frac{3}{4}$oz. Blue Curaçao, 1oz. Lemon Juice, 3oz. Apple Juice.
Stir and strain into an ice-filled old-fashioned glass.

Apple Brandy Cocktail

3oz. Applejack, $\frac{3}{4}$oz. Grenadine, $\frac{3}{4}$oz. Lemon Juice.
Shake and strain into a martini glass.

Applecar

1oz. Calvados, 1oz. Cointreau, 1oz. Lemon Juice.
Shake and strain into a martini glass.

Applejack Rabbit

3oz. Calvados, 1oz. Orange Juice, 1oz. Lemon Juice, 1 dash Grenadine.
Shake and strain into a martini glass.

Applejack Sour

3oz. Applejack, Juice of 1 Lemon, $\frac{3}{4}$oz. Gomme Syrup.
Shake and pour into an old-fashioned glass. Garnish with a lemon slice.

Apricot

2oz. Apricot Brandy, 1oz. Lemon Juice, 1oz. Orange Juice.
Shake and strain into a martini glass.

Apricot 2

3oz. Apricot Brandy, 2oz. Gin, 1/2oz. Lemon Juice, 1/2oz. Orange Juice.
Shake and pour into an old-fashioned glass.

Apricot Lady

2oz. White Rum, 1oz. Apricot Brandy, 1/2oz. Cointreau, 1oz. Lemon juice, 1 Egg White.
Shake and strain into a martini glass.

Apricot Lady 2

2oz. Gin, 1oz. Apricot Brandy, 1/2oz. Cointreau, 1oz. Lemon Juice, 1 Egg White.
Shake and strain into a martini glass.

Apricot Sour

2oz. Apricot Brandy, Juice of 1 Lemon, 1/2oz. Gomme Syrup, 1 Egg White.
Shake and strain into a martini glass.

Aquarius

3oz. Scotch, 1oz. Cherry Brandy, 2oz. Cranberry Juice.
Shake and pour into an old-fashioned glass.

Arack Cocktail

3oz. Arack, Juice of 1 Lime, 2 dashes Grenadine.
Shake and strain into a martini glass.

Argentina

1 1/2oz. Gin, 1 1/2oz. Dry Vermouth, 1/4oz. Cointreau, 1/4oz. Benedictine, 1 dash Orange Bitters, 2 dashes Angostura Bitters, 1/2oz. Orange Juice.
Shake and strain into a martini glass.

Armagnac Sour

2oz. Armagnac, Juice of 1 Lemon, 1oz. Gomme Syrup, 1 dash Angostura Bitters, 1 Egg White.

Shake and strain into a martini glass.

Arrowhead

3oz. Scotch, 1/4oz. Sweet Vermouth, 1/4oz. Dry Vermouth, 1/4oz. Lemon Juice, 1 Egg White.

Shake and strain into a martini glass.

Aviation

3oz. Gin, 1 1/2oz. Lemon Juice, 1/4oz. Crème de Violette, 1/4oz. Maraschino Liqueur.

Stir and strain into a martini glass.

Aviation 2

2oz. Bourbon, 2oz. Grape Juice.

Build into an old-fashioned glass.

Bacardi Blossom

2oz. Bacardi White Rum, 2oz. Orange Juice, 1 dash Lemon Juice.

Shake and strain into a martini glass.

Bacardi Cocktail

2oz. Bacardi White Rum, Juice of 1 Lime, 3 dashes Grenadine.

Shake and strain into a martini glass.

Bacardi Silver

2oz. Bacardi White Rum, 1oz. Gin, 1/2oz. Lemon Juice, 1 dash Pineapple Juice, 1 Egg White.

Shake and strain into a martini glass.

Bacardi Special

2oz. Bacardi White Rum, Juice of 1 Lime, 3 dashes Grenadine, 2 dashes Gin.

Shake and strain into a martini glass.

Badminton

1oz. Gin, 1oz. Midori Melon Liqueur, 1/2oz. Blue Curaçao, 1oz. Lemon Juice.
Shake and strain into a martini glass.

Balalaika

1oz. Vodka, 1oz. Cointreau, 1oz. Lemon Juice.
Shake and strain into a martini glass.

Barbara Eastern

2oz. Bourbon, 1oz. Grapefruit Juice, 1/2oz. Apricot Brandy.
Shake and strain into a martini glass.

Barmaster

1oz. Mandarine Napoléon, 2oz. Orange Juice, 1 dash Campari, 1/2oz. Vodka, 1 Egg White.
Shake and strain into a martini glass.

Baronial

2oz. Kina Lillet, 1oz. Lemon Juice, 1/2oz. Triple Sec 1 dash Angostura Bitters.
Shake and strain into a martini glass.

Bayou

2oz. Cognac, 2oz. Peach Juice, 1 dash Lime Juice.
Shake and strain into a martini glass.

Beachcomber

2oz. White Rum, 1oz. Cointreau, 1oz. Lime Juice, 1/4oz. Maraschino Liqueur.
Shake and strain into a martini glass.

Bebbo

3oz. Gin, 2oz. Lemon Juice, 1/4oz. Orange Juice, 1/4oz. Clear Honey
Shake and strain into a martini glass.

Bee's Knees

1oz. Gin, 1oz. Lemon Juice, 1oz. Clear Honey.
Shake and strain into a martini glass.

Belote

1oz. Anisette, 1oz. Calvados, 1oz. Grenadine, 1oz. Orange Juice.
Shake and strain into a martini glass.

Benedictine Cocktail

2oz. Benedictine, 1oz. Cognac, 1oz. Lemon Juice, 1 dash Grenadine.
Shake and strain into a martini glass.

Bengal

2oz. Cognac 1/2oz. Maraschino Liqueur, 1/2oz. Cointreau, 1oz. Pineapple Juice, 4 dashes Angostura Bitters.
Stir and strain into a martini glass.

Bennett

3oz. Gin, 1oz. Lime Juice, 1/4oz. Gomme Syrup, 2 dashes Angostura Bitters.
Shake and strain into a martini glass.

Bermuda

2oz. Gin, 1oz. Peach Brandy, 1/4oz. Grenadine, 1/2oz. Orange Juice.
Shake and strain into a martini glass.

Bermudan

2oz. Gin, 1oz. Apricot Brandy, 1oz. Grenadine, 1/2oz. Lemon Juice, 1 dash Gomme Syrup.
Shake and strain into a martini glass.

Bertolucci

1oz. Vodka, 1oz. Galliano, 2oz. Lime Juice.
Shake and strain into a martini glass.

Between The Sheets

1oz. Cognac, 1oz. White Rum, 1oz. Cointreau, 1 1/2oz. Lemon Juice.
Shake and strain into a martini glass.

Biffy

3oz. Gin, 1/2oz. Swedish Punsch, 1oz. Lemon Juice.
Shake and strain into a martini glass.

Big Apple

1oz. Apple Schnapps, 1oz. Drambuie, 1oz. Amaretto, 1oz. Lemon Juice.

Shake and strain into a martini glass.

Billy Taylor

2oz. Gin, 1oz. Lime Juice, Soda.

Build into an old-fashioned glass and top with the soda.

Birdie

2oz. Dark Rum, 1/2oz. Triple Sec, 1/2oz. Pineapple Juice, 1 dash Grenadine, 1 dash Orange Juice.

Shake and strain into a martini glass.

Bishop 2

2oz. Bourbon, 1oz. Sweet Vermouth, 1oz. Orange Juice, 1 dash Green Chartreuse.

Shake and strain into a martini glass.

Bitter

1oz. Gin, 1/2oz. Green Chartreuse, 1/2oz. Yellow Chartreuse, 1oz. Lemon Juice, 1 dash Anisette.

Shake and strain into a martini glass.

Black Jack

1oz. Cognac, 1oz. Kirschwasser, 2oz. Cold Coffee.

Stir and strain into a medium goblet.

Black Out

2oz. Gin, 1oz. Blackberry Brandy, Juice of 1 Lime.

Shake and strain into a martini glass.

Black Widow

2oz. Dark Rum, 1oz. Southern Comfort, 1oz. Lime Juice.

Shake and strain into a martini glass.

Blinker

2oz. Rye Whiskey, 3oz. Grapefruit Juice, 1/2oz. Grenadine.
Shake and pour into an old-fashioned glass.

Blister

1oz. Gin, 1oz. Crème de Noyaux, 1/2oz. Lemon Juice, 1/4oz. Gomme Syrup.
Shake and strain into a martini glass.

Blood and Sand

1oz. Scotch, 1oz. Cherry Brandy, 1oz. Sweet Vermouth, 1oz. Orange Juice.
Shake and strain into a martini glass.

Blood Bronx

2oz. Gin, 1/2oz. Dry Vermouth, 1/2oz. Sweet Vermouth,
Juice of 1/2 Blood Red Ruby Orange.
Shake and strain into a martini glass.

Blossom

2oz. Gin, 3oz. Orange Juice, 1 dash Grenadine.
Shake and pour into an old-fashioned glass.

Bluebird

2oz. Gin, 1oz. White Curaçao, 1/2oz. Lemon Juice.
Shake and strain into a martini glass.

Bluebottle

2oz. Gin, 1oz. Blue Curaçao, 1oz. Passion or Peach Juice.
Shake and strain into a martini glass.

Blue Devil

2oz. Gin, 1oz. Maraschino Liqueur, 1oz. Lime Juice, 1/2oz. Blue Curaçao.
Shake and strain into a martini glass.

Blue Lady

See the chapter three, The Classics, (pp 68–9).
Substitute blue curaçao for the Cointreau in the white lady.

Blue Margarita

2oz. Tequila, 1oz. Blue Curaçao, 1oz. Lime Juice.
Shake and strain into a coupette.

Blue Moon

2oz. Gin, 1oz. Parfait Amour, 1oz. Lemon Juice.
Shake and strain into a martini glass.

Bolo

3oz. Dark Rum, Juice of 1 Lime, Juice of $\frac{1}{2}$ Orange, $\frac{1}{2}$oz. Gomme Syrup.
Shake and pour into a highball glass.

Bonnie Prince Charlie

1oz. Drambuie, 1oz. Cognac, 1oz. Lemon Juice.
Shake and strain into a martini glass.

Booby

1oz. White Rum, 1oz. Gin, Juice of 1 Lime, 1 dash Grenadine.
Shake and strain into a martini glass.

Booster

1oz. Gold Tequila, 1oz. Grapefruit Juice, $\frac{1}{2}$oz. Grenadine, 1 Egg White.
Shake and strain into a martini glass.

Boston Sidecar

1oz. Dark Rum, 1oz. Cointreau, 1oz. Cognac, 1oz. Lime Juice.
Shake and strain into a martini glass.

Boston Sour

2oz. Scotch, 1oz. Lemon Juice, $\frac{1}{2}$oz. Gomme Syrup, 1 Egg White.
Shake and strain into a sour glass.

Boulevard

$1\frac{1}{2}$oz. Gin, $1\frac{1}{2}$oz. Sweet Vermouth, $1\frac{1}{2}$oz. Orange Juice.
Shake and strain into a martini glass.

Bourbon Sour

2oz. Bourbon, 1oz. Lemon Juice, 1/2oz. Gomme Syrup.
Shake and strain into a sour or martini glass.

Brandy Daisy

2oz. Cognac, 1oz. Lemon Juice, 1 dash Grenadine.
Shake and strain into an ice-filled tankard.
Garnish with seasonal fruit and sprigs of mint and marjoram.

Brandy Eclipse

1 1/2oz. Cognac, 1 1/2oz. White Crème de Cacao, 3/4oz. Orange Juice.
Shake and strain into a martini glass.

Brandy Fix

2oz. Cognac, 1oz. Lemon Juice, 1/2oz. Gomme Syrup.
Build over crushed ice in an old-fashioned glass.
Garnish with a slice of lemon.

Brandy Sour

2oz. Cognac, 1oz. Lemon Juice, 1/2oz. Gomme Syrup.
Shake and strain into a sour glass.

Bronx

2oz. Gin, 1oz. Sweet Vermouth, 1oz. Dry Vermouth, Juice of 1/4 Orange.
Shake and strain into a martini glass.

Bronx River

2oz. Gin, 1oz. Sweet Vermouth, 1 dash Lemon Juice, 1 tsp. powdered Sugar.
Shake and strain into a martini glass.

Bronx Silver

2oz. Gin, 1oz. Dry Vermouth, Juice of 1/4 Orange, 1 Egg White.
Shake and strain into a martini glass.

Bronx Terrace

2oz. Gin, 1oz. Dry Vermouth, 1/2oz. Rose's Lime Cordial.
Stir and strain into a martini glass.

Brooklyn

2oz. Bourbon, 1oz. Sweet Vermouth, 1oz. Orange Juice, 1 dash Maraschino Liqueur.

Stir and strain into a martini glass.

Brunelle

1oz. Pernod, 3oz. Lemon Juice, 1½oz. Gomme Syrup.

Shake and strain into a martini glass.

Bulldog

2oz. Cherry Brandy, 1oz. Gin, 1oz. Lime Juice.

Shake and strain into a martini glass.

Bustanoby

2½oz. White Crème de Menthe, ½oz. Orange Juice, 1 dash Angostura Bitters, 1 tsp. powdered Sugar.

Shake and strain into a martini glass.

Cadillac Lady

1oz. Gin, 1oz. Grand Marnier, 1oz. Lemon Juice, 1 Egg White.

Shake and strain into a martini glass.

Cadillac Margarita

1½oz. Tequila, 1oz. Grand Marnier, 1oz. Lime Juice.

Shake and strain into a salt-rimmed coupette.

Caipirinha

2oz. Cachaça, 1 Lime, 1 tsp. granulated Sugar.

Cut the lime into eighths and muddle with the sugar in an old-fashioned glass. Fill with crushed ice and add the cachaça. Invert another old-fashioned glass and place on top of the first glass to create an instant shaker. Shake the ingredients between the two glasses and serve into one of them.

Caipirisima

As above but substituting vodka for the cachaça.

Calvados

2oz. Calvados, 1oz. Orange Juice, 1/2oz. Cointreau, 4 dashes Orange Bitters.

Shake and strain into a martini glass.

Calvados Sour

2oz. Calvados, 1oz. Lemon juice, 1/2oz. Gomme Syrup,
1 dash Egg White (optional).

Shake and strain into a sour glass.

Cameron's Kick

2oz. Scotch, 1oz. Irish Whiskey, 1oz. Lemon Juice, 1 dash Orange Bitters.

Shake and strain into a martini glass.

Camparetto

(PAULO VIVEIROS)

1oz. Campari, 1oz. Amaretto, 1oz. Grapefruit Juice, 1 dash Egg White.

Shake and strain into a Champagne Flute.

Canadian Apple

2oz. Canadian Club Whisky, 1oz. Calvados, 1/2oz. Lime Juice,
1/2oz. Gomme Syrup.

Shake and strain into a martini glass.

Canadian Cocktail

2oz. Canadian Club Whiskey, 1/2oz. Lime Juice, 1 dash Cointreau,
1 dash Grenadine.

Shake and strain into a martini glass.

Canadian Sunset

2oz. Canadian Club Whisky, 1oz. Strega, 1oz. Galliano, 1oz. Lemon Juice,
1 dash Grenadine.

Shake all but the grenadine and strain into a martini glass.
Drop the grenadine into the drink to create the sunset effect.

Cancan

(DAVIDE CAMPARI MILANO)

2oz. Cognac, 1 1/2oz. Campari, 1oz. Apricot Brandy, 1/2oz. Orange Juice.
Shake and strain into a martini glass.

Canned Cocktail

2oz. Gin, 1oz. Vodka, 1oz. Lime Juice.
Shake and strain into a martini glass.

Captain's Blood

2oz. Dark Rum, 1oz. Rose's Lime Cordial, 1 dash Angostura Bitters.
Shake and strain into a martini glass.

Casa Blanca

2oz. White Rum, 1oz. Lime Juice, 1/2oz. Cointreau, 1 dash Orange Bitters.
Shake and strain into a martini glass.

Champs-Elysées

2oz. Cognac, 1oz. Yellow Chartreuse, 1/2oz. Lemon Juice,
1/2oz. Gomme Syrup, 1 dash Angostura Bitters.
Shake and strain into a martini glass.

Chapala

2oz. Tequila, 2oz. Orange Juice, 1oz. Lemon Juice,
1 dash Orange Flower Water, 1/2oz. Grenadine.
Shake and strain into a martini glass.

Charlie Chaplin

1oz. Apricot Brandy, 1oz. Sloe Gin, 1oz. Lemon Juice.
Shake and strain into a martini glass.

Chelsea Sidecar

1oz. Gin, 1oz. Triple Sec, 1oz. Lemon Juice.
Shake and strain into a martini glass.

Cherry Sour

2oz. Cherry Brandy, 1oz. Lemon Juice, 1/2oz. Orange Juice, 1/2oz. Grenadine.
Shake and strain into a sour glass.

Clamato

2oz. Vodka, 2oz. Clam Broth, 3oz. Tomato Juice.
Shake and pour into an old-fashioned glass.

Classic

2oz. Cognac, 1oz. Maraschino Liqueur, 1/2oz. Orange Curaçao, 1oz. Lemon Juice.
Shake and strain into a sugar-rimmed martini glass.

Clover Club

2oz. Gin, 1oz. Lemon Juice, 2 dashes Grenadine, 1 Egg White.
Shake and strain into a martini glass.

Clover Club Royal

2oz. Gin, 1oz. Lemon Juice, 2 dashes Grenadine, 1 Egg Yolk.
Shake and strain into a martini glass.

Clover Leaf

2oz. Gin, 1oz. Lime Juice, 2 dashes Grenadine, 1 Egg White.
Shake and strain into a martini glass.

Cocoteq

2oz. Silver Tequila, 1oz. Noix de Coco, 1oz. Lemon Juice, 1 dash Gomme Syrup.
Shake and strain into a martini glass.

Coffee Sour

2oz. Tia Maria, 1oz. Lemon Juice, 1/4oz. Gomme Syrup, 1 dash Egg White.
Shake and strain into a sour glass.

Cold Cactus

1oz. Vodka, 1oz. Tequila, 1/2oz. Blue Curaçao, 1oz. Lemon Juice. 1 dash Egg White.

Shake and strain into a martini glass.

Colonial

2oz. Gin, 3/4oz. Grapefruit Juice, 1 dash Maraschino Liqueur.

Shake and strain into a martini glass.

Comfortable Sour

2oz. Southern Comfort, 1oz. Lemon Juice, 1/2oz. Gomme Syrup, 1 dash Orange Juice.

Shake and pour into an old-fashioned glass.

Commodore

2oz. Scotch, 2 dashes Orange Bitters, 3/4oz. Lime Juice, 1/4oz. Gomme Syrup.

Shake and strain into a martini glass.

Conchita

2oz. Tequila, 2oz. Grapefruit Juice, 1/2oz. Lemon Juice.

Shake and strain into a martini glass.

Cranikazee

1oz. Vodka, 1/2oz. Triple Sec, 1/2oz. Rose's Lime Cordial, 1oz. Cranberry Juice.

Shake and pour into an old-fashioned glass.

Creole

2oz. White Rum, 4oz. Beef Bouillon, 1 dash Tabasco Sauce, 1 dash Lemon Juice.

Shake and pour into an old-fashioned glass.

Cuban

2oz. White Rum, 1 dash Apricot Brandy, Juice of 1/2 Lime, 1 dash Gomme Syrup.

Stir and strain into a martini glass.

Daily Mail

1oz. Bourbon, 1oz. Amer Picon, 1oz. Orange Juice/Squash, 2 dashes Angostura Bitters.

Shake and strain into a martini glass.

Daiquiri

See chapter three, The Classics, (p. 53).

Daiquiri Blossom

2oz. White Rum, 1oz. Orange Juice, 1 dash Gomme Syrup.

Shake and strain into a martini glass.

Daiquiri (Florida)

2oz. White Rum, 1oz. Lemon Juice, 1/2oz. Gomme Syrup.

Shake and strain into a martini glass.

Daiquiri (Florida) 2

2oz. White Rum, 1oz. Lemon Juice, 1/2oz. Gomme Syrup, 1 dash Grapefruit Juice, 1 dash Maraschino Liqueur.

Shake and strain into a martini glass.

Daiquiri (Florida) 3

2oz. White Rum, 1oz. Lemon Juice, 1/2oz. Gomme Syrup, 1 dash Orange Juice, 1 dash Orange Curaçao.

Shake and strain into a martini glass.

Damn the Weather

2oz. Gin, 1/2oz. Sweet Vermouth, 1/2oz. Orange Juice, 1 dash Triple Sec.

Shake and strain into a martini glass.

D'Amour

2oz. Gin, 1oz. Anisette, 1oz. Lime Juice, 1 Egg White.

Shake and strain into a martini glass.

Danny's Special

2oz. Jack Daniel's Whiskey, 1/2oz. Triple Sec, 1oz. Lemon Juice, 1 dash Orange Curaçao.

Stir and strain into a martini glass.

Dead Arm

1oz. Campari, 1oz. Sweet Vermouth, 1/2oz. White Crème de Cacao, 1/2oz. Orange Juice.

Shake and strain into a martini glass.

Dean's Gate

2oz. White Rum, 1oz. Drambuie, 1oz. Rose's Lime Cordial.

Shake and strain into a martini glass.

Deauville

1oz. Cognac, 1oz. Calvados, 1oz. Triple sec, 1/2oz. Lemon Juice.

Shake and strain into a martini glass.

Derby Daiquiri

2oz. White Rum, 1oz. Orange Juice, 1/4oz. Gomme Syrup, 1 dash Lime Juice.

Shake and strain into a martini glass.

De Rigeur

2oz. Bourbon, 1oz. Grapefruit Juice, 1oz. Clear Honey.

Shake and strain into a martini glass.

Devil's Disciple

1oz. Dubonnet, 1oz. White Crème de Menthe, 2oz. Tonic Water.

Build into an old-fashioned glass.

Devonia

2oz. Cider, 1oz. Gin, 1 dash Orange Bitters.

Shake lightly and strain into a martini glass.

Diki Diki

2oz. Calvados, 1oz. Swedish Punsch, 1oz. Grapefruit Juice.

Shake and strain into a martini glass.

Di'Lemma

(CRAIG DICKSON)

1oz. Campari, 1oz. Galliano, 2oz. Orange Juice, 1 Egg White.
Shake and strain into a deep-dish champagne saucer.
Garnish with a cherry and a twist of orange.

Dinah

2oz. Bourbon, 3/4oz. Lemon Juice, 1/4oz. Gomme Syrup, 1 Mint Leaf.
Shake and strain into a martini glass.

Dixie

2oz. Gin, 1oz. Dry Vermouth, 1oz. Orange Juice, 1 dash Anisette.
Shake and strain into a martini glass.

Doctor

1oz. Swedish Punsch, 1oz. Lime Juice, 1oz. Orange Juice.
Shake and strain into a martini glass.

Double Standard Sour

1oz. Gin, 1oz. Scotch, 1oz. Lime Juice, 1/2oz. Gomme Syrup.
Shake and strain into a martini glass.

Dragon Lady

1oz. Midori Melon Liqueur, 1oz. Cointreau, Juice of 1 Lemon, 1 Egg White.
Shake and strain into a martini glass.

Du Bon

2oz. Dubonnet, 1oz. Gin, 1oz. Lemon Juice.
Shake and strain into a martini glass.

Durango

2oz. Tequila, 2oz. Grapefruit Juice, 1/2oz. Orgeat.
Shake and strain into a martini glass.

Eagle

2oz. Gin, 1/4oz. Parfait Amour, 1/2oz. Lemon Juice, 1 dash Egg White.
Shake and strain into a wineglass.

Eagle's Dream

2oz. Gin, 3/4oz. Crème Yvette, 1oz. Lemon Juice, 1 Egg White, 1 dash Gomme Syrup.

Shake and strain into a martini glass.

Eastern Promise

1oz. White Crème de Cacao, 1 oz. Pisang Ambon, 1/4oz. Grenadine, 3oz. Pineapple Juice

Shake and pour into an old-fashioned glass.

Editor's Curse

1oz. Scotch, 1oz. Van der Hum, 1oz. Orange Juice.

Shake and strain into a martini glass.

Ed's Baby

2oz. White Rum, 3/4oz. Cherry Brandy, 1 dash Crème de Banane, Juice of 1 Lime.

Shake and strain into a martini glass.

Egg Sour

2oz. Cognac, 1oz. Lemon Juice, 1/2oz. Gomme Syrup, 1 Egg.

Shake and pour into an old-fashioned glass.

Eight Bells

2oz. Dark Rum, 1oz. Van der Hum, 1oz. Dry Vermouth, 1/2oz. Orange and Lemon Squash.

Shake and pour into an old-fashioned glass.
Sprinkle grated nutmeg over drink.

Ekko

2oz. Manderine Napoléon, 1oz. Vodka, 1oz. Lemon Juice, 1 dash Grenadine.

Shake and strain into a martini glass.

Eldorado

2oz. Gold Tequila, 1oz. Lemon Juice, 1 tsp. Clear Honey.

Shake and strain into a martini glass.

Elegant Lady

2oz. Gin, 1oz. Grand Marnier, Juice of 1 Lime, 1 dash Orgeat, 1 Egg White.

Shake and strain into a martini glass.

Elephant Walk

1oz. Gin, $^1/_2$oz. Tequila, $^1/_2$oz. Orange Juice, 1 dash Grenadine, 1 dash Angostura Bitters.

Build into an old-fashioned glass.

Garnish with lemon and orange slice and a stick of cucumber.

El Jardinero

3oz. White Rum, 2oz. Sambuca, 1oz. Lime Juice.

Shake and strain into a large goblet.

El Presidente

2oz. White Rum, 1oz. Lime Juice, 1 dash Grenadine, 1 dash Pineapple Juice.

Shake and strain into a martini glass.

Emerson

2oz. Gin, $1^1/_4$oz. Sweet Vermouth, $^1/_2$oz. Lime Juice, 1 dash Maraschino.

Shake and strain into a martini glass.

Eve's Apple

1oz. Calvados, 1oz. Swedish Punsch, 1oz. Grapefruit Juice.

Shake and strain into a martini glass.

Excise Duty

1oz. Dark Rum, 1oz. Golden Rum, 1oz. Peach Brandy, 2oz. Orange Juice, 1 dash Grenadine.

Shake and pour into a large goblet.

Exhibitionist

2oz. Kümmel, 1oz. Gin, 1 dash Blue Curaçao, Juice of 1 Lime.

Shake and strain into a martini glass.

Falcon Claw

2oz. Gin, 1oz. Peach Schnapps, 1/2oz. Rose's Lime Cordial, 1 dash Amaretto.
Stir and strain into a martini glass.

Fallen Angel

2oz. Gin, 1/4oz. White Crème de Menthe, Juice of 1 Lime, 1 dash Angostura Bitters.
Shake and strain into a martini glass.

Fantasia

1 1/4oz. Green Chartreuse, 1oz. Vodka, 3/4oz. Grapefruit Juice, 1/4oz. Cherry Brandy.
Shake and strain into a frosted martini glass.

Fig Leaf

1 1/2oz. Dry Vermouth, 1oz. White Rum, 1oz. Lime Juice, 1 dash Angostura Bitters.
Shake and strain into a martini glass.

Fine and Dandy

3oz. Gin, 1oz. Triple Sec, 1/2oz. Lemon Juice, 1 dash Angostura Bitters.
Shake and strain into a martini glass.

Flamingo

2oz. Gin, 3/4oz. Apricot Brandy, 1 dash Grenadine, 1/2oz. Lime Juice.
Shake and strain into a martini glass.

Fleur-de-Lys

2oz. Kümmel, 1 dash Peach Schnapps, 4oz. Tonic Water.
Build into an old-fashioned glass.

Florida

1oz. Gin, 1/4oz. Kirschwasser, 1/4oz. Triple Sec, 2oz. Orange Juice, 1 dash Lemon Juice.
Shake and strain into a martini glass.

Florida Daiquiri

2oz. White Rum, 1oz. Lime Juice, 1/2oz. Maraschino Liqueur.
Shake and strain into a sugar-rimmed martini glass.

Flu

2oz. Rye Whiskey, 1 dash Rock-Candy Syrup, 1 dash Ginger Brandy, 1/2oz. Lemon Juice.
Stir and strain into a martini glass.

Forester's Delight

1 1/2oz. Bourbon, 1 1/2oz. Cointreau, 2 dashes Blue Curaçao, 1/2oz. Lemon Juice.
Shake and strain into a sugar-rimmed champagne flute.

Fort Lauderdale

3oz. White Rum, 1oz. Sweet Vermouth, Juice of 1/2 Orange, Juice of 1/2 Lime.
Shake and strain into an ice-filled old-fashioned glass.

Fourth of July

1oz. Bourbon, 1oz. Galliano, 1oz. Kahlúa, 1oz. Orange Juice.
Flambé the spirits in a glass and pour the orange juice into the flaming concoction.

Foxtrot

2oz. White Rum, 1/2oz. Orange Curaçao, Juice of 1 Lime.
Shake and strain into a martini glass.

Frank Sullivan

1oz. Cognac, 1oz. Cointreau, 1oz. Kina Lillet, 1oz. Lemon Juice.
Shake and strain into a martini glass.

Friendship

1oz. Gin, 1oz. Orange Curaçao, 1oz. Lemon Juice.
Shake and strain into a martini glass.

Frisco Sour

2oz. Bourbon, 1/2oz. Benedictine, 1/2oz. Lemon Juice, 1/2oz. Lime Juice.
Shake and strain into a sour glass.

Funny Boy

2oz. Crème de Cassis, 1oz. Vodka, 2oz. Lemon Juice.
Shake and strain into a martini glass.

Furore

2oz. Aurum, 1 1/2oz. Cognac, 1oz. Kina Lillet, 1/2oz. Orange Juice.
Shake and strain into a martini glass.

Fuzz Buster

2oz. Peach Schnapps, 1oz. Vodka, 1oz. Orange Juice, 1 oz. Lemon Juice.
Build into an old-fashioned glass.

Gazette

1oz. Cognac, 1oz. Sweet Vermouth, 1/2oz. Gomme Syrup, 1/2oz. Lemon Juice.
Shake and strain into a martini glass.

Gilroy

1oz. Gin, 1oz. Cherry Brandy, 1/2oz. Lemon Juice, 1 dash Dry Vermouth, 1 dash Orange Bitters.
Shake and strain into a martini glass.

Gimlet

See chapter three, The Classics, (p. 54).

Gin Aloha

1 1/2oz. Cointreau, 1 1/2oz. Gin, 1/2oz. Pineapple Juice, 1 dash Orange Bitters.
Shake and strain into a martini glass.

Gin Daisy

2oz. Gin, 1oz. Lemon Juice, 1/2 tsp. powdered Sugar, 1 dash Grenadine.
Shake and strain into a tankard.
Fill with ice, stir and garnish with seasonal fruits.

Ginger Snap

2oz. Vodka, 1oz. Ginger Wine, Soda.

Shake and strain into an ice-filled old-fashioned glass.
Top with the soda.

Gin & Sin

1 1/2oz. Gin, 1 1/2oz. Lemon Juice, 1 dash Orange Juice, 1 dash Grenadine.

Shake and strain into a martini glass.

Gin Sling

2oz. Gin, 1oz. Lemon Juice, 1 tsp. powdered Sugar, 1oz. Water.

Stir the sugar, water and lemon in an old-fashioned glass.
Add ice and stir in the gin. Serve with a twist of orange.

Gin Sour

2oz. Gin, 1oz. Lemon Juice, 1/2oz. Gomme Syrup.

Shake and strain into a sour glass.

Gloom Chaser

1oz. Grand Marnier, 1oz. Cointreau, 1/2oz. Grenadine, 1oz. Lemon Juice.

Shake and strain into a martini glass.

Gloom Lifter

1oz. Scotch, 1oz. Cognac, 1oz. Lemon Juice, 1/4oz. Crème de Framboise, 1 dash Gomme Syrup, 1 dash Egg White.

Shake and strain into a martini glass.

Gloriana

2oz. Apricot Brandy, 1oz. Gin, 1oz. Lemon Juice.

Shake and strain into a martini glass.

Golden Dawn

1oz. Calvados, 1oz. Gin, 1/2oz. Apricot Brandy, 1oz. Orange Juice, 1 dash Grenadine.

Shake and strain into a martini glass.

Golden Daze

2oz. Gin, 3/4oz. Crème de Pêche, 1oz. Orange Juice.
Shake and strain into a martini glass.

Golden Gleam

1oz. Grand Marnier, 1oz. Cognac, 1oz. Orange Juice.
Shake and strain into a martini glass.

Golden Margarita

1 1/2oz. Gold Tequila, 1oz. Grand Marnier, 1oz. Lime Juice.
Shake and strain into a salt-rimmed coupette.

Golden Medallion

1oz. Cognac, 1oz. Galliano, 1oz. Orange Juice, 1 Egg White.
Shake and strain into a martini glass.

Golden Tang

2oz. Vodka, 1oz. Strega, 1/2oz. Crème de Banane, 1/2oz. Orange Squash.
Shake and strain into a martini glass.

Gold Fish

1oz. Gin, 1oz. Goldwasser, 1/2oz. Cointreau, 1/2oz. Lemon Juice.
Shake and strain into a martini glass.

Gold Time

1oz. Golden Rum, 1oz. Pineapple Juice, 1/2oz. Lemon Juice, 1 Egg Yolk.
Shake and strain into a martini glass.

Grand Bretagne

1 1/2oz. Gin, 1/2oz. Kirschwasser, 1/2oz. Lime Juice, 1 Egg White, 1 dash Orange Bitters.
Shake and strain into a martini glass.

Grand Prix

1oz. Vodka, 1oz. Crème de Pêche, 1oz. Lemon Juice, 1 Egg.
Shake and strain into a martini glass.

Grand Royal

2oz. Gin, 1oz. Lime Juice, 1/2oz. Grenadine, 1 Egg.

Shake and strain into a martini glass.

Grapefruit Cocktail

1oz. Gin, 1oz. Grapefruit Juice, 1 dash Maraschino Liqueur.

Shake and strain into a martini glass.

Grapevine

2oz. Gin, 1/2oz. White Grape Juice, 1/2oz. Lemon Juice.

Shake and strain into a martini glass.

Grape Vodka Froth

2oz. Vodka, 1oz. White Grape Juice, 1oz. Lemon Juice, 1 Egg White, 1 dash Grenadine.

Shake and strain into a martini glass.

Green Angel

1oz. Bourbon, 1oz. Green Crème de Menthe, 2oz. Orange Juice, 1oz. Lemon Juice.

Shake and strain into an old-fashioned glass.

Green Back

1 1/2oz. Gin, 1oz. Green Crème de Menthe, 1oz. Lemon Juice.

Shake and strain into an old-fashioned glass.

Green Devil

1oz. Green Crème de Menthe, 1oz. Gin, 1oz. Lime Juice.

Shake and pour into an old-fashioned glass.
Garnish with a sprig of mint.

Green Dragon

1 1/2oz. Gin, 1oz. Green Crème de Menthe, 1/2oz. Kümmel, 1oz. Lemon Juice, 3 dashes Orange Bitters.

Shake and strain into a martini glass.

Green Fantasy

2oz. Vodka, $1\frac{1}{4}$oz. Midori Melon Liqueur, 1oz. Dry Vermouth, $\frac{1}{2}$oz. Lime Juice.
Shake and pour into an old-fashioned glass.

Green Hope

1oz. Vodka, 1oz. Crème de Banane, $\frac{1}{2}$oz. Blue Curaçao, 1oz. Lemon Juice.
Shake and strain into a martini glass.

Green Iguana Margarita

$1\frac{1}{2}$oz. Tequila, 1oz. Midori Melon Liqueur, 1oz. Lime Juice.
Shake and strain into a salt-rimmed coupette.

Green Lady 2

1oz. Gin, 1oz. Green Curaçao, 1oz. Lemon Juice, 1 Egg White.
Shake and strain into a martini glass.

Green Peace

$1\frac{1}{2}$oz. Midori Melon Liqueur, $\frac{3}{4}$oz. Blue Curaçao, $\frac{1}{2}$oz. Pineapple Juice, $\frac{1}{2}$oz. Lemon Juice.
Shake and strain into a martini glass.

Grenadier

2oz. Cognac, 1oz. Ginger Wine, $\frac{1}{2}$oz. Gomme Syrup, 1oz. Lemon Juice.
Shake and strain into a martini glass.

Grenadine Cocktail

2oz. Gin, 1oz. Grenadine, 1oz. Lime Juice, 2 dashes Angostura Bitters.
Shake and strain into a martini glass.

Happy Horse

2oz. White Horse Whisky, 1oz. Lime Juice, 1 dash Grenadine, 1 dash Egg White.
Shake and strain into a martini glass.

Happy Medium

1oz. Pimm's No.1, 1oz. Gin, 1oz. Cointreau, 1/2oz. Kina Lillet, 1/2oz. Orange Squash.

Shake and pour into an old-fashioned glass.

Hard Candy

2oz. Midori Melon Liqueur, 1oz. White Crème de Menthe, 1oz. Lemon Juice.

Shake and strain into a martini glass.

Harlem

2oz. Gin, 1oz. Pineapple Juice, 1/4oz. Maraschino Liqueur.

Shake and strain into a martini glass.

Harrison

2oz. Gin, 1/2oz. Lemon Juice, 1/2oz. Lime Juice, 1 dash Angostura Bitters, 1 dash Gomme Syrup, 1 dash Egg White.

Shake and strain into a martini glass.

Harrovian

2oz. Gin, 1/4oz. Orange Juice, 1 dash Lemon Juice, 1 dash Angostura Bitters.

Shake and strain into a martini glass.

Havana

1oz. White Rum, 2oz. Pineapple Juice, 1/4oz. Lemon Juice.

Shake and strain into a martini glass.

Havana Beach

2oz. Cuban White Rum, 2oz. Pineapple Juice, 1/2oz. Gomme Syrup.

Shake and strain into a martini glass.

Have a Heart

1 1/2oz. Gin, 3/4oz. Swedish Punsch, 1 dash Grenadine, 1oz. Lime Juice.

Shake and strain into a martini glass.

Hawaii

1oz. Gin, 1 dash Orange Bitters, 1 dash Angostura Bitters, 1 Egg White, 1oz. Pineapple Juice.

Shake and strain into a martini glass.

Hawaiian

2oz. Gin, 1/2oz. Triple Sec, 1/4oz. Pineapple Juice.

Shake and strain into a martini glass.

Hawaiian Brandy

2oz. Calvados, 1/4oz. Maraschino Liqueur, 1oz. Pineapple Juice, 1 dash Lemon Juice.

Shake and strain into a martini glass.

Heart's Desire

1oz. White Rum, 1oz. Swedish Punsch, 1oz. Grapefruit Juice, 1 dash Orange Curaçao.

Shake and strain into a martini glass.

Helen's Own

1oz. Gin, 1oz. Dry Vermouth, 1/2oz. Apricot Brandy, 1/2oz. Orange Juice.

Shake and strain into a martini glass.

Hesitation

2oz. Swedish Punsch, 3/4oz. Bourbon, 1/2oz. Lemon Juice.

Shake and strain into a martini glass.

Hibernian

1oz. Gin, 1oz. Cointreau, 1oz. Green Curaçao, 1/2oz. Lemon Juice.

Shake and strain into a martini glass.

Hibiscus

2oz. Dark Rum, 1/4oz. Dry Vermouth, 1/4oz. Grenadine, 1/2oz. Lemon Juice.

Shake and strain into a martini glass.

High Hat

$1^1/_2$oz. Cognac, $1^1/_2$oz. Grapefruit Juice, $^1/_4$oz. Gomme Syrup.
Shake and strain into a martini glass.

Holland House

2oz. Gin, $^1/_2$oz. Dry Vermouth, $^1/_2$oz. Lemon Juice,
$^1/_4$oz. Maraschino Liqueur, 1 slice Pineapple.
Crush pineapple and add to shaker with remaining ingredients.
Shake and strain into an ice-filled old-fashioned glass.

Hollywood

2oz. Vodka, $^1/_2$oz. Cointreau, $^1/_2$oz. Lime Juice, $^1/_2$oz. Grenadine.
Shake and strain into a martini glass.

Honey Green Moon

2oz. Midori Melon Liqueur, 1oz. Vodka, 1oz. Rose's Lime Cordial.
Shake and strain into a martini glass.

Honeymoon

$^3/_4$oz. Calvados, $^3/_4$oz. Benedictine, 1oz. Lemon Juice, 1 dash Cointreau.
Shake and strain into a martini glass.

Hong Kong

1oz. Gin, 1oz. Dry Vermouth, $^1/_4$oz. Kirschwasser, 1oz. Orange Juice,
1 dash Lemon Juice.
Shake and strain into a martini glass.

Honi Honi

2oz. Dark Rum, 1oz. Apricot Brandy, 1oz. Lemon Juice.
Shake and strain into a martini glass.

Honolulu

2oz. Gin, $^1/_4$oz. Gomme Syrup, 2 dashes each of Lemon, Pineapple,
Orange Juice, 1 dash Angostura Bitters.
Shake and strain into a martini glass.

Hoopla

1oz. Cognac, 1oz. Cointreau, 1oz. Kina Lillet, 1oz. Lemon Juice.
Shake and strain into a martini glass.

Hop Toad

1oz. White Rum, 1oz. Apricot Brandy, 3/4oz. Lime Juice.
Stir and strain into a martini glass.

Hotel Plaza

1oz. Gin, 1oz. Sweet Vermouth, 1oz. Dry Vermouth, 1 Slice Pineapple.
Crush pineapple and add to shaker with remaining ingredients.
Shake and strain into a martini glass.

Hot Shot Margarita

2oz. Tequila, 1oz. Hot Shot Tropical Liqueur, 1oz. Lime Juice.
Shake and strain into a salt-rimmed coupette.

Hugo Bracer

1oz. Calvados, 1oz. Amer Picon, 1 dash Grenadine, 1oz. Lime Juice.
Shake and strain into a martini glass.

Hula-Hula

2oz. Gin, 1oz. Orange Juice, 1/4oz. Gomme Syrup.
Shake and strain into a martini glass.

Huntsman

1 1/2oz. Vodka, 1oz. Dark Rum, 1oz. Lime Juice, 1–3 dashes Gomme Syrup.
Shake and strain into a martini glass.

Ideal

1oz. Gin, 1oz. Dry Vermouth, 1/4oz. Maraschino Liqueur, 1/2oz. Grapefruit Juice.
Shake and strain into a martini glass.

Income Tax

1oz. Gin, 1 tsp. Dry Vermouth, 1 tsp. Sweet Vermouth,
1 dash Angostura Bitters, Juice of 1/2 Orange.
Shake and strain into a martini glass.

Indian Ocean

1oz. Crème de Banane, 1/2oz. Grenadine, 3 dashes Tabasco Sauce, 4oz. Orange Juice.

Shake and pour into an old-fashioned glass.

Inebriate Cocktail

1oz. Absolut Citron Vodka, 1oz. Absolut Kurrant Vodka, 1 Lime, 1 tsp. Granulated Sugar.

Cut the lime into eighths and muddle with the sugar in an old-fashioned glass. Fill with crushed ice and add the vodka. Invert another old-fashioned glass and place on top of the first glass to create an instant shaker. Shake the ingredients between the two glasses and serve in one of them.

Ink Street

1oz. Bourbon or Rye Whiskey, 1oz. Orange Juice, 1oz. Lemon Juice.

Shake and strain into a martini glass.

In Town Tonight

2oz. Vodka, 1oz. Campari, 1oz. Orange Juice, 1 Egg White.

Shake and strain into an ice-filled old-fashioned glass.

Irish Rose

3oz. Bourbon, 1oz. Lemon Juice, 1/4oz. Grenadine.

Stir and strain into a martini glass.

Irish Shillelagh

2oz. Irish Whiskey, 1/4oz. White Rum, 1/4oz. Sloe Gin, 1/2oz. Gomme Syrup, 1oz. Lemon Juice.

Shake and pour into a highball glass. Garnish with seasonal fruits.

Irish Sour

2oz. Irish Whiskey, 1oz. Lemon Juice, 1/2oz. Gomme Syrup, 1 Egg White.

Shake and pour into an old-fashioned glass.

Jackie O's Rose

2oz. White Bacardi Rum, 1 dash Cointreau, 1oz. Lime Juice.

Shake and strain into a martini glass.

Jack-in-the-Box

1½oz. Calvados, 1½oz. Pineapple Juice, 1 dash Angostura Bitters.
Shake and strain into a martini glass.

Jack Pine

1½oz. Gin, ½oz. Dry Vermouth, 1oz. Orange Juice, 1 slice Pineapple.
Muddle the pineapple and shake with remaining ingredients.
Strain into an ice-filled old-fashioned glass.

Jack Rose

2oz. Calvados, 1oz. Lime Juice, 1 dash Grenadine.
Shake and strain into a martini glass.

Jack Sloat

1½oz. Gin, ¼oz. Dry Vermouth, ¼oz. Sweet Vermouth, 1oz. Orange Juice, 3 Slices of Pineapple.
Muddle the pineapple and shake with remaining ingredients.
Strain into a martini glass.

Jack Withers

1oz. Gin, 1oz. Sweet Vermouth, 1oz. Dry Vermouth, Juice of ½ Orange.
Shake and strain into a martini glass.

Jade

2oz. White Rum, ¼oz. Green Crème de Menthe, ¼oz. Cointreau, ½oz. Lime Juice.
Shake and strain into a martini glass.

Jamaica Honey-Bee

2oz. Dark Jamaican Rum, 1oz. Clear Honey, 1oz. Lemon Juice.
Shake and strain into a martini glass.

Japanese

2oz. Cognac, ¼oz. Orgeat, ¼oz. Lime Juice, 1 dash Angostura Bitters.
Shake and strain into a martini glass. Serve with a twist of lime.

Japanese Slipper 3

1oz. Midori Melon Liqueur, 1oz. Cointreau, 1oz. Lemon Juice.

Shake and strain into a martini glass.

Jersey City

2oz. Calvados, 1/2oz. Pineapple Juice, 3 dashes Angostura Bitters.

Shake and strain into a martini glass.

Jersey Lightning

2oz. Calvados, 1/2oz. Sweet Vermouth, 1oz. Lime Juice.

Shake and strain into a martini glass.

Jimmie Walker

1 1/2oz. Bourbon, 1/2oz. Sweet Vermouth, 1 dash Grenadine, 1/4oz. Lime Juice.

Shake and strain into a martini glass.

John Wood

1 1/2oz. Sweet Vermouth, 3/4oz. Irish Whiskey, 1/2oz. Kümmel, 1 dash Angostura Bitters, 3/4oz. Lemon Juice.

Shake and strain into a martini glass.

Joulouville

2oz. Gin, 1oz. Calvados, 1/4oz. Sweet Vermouth, 1/4oz. Lemon Juice, 2 dashes Grenadine.

Shake and strain into a martini glass.

Journalist

2oz. Gin, 1/4oz. Dry Vermouth, 1 tsp. Sweet Vermouth, 1 dash Triple Sec, 1/2oz. Lemon Juice, 1 dash Angostura Bitters.

Shake and strain into a martini glass.

Jubilee

2oz. Gin, 1oz. Van der Hum, 1oz. Lime Juice.

Shake and strain into a martini glass.

Judge Jr.

1oz. Gin, 1oz. White Rum, 1oz. Lemon Juice, 1/4oz. Gomme Syrup, 1 dash Grenadine.

Shake and strain into a martini glass.

Judgette

1oz. Gin, 1oz. Crème de Pêche, 1oz. Dry Vermouth, 1/2oz. Lime Juice.

Shake and strain into a martini glass.

June Bride

2oz. Gin, 1/4oz. Crème de Fraises, 1/2oz. Lemon Juice, 1 dash Gomme Syrup, 1 Egg White.

Shake and strain into a martini glass.

Kahlúa Sour

2oz. Kahlúa, 1oz. Lemon Juice, 1 Egg White.

Shake and pour into an old-fashioned glass.

Kamikaze

1oz. Vodka, 1oz. Triple Sec, 1oz. Lime Juice.

Shake and pour into an old-fashioned glass.

Kanzler

(BILL DECK)

2oz. Bourbon, 1oz. Cointreau, 1oz. Lemon Juice.

Shake and strain into a martini glass.

Kempinski

1oz. White Rum, 1oz. Cointreau, 2oz. Grapefruit Juice.

Shake and strain into a martini glass.

Kentucky

2oz. Bourbon, 1oz. Pineapple Juice.

Shake and strain into a martini glass.

KGB

1 1/2oz. Gin, 1oz. Kümmel, 1 dash Apricot Brandy, 1/4oz. Lemon Juice.
Shake and strain into a martini glass.

King Cole

2oz. Bourbon, 1 tsp. granulated Sugar, 1 slice Orange, 1 slice Pineapple.
Muddle the sugar and fruit in an old-fashioned glass.
Fill with ice and stir in the bourbon.

King Cole 2

2oz. Bourbon, 1 dash Fernet Branca, 1 tsp. granulated Sugar,
1 slice Orange, 1 slice Pineapple.
Muddle fruit and sugar in shaker, add ice and remaining ingredients.
Shake and strain into a martini glass.

King George IV

1oz. Gin, 1oz. Cointreau, 1oz. Scotch, 1oz. Lemon Juice.
Shake and strain into a martini glass.

King Louis

2oz. Cognac, 1 1/2oz. Lemon Juice, 1/4oz. Gomme Syrup, 1/4oz. Clear Honey.
Shake and strain into a martini glass.

Kingston

1oz. Dark Jamaican Rum, 1oz. Orange Curaçao, 1/2oz. Grenadine,
1/2oz. Lemon Juice.
Shake and strain into a martini glass.

Kingston Heights

1oz. White Rum, 1/2oz. Kümmel, 1/2oz. Orange Juice, 1 dash Pimento Dram.
Shake and strain into a martini glass.
Dash the Pimento Dram on the top.

Kiss The Boys Goodbye

1oz. Cognac, 1oz. Sloe Gin, 1 Egg White, 1 1/2oz. Lemon Juice.
Shake and strain into a martini glass.

Manhasset

2oz. Bourbon, 1/4oz. Dry Vermouth, 1/4oz. Sweet Vermouth, 1/2oz. Lemon Juice.

Shake and strain into a martini glass.

Manyann

1oz. Gin, 1oz. Caperitif, 1/4oz. Orange Curaçao, 1oz. Lemon Juice.

Shake and strain into a martini glass.

Maple Leaf

2oz. Bourbon, 1oz. Lemon Juice, 1 tbsp. Maple Syrup.

Shake and strain into a martini glass.

Maragato

1oz. White Rum, 1oz. Dry Vermouth, 1oz. Sweet Vermouth, 1 dash Kirschwasser, 1oz. Lemon Juice, 1/2oz. Lime Juice.

Shake and strain into a martini glass.

Marble Hill

2oz. Gin, 1oz. Dubonnet, 1oz. Orange Juice.

Stir and strain into a martini glass.

Margarita

See chapter three, The Classics, (p. 56).

Mariposa

2oz. White Rum, 1oz. Cognac, 1/4oz. Orange Juice, 1/4z. Lemon Juice, 1 dash Grenadine.

Shake and strain into a martini glass.

Marvel

2oz. Dark Rum, 1oz. Grenadine, 1/2oz. Lemon Juice.

Shake and strain into a martini glass.

Mary Jane

1oz. Gin, 1oz. dry Vermouth, 1oz. Dubonnet, 1oz. Orange Juice.

Shake and pour into an old-fashioned glass.

Mary Pickford

2oz. White Rum, 1oz. Pineapple Juice, 1 dash Grenadine, 1 dash Maraschino Liqueur.

Shake and strain into a martini glass.

Maurice 2

1oz. Gin, 1/2oz. Dry Vermouth, 1/2oz. Sweet Vermouth, 1 dash Angostura Bitters, Juice of 1/4 Orange.

Shake and strain into a martini glass.

Mayfair

1oz. Apricot Brandy, 1oz. Gin, 1/4oz. Orange Juice, 1/4 tsp. ground Cloves.

Shake and strain into a martini glass.

Melba 2

1oz. White Rum, 1oz. Peach Schnapps, 1oz. Lime Juice, 1 dash Grenadine.

Shake and strain into a martini glass.

Mellow Tongue

(PETER LALA)

1oz. White Rum, 1/2oz. Midori Melon Liqueur, 1/2oz. Peach Tree, 3/4oz. Lime Juice, 2 dashes Egg White.

Shake and strain into a martini glass.

Melon Cocktail

2oz. Gin, 1/2oz. Maraschino Liqueur, 1/2oz. Lemon Juice.

Shake and strain into a martini glass.

Melon Daiquiri

1 1/2oz. White Rum, 1oz. Midori Melon Liqueur, 1oz. Lime Juice.

Shake and strain into a martini glass.

Melon Sour

2oz. Midori Melon Liqueur, 1oz. Lemon Juice, 1 dash Gomme Syrup, 1 Egg White.

Shake and strain into a martini glass.

Menlo Club

1/2oz. Gin, 1/2oz. Cointreau, 1oz. White Rum, 1/4oz. Gomme Syrup, 1oz. Lemon Juice.

Shake and strain into a martini glass.

Mexicana

2oz. Tequila, 1 dash Grenadine, 1oz. Lemon Juice.

Shake and pour into an old-fashioned glass.

Mexican Rose

2oz. Tequila, 1oz. Rose's Lime Cordial.

Stir and strain into a martini glass.

Miami

2oz. White Rum, 3/4oz. White Crème de Menthe, 1/4oz. Lemon Juice.

Shake and strain into a martini glass.

Miami 2

2oz. White Rum, 3/4oz. Cointreau, 1/4oz. Lemon Juice.

Shake and strain into a martini glass.

Miami Beach

1oz. Scotch, 1oz. Dry Vermouth, 1oz. Grapefruit Juice.

Shake and strain into a martini glass.

Midnight

2oz. Apricot Brandy, 1oz. Cointreau, 1/2oz. Lemon Juice.

Shake and strain into a martini glass.

Midori Slipper

1oz. Midori Melon Liqueur, 1oz. Cointreau, 1oz. Lemon Juice.

Shake and strain into a martini glass.

Milan

1oz. Bourbon, 1oz. White Rum, 1/4oz. Orange Juice.

Shake and strain into a martini glass. Serve with a twist of lemon.

Milan Dawn

(DAVIDE CAMPARI MILANO)

2oz. Gin, 1oz. Campari, 2oz. Orange Juice.

Shake and pour the gin and orange into a deep dish champagne saucer. Splash the Campari over the drink.

Million-Dollar

2oz. Gin, 1oz. Sweet Vermouth, 1/4oz. Pineapple Juice, 1 dash Grenadine, 1 Egg White.

Shake and strain into a martini glass.

Miracle

1oz. Gin, 1oz. Kina Lillet, 1oz. Cointreau, 1oz. Lemon Juice, 1 dash Pastis.

Shake and strain into a martini glass.

Mississippi Mule

1oz. Gin, 1oz. Crème de Cassis, 1oz. Lemon Juice.

Shake and pour into a sugar-rimmed salude grande glass.

Mr Manhattan

2oz. Gin, 1/4oz. Orange Juice, 1/2oz. Gomme Syrup, 6 Mint Leaves.

Shake all including the mint and strain into a martini glass.

Modern

2oz. Scotch, 1/4oz. Dark Rum, 1/4oz. Anisette, 1/2oz. Lemon Juice, 1 dash Angostura Bitters.

Shake and strain into a martini glass.

Monkey Gland

2oz. Gin, 1/4oz. Benedictine, 1/4oz. Grenadine, 1oz. Orange Juice.

Shake and strain into a martini glass.

Montreal Sour

2oz. Gin, 1oz. Lemon Juice, 1/2oz. Gomme Syrup, 1 Egg White.

Shake and strain into a sour glass.

Moonlight

2oz. Calvados, 1oz. Lemon Juice, 1/2oz. Gomme Syrup.

Shake and pour into an old-fashioned glass.

Moon Quake

2oz. Dark Rum 1oz. Kahlúa, 1oz. Lemon Juice.

Shake and strain into a martini glass.

Moon River

1oz. Gin, 1oz. Apricot Brandy, 1oz. Triple Sec, 1/2oz. Galliano, 1/2oz. Lime Juice.

Shake and strain into a martini glass.

Morning Glory

2oz. Gin, 1/4oz. Green Crème de Menthe, 1 dash Scotch, 1oz. Lime Juice, 1 Egg.

Shake and strain into a martini glass.

Mountain

2oz. Bourbon, 1/4oz. Dry Vermouth, 1 dash Sweet Vermouth, 1/2oz. Lemon Juice, 1 Egg White.

Shake and strain into a martini glass.

Mustapha

2oz. Gin, 1oz. Crème de Cassis, 1/4oz. Rose's Lime Cordial, 1 Egg White, 1 dash Tabasco Sauce.

Shake all but the tabasco and strain into a martini glass.
Dash the tabasco over the drink.

My Fair Lady

2oz. Gin, 1/2oz. Crème de Fraises, 1oz. Lemon Juice, 1oz. Orange Juice, 1 Egg White.

Shake and pour into an old-fashioned glass.

Naked Lady

1 1/2oz. White Rum, 1oz. Apricot Brandy, 1oz. Lemon Juice, 1 dash Grenadine, 1 Egg White.

Shake and strain into a martini glass.

Natural

2oz. White Rum, 1oz. Cognac, 1/4oz. Lemon Juice, 1 dash Orgeat Syrup.
Shake and strain into a martini glass.

Nevada

1 1/2oz. White Rum, 2 dashes Angostura Bitters, 1oz. Gomme Syrup, 1oz. Lime Juice, 1oz. Grapefruit Juice.
Shake and strain into a martini glass.

Nevins

2oz. Bourbon, 1/4oz. Apricot Brandy, 1/2oz. Lemon Juice, 1 dash Grapefruit Juice, 1 dash Angostura Bitters.
Shake and strain into a martini glass.

New York

2oz. Bourbon, 1oz. Lime Juice, 1/4oz. Gomme Syrup, 1 dash Grenadine.
Shake and strain into a martini glass. Serve with a twist of lemon.

Night Flight

2oz. Dark Rum, 1oz. Lime Juice, 1/2oz. Maple Syrup.
Shake and strain into a martini glass.

Nightmare Abbey

1oz. Gin, 1oz. Dubonnet, 1/2oz. Cherry Brandy, 1/2oz. Orange Juice.
Shake and strain into a martini glass.

Night Shade

1oz. Bourbon, 1oz. Sweet Vermouth, 1/4oz. Yellow Chartreuse, 1oz. Orange Juice.
Shake and strain into a martini glass.

Ninotchka

2oz. Vodka, 1 1/4oz. White Crème de Cacao, 1/4oz. Lemon Juice.
Shake and strain into a martini glass.

Nora

(DAVIDE CAMPARI MILANO)

2oz. Gin, 1oz. Campari, 2oz. Pineapple Juice.

Shake and strain into a martini glass. Serve with a twist of orange.

Normandy Golden Dawn

1oz. Calvados, 1oz. Apricot Brandy, 1/2oz. Grand Marnier, 1oz. Orange Juice, 2 dashes Grenadine.

Shake and pour into an old-fashioned glass.

Normandy Rose

2oz. Calvados, 1oz. White Rum, 1oz. Lime Juice, 2 dashes Grenadine.

Shake and strain into a martini glass.

Oddball

1oz. Midori Melon Liqueur, 1oz. Tequila, 1oz. Orange Juice, 1oz. Pineapple Juice.

Shake and pour into an old-fashioned glass.

Old Crow Cocktail

2oz. Old Crow Bourbon, 1/2oz. Sweet Vermouth, 1oz. Orange Juice, 1 dash Grenadine.

Shake and strain into a martini glass.

Old Tart

1oz. Tequila, 1oz. Cointreau, Juice of 1 Lime, Juice of 1 Lemon.

Shake and pour into an old-fashioned glass.

Old Tom Cocktail

2oz. Old Tom Gin, 1oz. Lime Juice, 1/2oz. Grenadine.

Shake and strain into a martini glass.

Olympic

1oz. Cognac, 1oz. Cointreau, 1oz. Orange Juice.

Shake and strain into a martini glass.

Olympic 2

2oz. Gin, 1oz. Sweet Vermouth, 1/2oz. Pastis, 1 dash Angostura Bitters, 1/4oz. Lemon Juice.

Stir and strain into a martini glass.

One Spot

2oz. Gin, 1oz. Pernod, 1oz. Lemon Juice.

Shake and strain into a martini glass.

Opal

2oz. Gin, 1oz. Cointreau, 1/4oz. Orange Juice, 1 tsp. powdered Sugar.

Shake and strain into a martini glass.

Orgeat Cocktail

2oz. Gin, 1oz. Orgeat Syrup, 1oz. Lemon Juice.

Shake and strain into a martini glass.

Oriental

2oz. Bourbon, 1oz. Cointreau, 1/2oz. Sweet Vermouth, 1oz. Lime Juice.

Shake and strain into a martini glass.

Outrigger

1oz. Crème de Pêche, 1oz. Absolut Citron Vodka, 1oz. Pineapple Juice.

Shake and strain into an ice-filled old-fashioned glass.

Paddy 2

2oz. Rye Whiskey, 1/4oz. Lemon Juice, 3 dashes Angostura Bitters.

Stir and strain into a martini glass.

Paediatrician

2oz. Gin, 1oz. Lemon Juice, 1oz. White Grape Juice, 1 dash Grenadine.

Shake and strain into a martini glass.

Palm Beach

2oz. Gin, 1/2oz. Dry Vermouth, 1oz. Grapefruit Juice.

Shake and strain into a martini glass.

Palmetto

1oz. White Rum, 1oz. Apricot Brandy, $^3/_4$oz. Cointreau, $^3/_4$oz. Lemon Juice.
Shake and strain into a martini glass.

Panther

1oz. Campari, 1oz. Cointreau, Juice of 1 Lime.
Shake and strain into a martini glass.

Paradise

1oz. Gin, 1oz. Apricot Brandy, 1oz. Orange Juice.
Shake and strain into a martini glass.

Parchment

2$^1/_2$oz. Gin, $^1/_2$oz. Cranberry Juice.
Stir and strain into a martini glass. Garnish with 3 whole cloves.

Park Avenue

2oz. Gin, 1oz. Sweet Vermouth, 1oz. Pineapple Juice.
Shake and strain into a martini glass.

Peking

2oz. Dark Rum, $^1/_4$oz. Pernod, $^3/_4$oz. Lemon Juice, 2 dashes Grenadine.
Shake and strain into a martini glass.

Pendennis

1oz. Gin, $^1/_2$oz. Apricot Brandy, $^1/_2$oz. Dry Vermouth, 1oz. Lime Juice, 1 dash Angostura Bitters.
Shake and strain into a martini glass.

Perfect Lady

1oz. Gin, 1oz. Crème de Pêche, 1oz. Lemon Juice, 1 Egg White.
Shake and strain into a martini glass.

Perfect Love

1oz. Vodka, 1oz. Parfait Amour, 1oz. Lemon Juice.
Shake and strain into a martini glass.

Persuasion

2oz. Vodka, 1oz. Rose's Lime Cordial, 1oz. Cranberry Juice.

Shake and strain into a martini glass.

Pet

1 1/2oz. White Rum, 3/4oz. Dark Rum, 1/4oz. Cointreau, 2 dashes Grenadine, 1/4oz. Lemon Juice.

Shake and strain into a martini glass.

Peter Pan

1oz. Gin, 1oz. Dry Vermouth, 1oz. Orange Juice, 1 dash Orange Bitters.

Shake and strain into a martini glass.

Petite Fleur

1oz. White Rum, 1oz. Triple Sec, 1oz. Grapefruit Juice.

Shake and strain into a martini glass.

Pig's Tail

1oz. Slivovitz, 1oz. Vodka, 2oz. White Grape Juice.

Stir and strain into a martini glass.

Pilgrim

1 1/2oz. White Rum, 1oz. Cointreau, 1oz. Lemon Juice, 2 dashes Maraschino Liqueur.

Shake and pour into an old-fashioned glass.

Pineapple

2oz. White Rum, 1oz. Pineapple Juice, 1/4oz. Lemon Juice.

Shake and strain into a martini glass.

Pineapple 2

1oz. Gin, 2oz. Pineapple Juice, 1 dash Grenadine.

Shake and strain into a martini glass.

Ping-Pong

2oz. Sloe Gin, 1oz. Lemon Juice, 1 Egg White.

Shake and strain into a martini glass.

Pink Garter

2oz. Gin, 1/2oz. Lemon Juice, 1/2oz. Orange Juice, 2 dashes Grenadine.
Shake and strain into a martini glass.

Pink Lady

1oz. Gin, 1oz. Cointreau, 1oz. Lemon Juice, 2 dashes Grenadine, 1 Egg White.
Shake and strain into a martini glass.

Pink Lady 3

1oz. Gin, 1oz. Calvados, 1oz. Lime Juice, 1 dash Grenadine.
Shake and strain into a martini glass.

Pink Margarita

1 1/2oz. Tequila, 1oz. Cointreau, 1oz. Lime Juice, 1 dash Grenadine.
Shake and strain into a salt-rimmed coupette.

Pink Panther 2

1oz. Campari, 1oz. Cointreau, 1oz. Tequila, 1/2oz. Cranberry Juice.
Shake and strain into a martini glass.

Pink Pussy

1oz. Campari, 1oz. Apricot Brandy, 1 Egg White, 2oz. Bitter Lemon.
Shake all but the bitter lemon and strain into an old-fashioned glass. Top with the bitter lemon.

Pisco Sour

2oz. Pisco, 2oz. Lime Juice, 3/4oz. Gomme Syrup, 1 Egg White, 2 dashes Angostura Bitters.
Shake and strain into a martini glass.

Planter's

2oz. Dark Jamaican Rum, Juice of 1 Lime, 1/2oz. Gomme Syrup.
Shake and strain into a martini glass.

Plaza

1oz. Gin, 1oz. Dry Vermouth, 1oz. Sweet Vermouth, 1 chunk Pineapple.
Muddle the pineapple and add to the remaining ingredients.
Shake and strain into a martini glass.

Polynesian

2oz. Vodka, 1oz. Cherry Brandy, 1oz. Lime Juice, 1 dash Grenadine.
Shake and strain into a sugar-rimmed martini glass.

President

2oz. Dark Cuban Rum, 1 dash Grenadine, Juice of 1/2 Ruby Orange, 1 dash Lemon Juice.
Shake and strain into a martini glass.

President 2

2oz. Dark Cuban Rum, 1oz. Orange Curaçao, 1 dash Grenadine, 1/4oz. Lemon Juice.
Shake and strain into a martini glass.

Presto

2oz. Cognac, 1/2oz. Sweet Vermouth, 1 dash Pernod, 1oz. Orange Juice.
Shake and strain into a martini glass.

Prince Charles

1oz. Cognac, 1oz. Drambuie, 1oz. Lemon Juice.
Stir and strain into a martini glass.

Prince of Wales

2oz. Gin, 1oz. Pineapple Juice, 1 Egg White.
Shake and strain into a martini glass.

Princeton

1oz. Gin, 1oz. Dry Vermouth, 1oz. Lime Juice.
Shake and strain into a martini glass.

Prunelle

2oz. Cognac, 1oz. Prunelle, 1oz. Lime Juice.
Shake and strain into a martini glass.

Puerto Rican

2oz. Puerto Rican White Rum, Juice of 1 Lime, 2 dashes Grenadine.
Shake and strain into a martini glass.

Purple Kiss

1oz. Gin, 1oz. Crème de Noyaux, 1/4oz. Cherry Brandy, 1/2oz. Lemon Juice, 1 Egg White.
Shake and pour into an old-fashioned glass.

Quaker

1oz. White Rum, 1oz. Cognac, 1/2oz. Crème de Framboise, 1/4oz. Gomme Syrup, 1/2oz. Lemon Juice.
Shake and strain into a martini glass.

Quality Cocktail

2oz. Beefeater Crown Jewel Gin, 1oz. Grapefruit Juice, 2 dashes Grenadine, 1 dash Angostura Bitters.
Shake and strain into a martini glass.

Queen Elizabeth 2

1oz. Gin, 1/2oz. Cointreau, 1/2oz. Lemon Juice, 2 dashes Pernod.
Shake and strain into a martini glass.

Ranger

1oz. White Rum, 1oz. Gin, 1oz. Lemon Juice, 1/4oz. Gomme Syrup.
Shake and strain into a martini glass.

Raspberry Sour

2oz. Crème de Framboise, 1oz. Lemon Juice, 1/2oz. Gomme Syrup, 1 Egg White.
Shake and strain into an ice-filled old-fashioned glass.

Rattlesnake

2oz. Bourbon, 1 dash Anisette, 1oz. Lemon Juice, 1/4oz. Gomme Syrup, 1 Egg White.

Shake and strain into a martini glass.

Rebel Charge

2oz. Bourbon, 1oz. Cointreau, 1 Egg White, 1/4oz. Lemon Juice, 1/4oz. Orange Juice.

Shake and strain into an old-fashioned glass. Garnish with a slice of orange.

Red Apple

1oz. Absolut 100 Vodka, 1oz. Apple Juice, 1 dash Grenadine.

Shake and strain into a martini glass.

Red Cloud

2 1/4oz. Gin, 3/4oz. Apricot Brandy, 1/4oz. Lemon Juice, 1 dash Grenadine.

Shake and strain into a martini glass.

Red Hot Willy

2oz. Tequila, 1oz. Tomato Juice, 4 dashes Tabasco Sauce.

Shake and strain into a martini glass.

Red Lion

1oz. Gin, 1oz. Grand Marnier, 1/2oz. Lemon Juice, 1/2oz. Orange Juice.

Shake and strain into a martini glass.

Red Raider

2oz. Bourbon, 1oz. Cointreau, 1oz. Lemon Juice, 1/4oz. Grenadine.

Shake and pour into an old-fashioned glass.

Resolute

2oz. Gin, 1oz. Apricot Brandy, 1/2oz. Lemon Juice.

Shake and strain into a martini glass.

Retreat From Moscow

1oz. Vodka, 1oz. Kümmel, 1oz. Lemon Juice.

Shake and strain into a martini glass.

Robson

2oz. Dark Jamaican Rum, 1/2oz. Orange Juice, 1/4oz. Lemon Juice, 2 dashes Grenadine.

Shake and strain into a martini glass.

Rococo

1oz. Cointreau, 1oz. Cherry Vodka, 1oz. Orange Juice.

Shake and strain into a martini glass.

Rolls-Royce 2

1oz. Cognac, 1oz. Cointreau, 1oz. Orange Juice.

Shake and strain into a martini glass.

Rose

1oz. Gin, 1oz. Apricot Brandy, 1/4oz. Dry Vermouth, 1/4oz. Lemon Juice, 3 dashes Grenadine.

Shake and strain into a martini glass.

Royal Bronx

1oz. Gin, 1/2oz. Dry Vermouth, 1/2oz. Sweet Vermouth, 3 dashes Grand Marnier, Juice of 1/4 Orange.

Shake all but the Grand Marnier and strain into a deep-dish champagne saucer half filled with crushed ice. Dash the Grand Marnier over the drink.

Royal Clover Club

2oz. Gin, 1oz. Lime Juice, 2 dashes Grenadine, 1 Egg Yolk.

Shake and strain into a martini glass.

Royal Cocktail

2oz. Gin, 1oz. Lemon Juice, 1/4oz. Gomme Syrup, 1 Egg.

Shake and strain into a martini glass.

Royal Mail

1oz. Sloe Gin, 1oz. Van der Hum, 1oz. Orange Juice, 1oz. Lemon Juice.

Shake and strain into a martini glass.

Royston's Revenge

(MICHAEL ROYSTON-YORKE)

1oz. Midori Melon Liqueur, 1oz. Monin Lime Liqueur, 1/2oz. Sake, 1/2oz. Lemon Juice.

Shake and strain into a martini glass. Garnish with slices of lemon and lime.

Rum Cobbler

2oz. Dark Rum, 1 tsp. powdered Sugar, 1oz. Soda Water.

In an old-fashioned glass, dissolve the sugar in the soda. Fill with crushed ice and stir in the rum. Garnish with seasonal fruits.

Rum Daisy

2oz. Dark Rum, 1oz. Lemon Juice, 1 tsp. powdered Sugar, 2 dashes Grenadine.

Shake very well and strain into an ice-filled tankard. Garnish with seasonal fruit and mint.

Rum Fix

2oz. Dark Rum, 1/2oz. Lemon Juice, 1oz. Gomme Syrup.

Stir ingredients into an old-fashioned glass three-quarters filled with crushed ice. Garnish with a slice of lemon.

Rum Sidecar

1oz. Golden Rum, 1oz. Cointreau, 1oz. Lemon Juice.

Shake and strain into a martini glass.

Rum Sour

2oz. White Rum, 1oz. Lemon Juice, 1/2oz. Gomme Syrup.

Shake and strain into a martini glass.

San Sebastian

1 1/2oz. Gin, 1/4oz. White Rum, 1/4oz. Triple Sec, 1/2oz. Grapefruit Juice, 1 dash Lemon Juice.

Shake and strain into a martini glass.

Santiago

2oz. White Rum, 1oz. Lime Juice, 1/4oz. Grenadine.

Shake and strain into a martini glass.

Satan's Whiskers (Straight)

1oz. Gin, 1/2oz. Dry Vermouth, 1/2oz. Sweet Vermouth, 1/2oz. Grand Marnier, 1oz. Orange Juice, 3 dashes Orange Bitters.

Shake and strain into a martini glass.

Satan's Whiskers (Curled)

1oz. Gin, 1/2oz. Dry Vermouth, 1/2oz. Sweet Vermouth, 1/2oz. Orange Curaçao, 1oz. Orange Juice, 3 dashes Orange Bitters.

Shake and strain into a martini glass.

Savannah

1oz. Gin, 1oz. White Crème de Cacao, 1oz. Orange Juice, 1 Egg White.

Shake and strain into a martini glass.

Saxon

2oz. White Rum, 1oz. Lime Juice, 1/2oz. Grenadine, 1 strip Orange Peel.

Shake all including the orange peel and strain into a martini glass.

Scotch Bishop

2oz. Scotch, 1/2oz. Dry Vermouth, 1/4oz. Cointreau, 1/4oz. Orange Juice, 1/4oz. Gomme Syrup.

Shake and strain into a martini glass.

Scotch Cobbler

2oz. Scotch, 1/4oz. Orange Curaçao, 2 dashes Gomme Syrup.

Pour ingredients into an ice-filled wine glass.
Garnish with seasonal fruit and mint.

Scotch Holiday Sour

2oz. Scotch, 1oz. Cherry Brandy, 1/2oz. Sweet Vermouth, 1oz. Lemon Juice.

Shake and pour into an old-fashioned glass.

Scotch Sour

2oz. Scotch, 1oz. Lemon Juice, 1/2oz. Gomme Syrup.

Shake and strain into a sour glass.

Screwball

1oz. Midori Melon Liqueur, 1oz. Vodka, 2oz. Orange Juice.
Shake and pour into an old-fashioned glass.

Sea Board

1oz. Bourbon, 1oz. Gin, 1oz. Lemon Juice, 1/2oz. Gomme Syrup.
Shake and pour into an old-fashioned glass. Garnish with a sprig of mint.

Serenissima

2oz. Vodka, 1 dash Campari, 2oz. Grapefruit Juice.
Shake and strain into an ice-filled wineglass.

Sex On The Beach

1oz. Vodka, 1oz. Amaretto, 2oz. Cranberry Juice.
Shake and pour into an old-fashioned glass.

Shalom

1oz. Absolut 100 Vodka, 1oz. Madeira, 1oz. Orange Juice.
Shake and pour into an old-fashioned glass.

Shamrock 2

1oz. Gin, 1oz. Green Crème de Menthe, 1/4oz. Lemon Juice, 1/4oz. Orange Juice, 1 Egg White.
Shake and strain into a martini glass.

Sidecar

See chapter three, The Classics, (pp 67–8).

Sir Walter

1oz. Cognac, 1oz. White Rum, 1/4oz. Orange Curaçao, 1/4oz. Lemon Juice, 1 dash Grenadine.
Shake and strain into a martini glass.

Skipper

1oz. Gin, 1oz. Maraschino Liqueur, 3/4oz. Lemon Juice, 1/4oz. Grenadine.
Shake and strain into a martini glass.

Slam
1oz. Cognac, 1oz. Cointreau, 1/2oz. Apricot Brandy, 1/2oz. Lime Juice.
Shake and strain into a martini glass.

Sloe Gin Cocktail
2oz. Sloe Gin, 1/2oz. Lemon Juice, 2 dashes Angostura Bitters.
Shake and strain into a martini glass.

Sloe Sour
2oz. Sloe Gin, 1oz. Lime Juice, 1/2oz. Gomme Syrup.
Shake and pour into an old-fashioned glass.

Sloe Tequila
1oz. Sloe Gin, 1oz. Tequila, 1oz. Lime Juice.
Shake and pour into an old-fashioned glass.

Sloppy Joe
1oz. Cognac, 1oz. Port, 1 dash Cointreau, 1oz. Pineapple Juice, 1 dash Grenadine.
Shake and strain into a martini glass.

Smile
1oz. Gin, 1oz. Grenadine, 1 Egg Yolk, 1/4oz. Lime Juice.
Shake and strain into a martini glass.

Soul Kiss
1oz. Dubonnet, 1/2oz. Dry Vermouth, 1/2oz. Sweet Vermouth, 2oz. Orange Juice.
Shake and pour into a medium goblet.

South of The Border
1oz. Tequila, 1oz. Kahlúa, 1oz. Lime Juice.
Shake and strain into a martini glass.

South Side
2oz. Gin, 1oz. Lemon Juice, 1/2oz. Gomme Syrup, 2 sprigs Mint.
Shake all including the mint and strain into a martini glass.

Spartan

2oz. Gin, 1oz. Orange Juice, 1/4oz. Orgeat Syrup.

Shake and strain into a martini glass.

Spring Buck

(MARK C. SUTTON)

1 1/2oz. Gin, 1/2oz. Midori Melon Liqueur, 1/2oz. Apricot Brandy, 1oz. Orange Juice.

Shake and strain into a martini glass filled with crushed ice.

Stanley

2oz. Gin, 3/4oz. White Rum, 1/2oz. Lemon Juice, 1 dash Grenadine.

Shake and strain into a martini glass.

Star Daisy

1oz. Gin, 1oz. Calvados, 1/2oz. Gomme Syrup, 1/4oz. Grenadine, 1oz. Lemon Juice.

Shake and strain into an ice-filled tankard.
Garnish with mint and seasonal fruit.

Star of Brazil

1oz. Midori Melon Liqueur, 1oz. White Rum, 1/2oz. Gin, 1/2oz. Apricot Brandy, 1/2oz. Lime Juice.

Shake and strain into a martini glass.

Stella Roma

(DAVE BARNWELL)

1oz. Galliano, 1oz. Campari, 1oz. Gin, 1oz. 7Up, 1 dash Egg White.

Shake and strain into a champagne flute.

Stiletto

2oz. Bourbon, 1/4oz. Amaretto, 1/2oz. Lemon Juice.

Shake and strain into an ice-filled old-fashioned glass.

Stone Sour

2oz. Amaretto, 1oz. Lemon Juice, 1/2oz. Gomme Syrup, 1 Egg White.

Shake and strain into a martini glass.

Strawberry Sour

2oz. Crème de Fraises, 1oz. Lemon Juice, $^{1}/_{2}$oz. Gomme Syrup, 1 Egg White.

Shake and strain into an ice-filled old-fashioned glass.

Sunshine

1oz. White Rum, 1oz. Maraschino Liqueur, 1oz. Crème de Cassis, $^{1}/_{2}$oz. Lemon Juice.

Shake and strain into a martini glass.

SW1

1oz. Campari, 1oz. Vodka, 1oz. Orange Juice, 1 dash Egg White.

Shake and strain into a martini glass. Serve with a twist of orange.

Sweet Dreams

1oz. Gin, 1oz. Apricot Brandy, 1oz. White Rum, 1oz. Pineapple Juice.

Shake and pour into an old-fashioned glass.

Sweet Patootie

2oz. Gin, 1oz. Triple Sec, $^{1}/_{2}$oz. Orange Juice.

Shake and strain into a martini glass.

Tahoe

$2^{1}/_{2}$oz. White Rum, $^{1}/_{4}$oz. Lime Juice, $^{1}/_{4}$oz. Gomme Syrup.

Shake and strain into a martini glass.

Take It Or Leave It

$1^{1}/_{2}$oz. Gin, $^{3}/_{4}$oz. Dry Vermouth, $^{3}/_{4}$oz. Apricot Brandy, $^{1}/_{4}$oz. Grenadine, $^{1}/_{4}$oz. Lemon Juice.

Shake and strain into a martini glass.

Tanglefoot

1oz. White Rum, 1oz. Swedish Punsch, $^{1}/_{2}$oz. Lemon Juice, $^{1}/_{2}$oz. Orange Juice.

Shake and strain into a martini glass.

Tango 2

1oz. White Rum, 1/2oz. Sweet Vermouth, 1/2oz. Dry Vermouth, 1/4oz. Benedictine, 1/2oz. Orange Juice.

Shake and strain into a martini glass.

Tantalus

1oz. Forbidden Fruit Liqueur, 1oz. Cognac, 1oz. Lemon Juice.

Shake and strain into a martini glass.

Tennessee Cocktail

2oz. Bourbon, 1/2oz. Maraschino Liqueur, 1/2oz. Lemon Juice.

Shake and strain into a martini glass.

Tennis Girl

2oz. Dry Vermouth, 1oz. Scotch, 1/4oz. Lime Juice.

Shake and strain into a martini glass.

Tequila Cocktail

2oz. Tequila, 1oz. Lime Juice, 1/4oz. Grenadine.

Shake and strain into a martini glass.

Tequila Mockingbird

2oz. Tequila, 1oz. Green Crème de Menthe, 1oz. Lime Juice.

Shake and strain into a martini glass.

Tequila Sour

2oz. Tequila, 1oz. Lemon Juice, 1/2oz. Gomme Syrup, 1 Egg White.

Shake and strain into a sour glass.

Testarossa

(DAVIDE CAMPARI MILANO)

1oz. Campari, 1oz. Vodka, 1/2oz. Tonic Water.

Build into an old-fashioned glass and garnish with a slice of orange.

Three Stripes

2oz. Gin, 1oz. Dry Vermouth, Juice and pulp of 1/4 Orange.

Shake and strain into a martini glass.

Tipperary 2

1oz. Gin, 1oz. Dry Vermouth, 1/4oz. White Crème de Menthe, 1/4oz. Grenadine, 1/2oz. Orange Juice.

Shake and strain into a martini glass. Garnish with a sprig of mint.

TNT 2

2oz. Tequila, 2oz. Tonic.

Build into an old-fashioned glass. Serve with a twist of lemon.

Tokyo Lady

1 1/2oz. Gin, 1oz. Midori Melon Liqueur, 1oz. Lime Juice, 1 Egg White.

Shake and strain into a martini glass.

Top Hat 2

5oz. Guinness Stout, 5oz. Ginger Beer.

Pour into a half-pint beer glass.

Tovarich

2oz. Vodka, 1oz. Kümmel, 1oz. Lime Juice.

Shake and strain into a martini glass.

Trinidad Cocktail

2oz. Trinidad Rum, Juice of 1/2 Lime, 1/2oz. Gomme Syrup, 3 dashes Angostura Bitters.

Shake and strain into a martini glass.

Tropical 2

2oz. White Rum, 1/4oz. Cointreau, Juice of 1/2 Lime.

Shake and strain into a martini glass.

Tropical Dawn

2oz. Gin, 1oz. Campari, 2oz. Orange Juice.

Shake gin and orange and strain into an old-fashioned glass half filled with crushed ice. Pour the Campari over the top.

Turret

1oz. Gin, 1/2oz. Swedish Punsch, 1/2oz. Calvados, 1/2oz. Grenadine, 1/2oz. Lemon Juice.

Shake and strain into a martini glass.

Twentieth Century

1 1/2oz. Gin, 3/4oz. Kina Lillet, 3/4oz. White Crème de Cacao, 1oz. Lemon Juice.

Shake and strain into a martini glass.

Twin Six

1 1/2oz. Gin, 1oz. Sweet Vermouth, 1/4oz. Grenadine, Juice of 1/4 Orange, 1 Egg White.

Shake and strain into a martini glass.

Unusual

1oz. Gin, 1oz. Swedish Punsch, 1oz. Cherry Brandy, 1/2oz. Lime Juice.

Shake and strain into a martini glass.

Up In The Air

2oz. Gin, 1/4oz. Maraschino Liqueur, 1oz. Lemon Juice.

Shake and strain into a martini glass.

Vacuum

2oz. Grand Marnier, 3/4oz. Dubonnet, Juice of 1/2 Ruby Grapefruit.

Shake and strain into a martini glass.

Valencia

2oz. Apricot Brandy, 1/4oz. Orange Juice, 2 dashes Orange Bitters.

Shake and strain into a martini glass.

Van Fleet

3oz. White Rum, 1oz. Lemon Juice, 1oz. Maple Syrup.

Shake and strain into an ice-filled old-fashioned glass.

Venticello di Carnevale

(TONY NGUYEN)

1oz. Campari, 1oz. Golden Rum, 1/2oz. Lemon Juice, 1/2oz. Lime Juice, 1 dash Gomme Syrup.
Shake and strain into a martini glass.

Versace

1oz. Campari, 1oz. Tequila, 1oz. Orange Juice, 1 dash Grenadine.
Stir and pour into a highball glass.

Vesper 2

2oz. Gin, 1oz. Crème de Noyaux, 1/4oz. Orange Juice, 2 dashes Angostura Bitters.
Shake and strain into a martini glass.

Victory

1 1/2oz. Dry Vermouth, 1 1/2oz. Sweet Vermouth, 1/4oz. Lemon Juice, 1/4oz. Orange Juice, 2 dashes Grenadine.
Shake and strain into a martini glass.

Viva Villa

2oz. Tequila, 1oz. Lime Juice, 1/2oz. Gomme Syrup.
Shake and pour into a salt-rimmed old-fashioned glass.

Vladivostok Virgin

1oz. Vodka, 1oz. Gin, 1oz. Grapefruit Juice, 2 dashes Angostura Bitters.
Shake and strain into a martini glass. Garnish with a thin slice of cucumber.

Vodka Daisy

2oz. Vodka, 1oz. Lemon Juice, 1/4oz. Grenadine, Soda Water.
Shake all but the soda and strain into an ice-filled tankard.
Stir in required amount of soda and garnish with seasonal fruits.

Vodka Fix

2oz. Vodka, 1oz. Lemon Juice, 1/2oz. Gomme Syrup.
Stir into an old-fashioned glass three-quarters filled with crushed ice.
Garnish with a slice of lemon.

Vodka Gimlet

See chapter three, The Classics, (p. 54).
Substitute vodka for the gin in the gimlet.

Vodka Sling

2oz. Vodka, 1oz. Lemon Juice, 1 tsp. granulated Sugar, 1oz. Water.
Stir the sugar and water together in an old-fashioned glass.
Fill with ice and stir in the vodka and lemon juice.

Vodka Sour

2oz. Vodka, 1oz. Lemon Juice, 1/2oz. Gomme Syrup, 1 Egg White.
Shake and strain into a martini glass.

Waikiki Beachcomber

1 1/2oz. Gin, 1 1/2oz. Cointreau, 1/4oz. Pineapple Juice.
Shake and strain into a martini glass.

Wallis Blue

1oz. Gin, 1oz. Cointreau, 1oz. Lime Juice.
Shake and strain into a sugar-rimmed martini glass.

Waterbury

2oz. Cognac, 1oz. Lime Juice, 1 Egg White, 1/4oz. Grenadine, 1/4oz. Gomme Syrup.
Shake and strain into a martini glass.

Webster

2oz. Gin, 3/4oz. Dry Vermouth, 2 dashes Apricot Brandy, 1oz. Lime Juice.
Shake and strain into a martini glass.

Wedding Belle

1oz. Gin, 1oz. Dubonnet, 1/2oz. Cherry Brandy, 1/2oz. Orange Juice.
Shake and strain into a martini glass.

Welcome

1/2oz. Gin, 1/2oz. Swedish Punsch, 1/2oz. Cognac, 1/2oz. Grenadine, 1/2oz. Lemon Juice, 1/2oz. Orange Juice.

Shake and strain into a martini glass.

Wembley 2

1oz. Scotch, 1oz. Dry Vermouth, 1oz. Pineapple Juice.

Shake and strain into a martini glass.

Western Rose

1oz. Gin, 1oz. Bourbon, 1/2oz. Apricot Brandy, 1/4oz. Grenadine, 1/4oz. Lemon Juice.

Shake and strain into a martini glass.

Western Rose 2

1 1/2oz. Gin, 3/4oz. Apricot Brandy, 3/4oz. Dry Vermouth, 1/4oz. Lemon Juice.

Shake and strain into a martini glass.

Whisky Daisy

2oz. Scotch, 1oz. Lemon Juice, 1/4oz. Grenadine, Soda Water.

Shake all but the soda and strain into an ice-filled tankard. Stir in required amount of soda and garnish with seasonal fruits.

Whisky Fix

2oz. Scotch, 1oz. Lemon Juice, 1/2oz. Gomme Syrup.

Stir into an old-fashioned glass three-quarters filled with crushed ice. Garnish with a slice of lemon.

Whisky Sling

2oz. Scotch, 1oz. Lemon Juice, 1 tsp. granulated Sugar, 1oz. Water.

Stir the sugar and water together in an old-fashioned glass. Fill with ice and stir in the Scotch whisky and lemon juice.

Whisky Sour

2oz. Scotch, 1oz. Lemon Juice, 1/2oz. Gomme Syrup, 1 Egg White.

Shake and strain into a martini glass.

White Baby

2oz. Gin, 1oz. Cointreau, 1oz. Lemon Syrup.
Stir and strain into a martini glass.

White Cactus

2oz. Tequila, 1oz. Lime Juice, 1/2oz. Gomme Syrup, 1 Egg White.
Shake and strain into a martini glass.

White Lamp

1oz. Vodka, 1oz. Kümmel, 1oz. Lime Juice, 1 Egg White.
Shake and strain into a martini glass.

White Lion

2oz. White Rum, 2 dashes Angostura Bitters, 1oz. Lemon Juice, 1 Egg White, 1/2oz. Gomme Syrup.
Shake and strain into a martini glass.

White Rose

2oz. Gin, 1/4oz. Maraschino Liqueur, 1 dash Orange Juice, 1oz. Lime Juice, 1 Egg White.
Shake and strain into a martini glass.

Why Not?

1oz. Gin, 1oz. Apricot Brandy, 1/2oz. Dry Vermouth, 1/4oz. Lemon Juice.
Shake and strain into a martini glass.

Wild Screw

2oz. Wild Turkey 101 Bourbon, 2oz. Orange Juice.
Shake and pour into an old-fashioned glass.

Wild Screw 2

1 1/4oz. Wild Turkey 101 Bourbon, 1oz. Vodka, 2 1/2oz. Orange Juice.
Shake and pour into an old-fashioned glass.

Willie Smith

2oz. Cognac, 1oz. Maraschino Liqueur, 1/4oz. Lemon Juice.
Shake and strain into a martini glass.

Will Rogers

$1^1/_2$oz. Gin, $^3/_4$oz. Dry Vermouth, Juice of $^1/_4$ Orange, $^1/_4$oz. Triple Sec.
Shake and strain into a martini glass.

Woodward

2oz. Scotch, $^1/_2$oz. Dry Vermouth, $^1/_4$z. Grapefruit Juice.
Shake and strain into a martini glass.

Woo Woo

1oz. Vodka, 1oz. Peach Schnapps, 3oz. Cranberry Juice.
Shake and pour into an old-fashioned glass.

XYZ

2oz. White Rum, $^1/_2$oz. Cointreau, $^1/_4$oz. Lemon Juice.
Shake and strain into a martini glass.

Yellow Bird

2oz. White Rum, $^1/_2$oz. Cointreau, $^1/_2$oz. Galliano, $^3/_4$oz. Lime Juice.
Shake and strain into a martini glass.

Yellow Rattler

2oz. Gin, $^1/_2$oz. Dry Vermouth, $^1/_2$oz. Sweet Vermouth, $^1/_4$oz. Orange Juice.
Shake and strain into a martini glass.
Garnish with a silver-skin cocktail onion.

Yellow Sea

1oz. Vodka, 1oz. Galliano, $^3/_4$oz. Crème de Banane,
$^1/_2$oz. Rose's Lime Cordial.
Shake and strain into a martini glass.

Yokohama

1oz. Gin, $^1/_2$oz. Vodka, $^1/_2$oz. Grenadine, 1oz. Orange Juice.
Shake and strain into a martini glass.

Yukon Gold

1oz. Yukon Jack Whiskey, 1oz. Crème de Banane, 2oz. Orange Juice.

Shake and pour into an old-fashioned glass.

Garnish with an orange peel spiral.

Zanzibar

2oz. Dry Vermouth, 1/4oz. Gin, 2 dashes Gomme Syrup, 2 dashes Lemon Juice.

Shake and strain into a martini glass. Serve with a twist of lemon.

El Zoral

1oz. White Rum, 1/2oz. Anisette, 2oz. Orange Juice, 1 dash Grenadine.

Shake and strain into an ice-filled old-fashioned glass.

BLENDED COCKTAILS

▼

The modern use of the blender for mixing cocktails makes it possible to include a myriad ingredients that were previously beyond the cocktail bartender's range. Now we are able to combine traditional spirits and liqueurs with fruits, nuts, ice-cream and a variety of other ingredients which could not amalgamate by classical methods such as shaking and stirring. In addition, we can effortlessly create the contemporary frozen (sorbet) style of cocktail and fashion icy variations of old favourites. The blender has been a revelation in the cocktail world. The following list is testimony.

Apple Colada

2oz. Calvados, 1oz. White Rum, 1oz. Sweetened Coconut Cream, 2oz. Apple Juice.

Blend until smooth and pour into a large goblet.
Garnish with slice of apple.

Apricot Daiquiri

1oz. White Rum, 1oz. Apricot Brandy, 1oz. Lime Juice, 1/2oz. Gomme Syrup, Flesh of 3 Apricots.

Blend until frozen and pour into a large goblet.

Aristocrat

2oz. Poire Williams, 1oz. White Rum, 3oz. Pineapple Juice, 1 dash Orgeat, 1/2 Pear (canned).

Blend until smooth and pour into a large goblet. Garnish with slices of pear.

Aztec

2oz. Tequila, 1oz. Lime Juice, 1/4 fresh Mango.

Blend until smooth and pour into a medium goblet.

Bahia

2oz. White Rum, 1oz. Sweetened Coconut Cream, 2oz. Pineapple Juice, 1oz. Grapefruit Juice, 1oz. Double Cream.

Blend until smooth and pour into a large goblet.

Banana Daiquiri

1oz. Crème de Banane, 1oz. White Rum, 1oz. Lime Juice, 3/4oz. Gomme Syrup, 1/2 ripe Banana.

Blend until frozen and pour into a large goblet.
Garnish with slices of banana.

Batida Abaci

2oz. Cachaça, 1 large piece of fresh Pineapple (approx 2oz.) 1/2oz. Gomme Syrup.

Blend until frozen and pour into a large goblet.

Batida Caju

2oz. Cachaça, 1 large tbsp Cashew Nuts, 1/2oz. Gomme Syrup.

Blend until frozen and pour into a large goblet.

Batida Goiaba

2oz. Cachaça, 1 large piece of fresh Guava (approx 2oz.) 1/2oz. Gomme Syrup.

Blend until frozen and pour into a large goblet.

Batida Limão

2oz. Cachaça, Juice of 1 Lime, 1/2oz. Gomme Syrup.

Blend until frozen and pour into a large goblet.

Batida Mango

2oz. Cachaça, 1 large piece of fresh Mango (approx 2oz.) 1/2oz. Gomme Syrup.

Blend until frozen and pour into a large goblet.

Batida Maracuja

2oz. Cachaça, flesh of 1 Passion Fruit, 1/2oz. Gomme Syrup.

Blend until frozen and pour into a large goblet.

Batida Morango

2oz. Cachaça, 4 fresh Strawberries, 1/2oz. Gomme Syrup.

Blend until frozen and pour into a large goblet.

Blue Hawaiian

1oz. Blue Curaçao, 1oz. White Rum, 3oz. Pineapple Juice, 1oz. Sweetened Coconut Cream.

Blend until smooth and pour into a large goblet.

Bronco-Buster

1oz. Midori Melon Liqueur, 1oz. fresh Blueberries/1oz. Mango Liqueur, 1/2oz. Lemon Juice, 2 chunks of Rock Melon.

Blend the first two ingredients until frozen and pour into a highball glass. Blend the remaining ingredients until smooth and float on top.

Calm Voyage

1oz. White Rum, 1oz. Strega, 1/2oz. Lemon Juice, 1 dash Passion Syrup, 1 dash Egg White.

Blend until smooth and pour into a champagne saucer.

Campari Colada

(NORMAN BUKOFZER)

1 1/2oz. Campari, 5oz. Pineapple Juice, 1oz. sweetened Coconut Cream.

Blend until smooth and pour into a large goblet.
Garnish with a slice of orange.

Carioca

2oz. Cognac, 1oz. Kahlúa, 1 Egg Yolk, 1 dash Double Cream.

Blend until smooth and pour into a deep-dish champagne saucer.
Sprinkle ground cinnamon over drink.

Casa Blanca 2

2oz. White Rum, 1oz. Sweetened Coconut Cream, 3oz. Pineapple Juice, 1/2oz. Grenadine.

Blend until smooth and pour into a large goblet.

Cherry Daiquiri

1oz. White Rum, 1oz. Cherry Brandy, 1oz. Lime Juice, 1 dash Grenadine, flesh of 6–8 fresh Cherries.

Blend until frozen and pour into a large goblet.

Cherry Frappé

2oz. Cherry Brandy, 1 dash Grenadine.

Blend with a regular scoop of ice until frozen and pour into an old-fashioned glass.

Chi Chi

2oz. Vodka, 1oz. Sweetened Coconut Cream, 3oz. Pineapple Juice.

Blend until smooth and pour into a large goblet.

Chocolate Ant

1oz. Kahlúa, 1oz. Brown Crème de Cacao, 1 scoop Chocolate Ice-Cream, 3oz. Milk.

Blend without additional ice and pour into a large goblet.
Garnish with crumbled chocolate flake.

Chocolate Frappé

2oz. White Crème de Cacao.

Blend with a regular scoop of ice until frozen and pour into an old-fashioned glass.

Ciao Baby

2oz. Cointreau, 1oz. Campari, 2oz. Banana Juice.

Blend until smooth and pour into a large goblet.
Garnish with a slice of banana.

Classic Hummer

1oz. Canadian Club Whisky, 1oz. Kahlúa, 2 scoops Vanilla Ice-Cream.

Blend until smooth and pour into a medium goblet.

Cocoloco

1oz. White Rum, 1oz. Vodka, 1oz. Tequila, 1oz. Lemon Juice, 1oz. Sweetened Coconut Cream.

Blend until smooth and pour into a large goblet.

Coconut Breeze

2oz. Dark Rum, 1oz. Sweetened Coconut Cream, 4oz. Fresh Pineapple, 1 dash Grenadine, 1 dash Orgeat.

Blend until smooth and pour into a large goblet.

Coconut Daiquiri

1oz. White Rum, 1oz. Noix de Coco, 1oz. Lime Juice, 2oz. Fresh Coconut, 1/2oz. Gomme Syrup.

Blend until frozen and pour into a large goblet.

Coffee Colada

1oz. White Rum, 1oz. Kahlúa, 1oz. Sweetened Coconut Cream, 2oz. Pineapple Juice.

Blend until smooth and pour into a large goblet.

Coffee Frappé

2oz. Tia Maria.

Blend with a regular scoop of ice until frozen and pour into an old-fashioned glass.

Coffee Fudge

1oz. Kahlúa, 1/2oz. Bailey's, 1/2oz. Grand Marnier, 2 tbsp. Toffee-Flavoured Yoghurt.

Blend until smooth and pour into an old-fashioned glass.

Daiquiri (frozen)

2oz. White Rum, Juice of 1 Lime, $^1/_2$oz. Gomme Syrup, $^1/_2$oz. Maraschino Liqueur.

Blend until frozen and pour into a large goblet.

Devil's Tail

$1^1/_2$oz. Overproof Rum, 1oz. Vodka, $^1/_2$oz. Lime Juice, $^1/_2$oz. Apricot Brandy, 1 dash Grenadine.

Blend until smooth and pour into a large goblet.

Dextrose

2oz. Absolut Citron Vodka, 1 large scoop Lemon Water-Ice, 2oz. Orange Juice, 1 dash Gomme Syrup.

Blend without ice until smooth and pour into a coupette.

Drambuie Mist

2oz. Drambuie.

Blend with a scoop of ice and pour into an old-fashioned glass.

Earthquake 2

2oz. Tequila, 1 dash Campari, $^1/_4$oz. Grenadine, 2 fresh Strawberries.

Blend until smooth and pour into a medium goblet.
Garnish with additional strawberries.

Farmer's Daughter

2oz. Crème de Banane, 1oz. Bailey's, 1oz. Amaretto, 1oz. Double Cream.

Blend until smooth and pour into a large goblet.

Flash Gordon

2oz. Dark Rum, 1oz. Lime Juice.

Blend until frozen and pour into a wineglass.

Fraises Royale

1oz. Crème de Fraises, 2 Strawberries, Chilled Champagne.

Blend the strawberries and liqueur without ice and pour into a champagne flute.
Top with the champagne.

Frozen Apple

2oz. Calvados, 1oz. Lime Juice, 1 dash Gomme Syrup, 1 Egg White.
Blend until frozen and pour into a large goblet.

Frozen Berkeley

2oz. White Rum, 1/2oz. Cognac, 1 dash Lemon Juice, 1 dash Passion Syrup.
Blend until frozen and pour into a champagne flute.

Frozen Blue Margarita

2oz. Tequila, 1oz. Blue Curaçao, 1oz. Lime Juice.
Blend until frozen and pour into a coupette.

Frozen Mango Daiquiri

2oz. White Rum, 1oz. Lime Juice, 1/2oz. Gomme Syrup, 4oz. Fresh Mango.
Blend until frozen and pour into a large goblet.

Frozen Margarita

2oz. Tequila, 1oz. Cointreau, 1oz. Lime Juice.
Blend until frozen and pour into a coupette.

Frozen Matador

2oz. Tequila, 1oz. Lime Juice, 4oz. Fresh Pineapple.
Blend until frozen and pour into a large goblet.

Frozen Mint Daiquiri

2oz. White Rum, 1oz. Lime Juice, 1/2oz. Gomme Syrup, 8 fresh Mint Leaves.
Blend until frozen and pour into a large goblet.

Frozen Peach Daiquiri

1oz. White Rum, 1oz. Crème de Pêche, 1oz. Lime Juice,
1/2oz. Gomme Syrup, 4oz. Fresh Peach.
Blend until frozen and pour into a large goblet.

Frozen Pineapple Daiquiri

2oz. White Rum, 1oz. Lime Juice, 1/2oz. Gomme Syrup,
4oz. Fresh Pineapple.
Blend until frozen and pour into a large goblet.

Frozen Raspberry Daiquiri

1oz. White Rum, 1oz. Crème de Framboise, 1oz. Lime Juice, 1/2oz. Gomme Syrup, 4oz. Fresh Raspberries.

Blend until frozen and pour into a large goblet.

Frozen Steppes

1oz. Vodka, 1oz. White Crème de Cacao, 1 scoop Vanilla Ice Cream.

Blend without additional ice until smooth and pour into a coupette.

Frozen Strawberry Daiquiri

1oz. White Rum, 1oz. Crème de Fraises, 1oz. Lime Juice, 1/2oz. Gomme Syrup, 4oz. Fresh Strawberries.

Blend until frozen and pour into a large goblet.

Frozen Strawberry Margarita

2oz. Tequila, 1oz. Cointreau, 1/2oz. Crème de Fraises, 1oz. Lime Juice, 4 fresh Strawberries.

Blend until frozen and pour into a large goblet.

Gauguin

2oz. White Rum, 1 dash Passion Syrup, 1 dash Lime Juice, 1 dash Lemon Juice.

Blend until frozen and pour into an old-fashioned glass.

Geisha Delight

1 1/2oz. Midori Melon Liqueur, 3/4oz. Galliano, 3/4oz. Cointreau, 1/4oz. Malibu, 2 1/2oz. Pineapple Juice.

Blend until smooth and pour into a brandy balloon.

Glad Eye

1oz. Pernod, 1/2oz. White Crème de Menthe.

Blend with a regular scoop of ice until frozen and pour into an old-fashioned glass.

Golden Gloves

2oz. Dark Rum, 1oz. Lemon Juice, 1 dash Cointreau.

Blend until frozen and pour into an old-fashioned glass.
Serve with a twist of orange.

Green Eyes

1oz. White Rum, 1oz. Midori Melon Liqueur,
1oz. Sweetened Coconut Cream, $\frac{1}{2}$oz. Rose's Lime Cordial,
1oz. Pineapple Juice.

Blend until smooth and pour into a large goblet.

Green Tingle

$1\frac{1}{2}$oz. Midori Melon Liqueur, $\frac{3}{4}$oz. Lena Liqueur, $\frac{3}{4}$oz. Blue Curaçao,
$2\frac{1}{2}$oz. Orange Juice, $\frac{3}{4}$oz. Lemon Juice.

Blend until smooth and pour into a large goblet.

Hazel's Wonder

1oz. Kahlúa, 1oz. Bailey's, 2oz. Double Cream, 2oz. Shelled Hazelnuts.

Blend until smooth and pour into a medium goblet.

Hazy Cuban

2oz. White Rum, 1oz. Sweetened Coconut Cream, 1oz. Double Cream,
2oz. Pineapple Juice, 1 slice fresh Pineapple.

Blend until smooth and pour into a large goblet.

Heavenly Cloud

$1\frac{1}{2}$oz. Kahlúa, $1\frac{1}{2}$oz. Crème de Cassis, 2oz. Double Cream,
$\frac{1}{2}$ fresh Banana, 3 fresh Strawberries.

Blend until smooth and pour into a large goblet.

Hocus-Pocus

1oz. Gin, 1oz. Cointreau, 1oz. Lemon Juice.

Blend until frozen and pour into a champagne flute.

Honey Dew

$1\frac{1}{2}$oz. Gin, 1 dash Pernod, $\frac{3}{4}$oz. Lemon Juice, 4oz. Diced Honeydew Melon.

Blend until frozen and pour into a deep-dish champagne saucer.

Hummer

1oz. White Rum, 1oz. Kahlúa, 1 large scoop Vanilla Ice-Cream.

Blend without additional ice until smooth and pour into a medium goblet.

Hydraulic

1oz. Campari, 1oz. Grand Marnier, 1oz. Peach Schnapps, 1oz. Cranberry Juice.

Blend until frozen and pour into a large goblet.

Icebreaker

1oz. Tequila, 1oz. Blue Curaçao, 1/2oz. Vodka, 1oz. Lime Juice.

Blend until frozen and pour into a coupette.

Ice Peak

1oz. Peach Schnapps, 1oz. Midori Melon Liqueur, 1/2oz. Pernod, 1oz. Cranberry Juice.

Blend until frozen and pour into a large goblet.

Igloo

1oz. Cointreau, 1oz. White Crème de Cacao, 1oz. White Crème de Menthe, 1oz. Double Cream.

Blend until frozen and pour into a coupette.

Irish Banana

1oz. Bailey's, 1oz. Crème de Banane, 1oz. Double Cream, 1/2 fresh Banana.

Blend until smooth and pour into a highball glass.

Jagged Edge

1oz. Cointreau, 1oz. Kümmel, 1 dash Lime Juice.

Blend until frozen and pour into an old-fashioned glass.

Jamaican Melon

1oz. Midori Melon Liqueur, 1oz. Tia Maria, 1oz. Dark Rum, 1oz. Sweetened Coconut Cream, 3oz. Pineapple Juice.

Blend until smooth and pour into a large goblet.

Jocose Julep

2oz. Bourbon, $^1/_2$oz. Green Crème de Menthe, 1oz. Gomme Syrup, 1oz. Lime Juice, 8–10 fresh Mint Leaves.

Blend until frozen and pour into a large goblet. Garnish with a sprig of mint.

Jungle Juice

1oz. Drambuie, 1oz. White Rum, 1oz. Sweetened Coconut Cream, 2oz. Pineapple Juice, 1oz. Double Cream.

Blend until smooth and pour into a large goblet.

Kahlúa Colada

1oz. Kahlúa, 1oz. White Rum, 1oz. Sweetened Coconut Cream, 2oz. Pineapple Juice.

Blend until smooth and pour into a large goblet.

Kailua

2oz. Dark Rum, $^1/_2$oz. Lemon Juice, $^1/_4$oz. Grenadine, 1 slice Pineapple.

Blend until smooth and pour into an old-fashioned glass.

Kandy Kane

1oz. White Crème de Cacao, 1oz. White Crème de Menthe, 2 scoops Vanilla Ice-Cream.

Blend without additional ice until smooth and pour into a medium goblet.

Kermit's Undivided Attention

1$^1/_2$oz. Midori Melon Liqueur, 1oz. Malibu, 2$^1/_2$oz. Pineapple Juice, Flesh of $^1/_2$ Kiwi Fruit.

Blend until smooth and pour into a highball glass.

Kings Daiquiri

1oz. White Rum, 1oz. Cointreau, 1oz. Parfait Amour, 1oz. Lime Juice, $^1/_2$oz. Gomme Syrup.

Blend until frozen and pour into a large goblet.

Kiwi Margarita

2oz. Tequila, 1oz. Cointreau, 1oz. Lime Juice, Flesh of 1 Kiwi Fruit.

Blend until frozen and pour into a salt-rimmed salude grande glass.

Lady In Red

1 1/2oz. Vodka, 1oz. Cherry Brandy, 1oz. Crème de Fraises, 1 dash Grenadine, 3 Strawberries.

Blend until smooth and pour into a large goblet.

Le Paris

1 3/4oz. White Rum, 3/4oz. Cointreau, 1/4oz. Campari, 1oz. Lemon Juice, 4 Strawberries.

Blend until frozen and pour into a medium goblet.

Limey

2oz. White Rum, 1oz. Rose's Lime Cordial, 1oz. Triple Sec, 1/2oz. Lime Juice.

Blend until frozen and pour into a deep-dish champagne saucer.

Lion Tamer

2oz. Gin, 6 Raspberries.

Blend until frozen and pour into a martini glass.
Garnish with a fresh raspberry.

London Fog

2 1/2oz. Gin, 1/2oz. Pernod.

Blend until frozen and pour into an old-fashioned glass.

Long Neck

1 1/2oz. Vodka, 1oz. Midori Melon Liqueur, 1oz. Lemon Juice, 1 dash Grenadine.

Blend until smooth and pour into a champagne flute.
Dash grenadine on top.

Love Cocktail

2oz. Sloe Gin, 1/2oz. Lemon Juice, 4 Raspberries, 1 Egg White.

Blend until smooth and pour into a champagne flute.

Mandingo

1oz. Midori Melon Liqueur, 1oz. Mango Liqueur, 1oz. Lemon Juice, 2oz. Fresh Mango.

Blend until smooth and pour into a medium goblet.

Mango Colada

2oz. White Rum, 1oz. Sweetened Coconut Cream, 3oz. Pineapple Juice, 3oz. fresh Mango.

Blend until smooth and pour into a large goblet.

Mango's Comfort

1oz. Southern Comfort, 1oz. Mango Liqueur, 1/2oz. Midori Melon Liqueur, 3oz. Orange Juice, 2oz. fresh Mango.

Blend until smooth and pour into a large goblet.

Margo's Comfort

1oz. Southern Comfort, 1oz. Kiwi Liqueur, 1/2oz. Midori Melon Liqueur, 3oz. Pineapple Juice, 1 Kiwi Fruit.

Blend until smooth and pour into a large goblet.

Melon Colada

1oz. Midori Melon Liqueur, 1oz. White Rum, 1oz. Sweetened Coconut Cream, 2oz. Pineapple Juice.

Blend until smooth and pour into a medium goblet.

Midori Paradise

2oz. Midori Melon Liqueur, 1oz. Noix de Coco, 1oz. Sweetened Coconut Cream, 2oz. Double Cream.

Blend until smooth and pour into a large goblet.

Midori Strawberry Colada

1oz. Midori Melon Liqueur, 1oz. White Rum, 1/2oz. Crème de Fraises, 1oz. Sweetened Coconut Cream, 2oz. Pineapple Juice, 4 Strawberries.

Blend until smooth and pour into a large goblet.

Montezuma

2oz. Motezuma Silver Tequila, 1oz. Madeira, 1 Egg Yolk.

Blend until smooth and pour into a champagne flute.

Musk Melon

1oz. White Rum, 3/4oz. Midori Melon Liqueur, 1/2oz. Lemon Juice, 1/2oz. Orange Juice, 1 dash Gomme Syrup.

Blend until frozen and pour into a coupette.

Naked Jay Bird

2oz. Blue Curaçao, 1oz. Crème de Mûre, 1oz. Lemon Juice.

Blend until smooth and pour into a medium goblet.

Napa Fraises

1oz. Crème de Fraises, 2 Strawberries, Chilled Cuvée Napa.

Blend the strawberries with the liqueur and pour into a champagne flute. Top with the Cuvée Napa.

Nutty Banana 2

1oz. Crème de Banane, 1/2oz. Frangelico, 1/2oz. Tia Maria, 1oz. Single Cream, 1/2 fresh Banana, 1 dash Orgeat Syrup.

Blend until smooth and pour into a large goblet.

Nutty Colada

2oz. Amaretto, 1oz. White Rum, 1oz. Sweetened Coconut Cream, 2oz. Pineapple Juice.

Blend until smooth and pour into a large goblet.

Nutty Margarita

1oz. Frangelico, 1oz. Tequila, 1oz. Lime Juice, 1 tbsp. crushed Hazel Nuts.

Blend until frozen and pour into a salt-rimmed goblet.

Orange Chi-Chi

1oz. Vodka, 1oz. Cointreau, 1oz. Sweetened Coconut Cream, 1oz. Pineapple Juice, 1oz. Orange Juice.

Blend until smooth and pour into a goblet.

Passport

1oz. Peach Schnapps, 1 1/4oz. Tequila, 2oz. Passion Fruit Juice, 1/2oz. Lime Juice, 2 Strawberries.

Blend until smooth and pour into a deep-dish champagne saucer.

Peach Colada

1oz. White Rum, 1oz. Crème de Pêche, 1oz. Sweetened Coconut Cream, 1oz. Pineapple Juice, 1oz. Peach Nectar.

Blend until smooth and pour into a large goblet.

Peach Daiquiri

1oz. White Rum, 1oz. Crème de Pêche, 1oz. Lime Juice, 1/2oz. Gomme Syrup, 2 slices Peach.

Blend until smooth and pour into a medium goblet.

Peach Fuzz

2oz. Peach Schnapps, 2oz. Peach Nectar, 1/2oz. Double Cream.

Blend until frozen and pour into a salude grande glass.

Peach Margarita

1 1/2oz. Tequila, 1oz. Cointreau, 1oz. Lime Juice, 3 slices Peach.

Blend until frozen and pour into a salt-rimmed coupette.

Penang

1oz. Gin, 1/2oz. Green Crème de Menthe, 2oz. Pineapple Juice.

Blend until frozen and pour into a large goblet.

Petank

2oz. Crème de Fraises, 3oz. Cranberry Juice, 2 Strawberries, 2oz. Double Cream, 1/2oz. Gomme Syrup.

Blend until smooth and pour into a deep-dish champagne saucer.

Pina Colada

2oz. White Rum, 1oz. Sweetened Coconut Cream, 2oz. Pineapple Juice.

Blend until smooth and pour into a medium goblet.

Pina Colada 2

2oz. White Rum, 1oz. Sweetened Coconut Cream, 1oz. Double Cream, 2oz. Pineapple Juice.

Blend until smooth and pour into a large goblet.

Pina Colada 3

2oz. Golden Rum, 1oz. Sweetened Coconut Cream, 3oz. fresh Pineapple.
Blend until smooth and pour into a medium goblet.

Pooh-Bah

1oz. Gin, 1oz. Swedish Punsch, 1oz. White Rum, 2 Apricots.
Blend until smooth and pour into a wineglass.

Public Domain

1oz. Poire Williams, 1oz. Cointreau, 2oz. Pineapple Juice, Flesh of 1/2 Pear.
Blend until smooth and pour into a large goblet.

Queen's

1oz. Gin, 1oz. Dry Vermouth, 1oz. Sweet Vermouth, 2oz. fresh Pineapple.
Blend until smooth and pour into a wineglass.

Raspberry Chi-Chi

1oz. Vodka, 1oz. Absolut Kurrant Vodka, 1oz. Sweetened Coconut Cream, 2oz. Pineapple Juice, 6 fresh Raspberries.
Blend until smooth and pour into a large goblet.

Raspberry Colada

1oz. White Rum, 1oz. Crème de Framboise, 1oz. Sweetened Coconut Cream, 2oz. Pineapple Juice, 6 fresh Raspberries.
Blend until smooth and pour into a large goblet.

Raspberry Daiquiri

1oz. White Rum, 1oz. Crème de Framboise, 1oz. Lime Juice, 1/2oz. Gomme Syrup, 6 fresh Raspberries.
Blend until smooth and pour into a highball glass.

Raspberry Frappé

2oz. Crème de Framboise, 4 fresh Raspberries.
Blend until frozen and pour into a martini glass.

Raspberry Margarita

1½oz. Tequila, ½oz. Crème de Framboise, ½oz. Cointreau, 1oz. Lime Juice, 6 fresh Raspberries.

Blend until frozen and pour into a salt-rimmed coupette.

Red Hot Kiss

(JOHN GILCHRIST)

3oz. Campari, 1oz. Pineau des Charentes, 1oz. Plum Syrup.

Blend until smooth and strain into a champagne flute. Garnish with a slice of orange.

Relax

(LEE RUSSELL)

1oz. Midori Melon Liqueur, 1oz. Crème de Banane, ½oz. Frangelico, 2oz. Pineapple Juice, 1oz. Double Cream.

Blend until smooth and pour into a salude grande glass. Garnish with a strawberry and a slice of pineapple.

Roadrunner

1oz. Vodka, 1oz. Amaretto, 1oz. Sweetened Coconut Cream.

Blend until smooth and pour into a sugar-rimmed salude grande glass.

Royal Shaker

2oz. Royal Mint Chocolate Liqueur, 1 scoop Vanilla Ice-Cream, 10oz. Milk.

Blend without ice and pour into 2 highball glasses.

Rum Frappé

2oz. Dark Rum, ½oz. Gomme Syrup.

Blend until frozen and pour into an old-fashioned glass. Serve with a twist of orange.

Russian Roulette

1oz. Vodka, 1oz. Lemon Vodka, 1oz. Lime Juice, ½oz. Gomme Syrup.

Blend until frozen and pour into a martini glass.

Seasons Of Spring

(TAK WING WONG)

1 1/2oz. Midori Melon Liqueur, 1/2oz. Crème de Fraises, 3oz. Pineapple Juice, 1oz. Lemon Juice, 1 slice Honeydew Melon.

Blend until smooth and pour into a highball glass.
Garnish with a strawberry.

Snowbird

2oz. Amaretto, 1 Scoop Vanilla Ice-Cream.

Blend without additional ice and pour into an old-fashioned glass.

Sour Kiss

1oz. Gin, 1oz. Dry Vermouth, 1/4oz. Dubonnet, 1 dash Grapefruit Juice, 1 dash Lemon Juice.

Blend until frozen and pour into a large goblet.

Strawberries & Cream

2oz. Crème de Fraises, 1oz. Vodka, 2oz. Double Cream, 4 fresh Strawberries.

Blend until smooth and pour into a medium goblet.
Garnish with a sliced strawberry.

Strawberry Chi-Chi

2oz. Vodka, 1oz. Sweetened Coconut Cream, 2oz. Pineapple Juice, 6 fresh Strawberries.

Blend until smooth and pour into a large goblet.

Strawberry Colada

1oz. White Rum, 1oz. Crème de Fraises, 1oz. Sweetened Coconut Cream, 2oz. Pineapple Juice, 6 fresh Strawberries.

Blend until smooth and pour into a large goblet.

Strawberry Daiquiri

1oz. White Rum, 1oz. Crème de Fraises, 1oz. Lime Juice, 1/2oz. Gomme Syrup, 6 fresh Strawberries.

Blend until smooth and pour into a highball glass.

Strawberry Dawn

1oz. Gin, 1oz. Crème de Fraises, 1oz. Sweetened Coconut Cream, 6 fresh Strawberries.

Blend until smooth and pour into a salude grande glass.

Strawberry Frappé

2oz. Crème de Fraises, 4 fresh Strawberries.

Blend until frozen and pour into a martini glass.

Strawberry Margarita

1½oz. Tequila, 1oz. Cointreau, 1oz. Lime Juice, 6 fresh Strawberries.

Blend until frozen and pour into a salt-rimmed coupette.

Strawberry Rita

1oz. Tequila, 1oz. Crème de Fraises, 1oz. Lime Juice, 1oz. Double Cream, 3 fresh Strawberries, ½oz. Gomme Syrup.

Blend until smooth and pour into a sugar-rimmed salude grande glass.

Suntorian Star

(INGRAM JUNG)

1oz. Midori Melon Liqueur, ½oz. Lena Banana Liqueur, 4 chunks fresh Pineapple, flesh of ½ Passionfruit, 2 Strawberries.

Blend until smooth and pour into a deep-dish champagne saucer.

Superior

2oz. White Rum, 1oz. Sweet Vermouth, 1oz. Lemon Juice, 2 fresh Apricots.

Blend until frozen and pour into a large goblet.

Garnish with an orange slice.

Tabu

2oz. Dark Rum, 1oz. Gomme Syrup, 1oz. Cranberry Juice, ½oz. Lemon Juice, 3oz. fresh Pineapple.

Blend until smooth and pour into a large goblet.

Talisman

1oz. White Rum, 1oz. Golden Rum, 1/2oz. Grand Marnier, 1/2oz. Vodka, 1/2oz. Lime Juice, 1/2 tinned Pear.

Blend until smooth and pour into an old-fashioned glass.

Tequila Matador

2oz. Tequila, 2oz. Pineapple Juice, 1/2oz. Lime Juice.

Blend until frozen and pour into a champagne flute.

Top Hat

2oz. Dark Rum, 1/4oz. Grenadine, 1/4oz. Lemon Juice, 1/4oz. Orange Juice, 4oz. fresh Pineapple.

Blend until smooth and pour into a large goblet.

Tropical Cocktail

1oz. Vodka, 1oz. Peach Schnapps, 1oz. Crème de Fraises, 2oz. Pineapple Juice, 1/4oz. Double Cream, 4 fresh Strawberries.

Blend until smooth and pour into a highball glass.

Tropical Paradise

1oz. White Rum, 1oz. Mango Liqueur, 1oz. Peach Schnapps, 1/2oz. Midori Melon Liqueur, 1/4oz. Lemon Juice, 2oz. fresh Mango.

Blend until smooth and pour into a medium goblet.

Tropical Storm

2oz. Golden Rum, 1oz. Vodka, 1oz. Orange Juice, 1/2oz. Lime Juice, 1/2oz. Pineapple Juice, 1 dash Grenadine, 1 dash Angostura Bitters.

Blend until smooth and pour into a highball glass.

Tropical Surprise

1oz. Vodka, 1oz. Peach Schnapps, 1oz. Double Cream, 2oz. Peach Nectar, 2oz. fresh Mango.

Blend until smooth and pour into a large goblet.

Tumbleweed

1oz. Kahlúa, 1oz. Vodka, 1 scoop Chocolate Ice-Cream.

Blend without additional ice and pour into a wineglass.

Virgin's Answer

1/2oz. White Rum, 1/2oz. Kahlúa, 1/2oz. Brown Crème de Cacao, 1/2oz. Crème de Banane, 1oz. Lemon Juice, 1oz. Orange Juice, 1/2 fresh Banana.

Blend until smooth and pour into a large goblet.

Vodka Colada

2oz. Vodka, 1oz. Sweetened Coconut Cream, 2oz. Pineapple Juice.

Blend until smooth and pour into a medium goblet.

Voodoo

1oz. White Rum, 1oz. Crème de Banane, 1/2oz. Malibu, 2oz. Orange Juice, 1/2 fresh Banana.

Blend until smooth and pour into a medium goblet.

Zooper Dooper

1oz. Frangelico, 3/4oz. Amaretto, 1/2oz. Brown Crème de Cacao, 2oz. Double Cream, 2oz. Pineapple Juice.

Blend until smooth and pour into a large goblet.

DAIRY COCKTAILS

▼

The cocktails in this category are often consumed as after dinner drinks and have either milk or cream as one of their ingredients. The inclusion of dairy products imparts a smooth coherence, which in most cases camouflages the alcoholic content of the cocktail. The majority of recipes are sweet although there are a number of sour and bitter versions. I have excluded milk or cream drinks that fall within the Shooter, Blended or Hot Drink domain as these have sections of their own.

Ace

2oz. Gin, 3/4oz. Grenadine, 3/4oz. Double Cream, 1/4oz. Lemon Juice, 1 dash Egg White.

Shake and strain into a martini glass and sprinkle grated nutmeg on the top.

Alexander Baby

1oz. Navy Rum, 1oz. Brown Crème de Cacao, 1oz. Double Cream.

Shake and strain into a martini glass.

Alexander (Brandy)

1oz. Cognac, 1oz. Brown Crème de Cacao, 1oz. Double Cream.

Shake and strain into a martini glass.

Alexander (Gin)

1oz. Gin, 1oz. Brown Crème de Cacao, 1oz. Double Cream.

Shake and strain into a martini glass.

Alexander's Brother

1oz. Gin, 1oz. White Crème de Menthe, 1oz. Double Cream.
Shake and strain into a martini glass.

Alexander's Sister

1oz. Gin, 1oz. Green Crème de Menthe, 1oz. Double Cream.
Shake and strain into a martini glass.

Amaretto Comfort

2oz. Amaretto, 2oz. Southern Comfort, 1oz. Double Cream.
Stir and strain the Amaretto and Southern Comfort into a martini glass. Float the cream on top and serve.

Angelic

3oz. Bourbon, 1oz. Crème de Cacao, 1oz. Grenadine, 1oz. Double Cream.
Shake and strain into a martini glass and serve with sprinkled nutmeg on the top.

Atom Bomb

1oz. Polish Pure Spirit, 2oz. Clear Honey, 1oz. Kahlúa, 2oz. Double Cream.
Shake and pour into an old-fashioned glass.
(Note: Beware, this is extremely potent.)

Auld Man's Milk

1oz. Dark Rum, 1oz. Cognac, 1 Egg, 1 tsp. Sugar, 2oz. Very Hot Milk.
Shake and pour into a large goblet. Top with grated nutmeg.

Aziz Fizz

3oz. Gin, Juice of 1 Lemon, 1 tsp. powdered Sugar, 1 Egg White, 1oz. Double Cream, Soda Water.
Shake and strain into a highball glass add a dash of orange flower water (if available) and top with the soda.

Babbie's Special

3oz. Apricot Brandy, 1/2oz. Double Cream, 1 dash Gin.
Shake and strain into a martini glass.

Banana Bird

2oz. Bourbon, 1oz. Double Cream, 1/2oz. Crème de Banane, 1 dash Cointreau.

Shake and strain into a martini glass.

Banana Cow

2oz. Crème de Banane, 1oz. Dark Rum, 5oz. Milk, 1/2oz. Gomme Syrup.

Shake and strain into an ice-filled highball glass.

Banana Menthe

2oz. Crème de Banane, 1oz. White Crème de Menthe, 1oz. Double Cream.

Shake and strain into a martini glass.

Banshee

2oz. Crème de Banane, 1oz. White Crème de Cacao, 2oz. Double Cream.

Shake and strain into a medium goblet.

Barbary Coast

1oz. Scotch, 1oz. White Crème de Cacao, 1oz. Gin, 1/2oz. Double Cream, 1 dash White Rum.

Shake and strain into a martini glass.

Belmont

3oz. Gin, 1oz. Raspberry Syrup, 1oz. Double Cream.

Shake and strain into a martini glass.

Bikini

2oz. Vodka, 1oz. White Rum, 4oz. Milk, 1/2oz. Gomme Syrup.

Shake and pour into a highball glass.

Black & White

1oz. Kahlúa, 1oz. Green Crème de Menthe, 1/2oz. White Crème de Menthe, 1oz. Double Cream.

Stir the Kahlúa and green menthe into an ice-filled old-fashioned glass. Mix the white menthe and cream together and float on the top.

Black Sheep

2oz. Guinness, 1oz. Kahlúa, 1oz. Glayva, 1oz. Double Cream.
Build into an old-fashioned glass and float the cream on top.

Brandy Alexander

1oz. Brown Crème de Cacao, 1oz. Cognac, 1oz. Double Cream.
Shake and strain into a martini glass.

Brandy Egg-Nog

2oz. Cognac, 1oz. Dark Rum, 4oz. Milk, 1oz. Gomme Syrup, 1 Egg.
Shake all but the milk and strain into a medium goblet.
Stir in the milk and sprinkle grated nutmeg over the drink.

Breakfast Egg-Nog

1oz. Cognac, 1oz. Apricot Brandy, 1/2oz. Orange Curaçao, 6oz. Milk, 1 Egg.
Shake and strain into a highball glass.
Sprinkle grated nutmeg over drink.

Brighton Rock

2oz. Crème de Fraises, 3oz. Cranberry Juice, 1oz. Double Cream.
Shake and pour into a highball glass.

Brunette

2oz. Bourbon, 1oz. Kahlúa, 1oz. Double Cream.
Shake and pour into an old-fashioned glass.

Bud's Cocktail

2oz. Cointreau, 1oz. Double Cream, 2 dashes Angostura Bitters.
Shake and strain into a martini glass.

Bulldog 2

1 1/2oz. Kahlúa, 1 1/2oz. White Rum, 6oz. Single Cream, Cola.
Shake and pour into a highball glass, top with a splash of cola.

Bullfrog 2

2oz. Vodka, 1oz. Green Crème de Menthe, 1oz. Double Cream.
Shake and pour into an old-fashioned glass.

Burnt Toasted Almond

1oz. Vodka, 1oz. Kahlúa, 1oz. Amaretto, 2oz. Double Cream.

Shake and pour into a highball glass.

Cadiz

1oz. Dry Sherry, 1oz. Crème de Mûre, 1/2oz. Triple Sec, 1/2oz. Double Cream.

Shake and strain into an ice-filled old-fashioned glass.

Café Curaçao

1oz. Kahlúa, 1oz. Grand Marnier.

Build into an old-fashioned glass.

Café de Paris

2oz. Gin, 1/2oz. Single Cream, 1/2oz. Anisette, 1 Egg White.

Shake and strain into a martini glass.

Caledonia

1oz. Cognac, 1oz. Brown Crème de Cacao, 1oz. Single Cream, 1 Egg Yolk.

Shake and strain into a martini glass.

Candida

1oz. Cognac, 1oz. Anisette, 1oz. Double Cream.

Shake and strain into a martini glass.

Capri

1oz. Crème de Banane, 1oz. White Crème de Cacao, 1oz. Double Cream.

Shake and strain into a martini glass.

Cara Sposa

11/2oz. Kahlúa, 1oz. Cointreau, 1oz. Double Cream.

Shake and strain into a martini glass.

Cherry Alexander

2oz. Cherry Brandy, 1oz. White Crème de Cacao, 1oz. Double Cream.

Shake and strain into a martini glass.

Chocolate-Chip Mint

1oz. White Crème de Menthe, 1oz. Brown Crème de Cacao, 1oz. Tia Maria, 1/2oz. Vodka, 2oz. Double Cream.

Shake and strain into an ice-filled highball glass.

Climax

2oz. Southern Comfort, 1oz. Kahlúa, 1/2oz. Double Cream.

Shake and strain into a martini glass.

Coffee Grasshopper

1oz. Kahlúa, 1oz. Green Crème de Menthe, 1oz. Double Cream.

Shake and strain into a martini glass.

Cold Shower

2oz. Vodka, 1oz. Double Cream, 1 dash Grenadine, Lemonade.

Build into a highball glass, topping with the lemonade.

Colorado Bulldog

1oz. Vodka, 1oz. Kahlúa, 2oz. Double Cream, 1 splash Cola.

Shake and pour into an old-fashioned glass.

Concorde

2oz. Vodka, 1oz. White Crème de Cacao, 1oz. Triple Sec, 3oz. Single Cream.

Shake and pour into a highball glass.

Cool Banana

1oz. Crème de Banane, 1oz. Triple Sec, 1oz. Double Cream, 1 dash Grenadine.

Shake and strain into a martini glass.

Copperino

1oz. Kahlúa, 1oz. Galliano, 1oz. Double Cream.

Shake and strain into a martini glass.

Cowboy

2oz. Scotch, 1/4oz. Single Cream.

Shake and pour into an old-fashioned glass.

Cowpuncher

3oz. Galliano, 5oz. Milk.

Shake and pour into a highball glass.

Cream Fizz

2oz. Gin, 1oz. Lemon Juice, 1/2oz. Gomme Syrup, 1oz. Single Cream, Soda Water.

Shake all but the water and strain into an ice-filled highball glass. Top with the soda and stir.

Cream Puff

2oz. White Rum, 1oz. Peach Schnapps, 1oz. Double Cream.

Stir and strain into a martini glass.

Creamsicle

2oz. Galliano, 2oz. Double Cream, 3oz. Orange Juice.

Shake and pour into an old-fashioned glass.

Crème de Café

2oz. Tia Maria, 1oz. Dark Rum, 1oz. Anisette, 2oz. Double Cream.

Shake and pour into a highball glass.
Sprinkle grated cinnamon over drink.

Dairy Dream

2oz. Strega, 1oz. Vodka, 1oz. Galliano, 3oz. Double Cream.

Shake and pour into a highball glass.

Desert Island

1 1/2oz. Midori Melon Liqueur, 1oz. White Rum, 2oz. Pineapple Juice, 2oz. Double Cream.

Shake all but the cream and strain into a deep-dish champagne saucer. Float the cream on top.

Dirty Banana

1oz. Kahlúa, 1oz. Crème de Banane, 3oz. Single Cream.

Shake and pour into an old-fashioned glass.

Dirty Mother

1oz. Tequila, 1oz. Kahlúa, 1oz. Bailey's, 5oz. Milk.

Shake and pour into a highball glass.

Dirty White Mother

1oz. Tequila, 1oz. Cognac, 1/2oz. Kahlúa, 2oz. Double Cream.

Shake and strain into a martini glass.

Doctor Dangerous

1 1/2oz. Cognac, 1 1/2oz. Bailey's, 2oz. Double Cream.

Shake and strain into a martini glass.

Dreamsickle

2oz. Kahlúa, 1oz. Triple Sec, 1 dash Orange Juice, 1oz. Double Cream.

Shake all but the cream and strain into a sugar-rimmed coupette.
Float the cream on top.

Egg-Nog

2oz. Cognac, 1 Egg, 1/2oz. Gomme Syrup, 1 dash Dark Rum, 5oz. Milk.

Shake and pour into a highball glass. Sprinkle grated nutmeg over drink.

Egg-Nog Supreme

1 bottle Cognac, 3 pints Milk, 1 pint Double Cream, 1/4lb Sugar, 12 Eggs separated.

Stir the sugar into the egg yolks. Mix in the cream, milk and cognac in that order. Chill for at least 1 hour. Beat the egg whites until stiff and mix into the egg-nog just before serving.
Sprinkle ground nutmeg over bowl.

Festival

1oz. Kahlúa, 1oz. Noix de Coco, 2oz. Double Cream.

Shake and pour into an old-fashioned glass.

Fifth Avenue

1oz. Brown Crème de Cacao, 1oz. Apricot Brandy, 1 tsp. Double Cream.

Layer into a liqueur glass.

First Night

2oz. Cognac, 1oz. Tia Maria, 1oz. Van der Hum, 1oz. Double Cream.
Shake and pour into an old-fashioned glass.

Five-Fifteen

1oz. Cointreau, 1oz. Dry Vermouth, 1oz. Single Cream,
1 dash Gomme Syrup.
Shake and strain into a martini glass.

Fixer

1oz. Cognac, 1oz. Crème de Noyau, 1oz. Prunelle, 1/2oz. Double Cream.
Shake and strain into a martini glass.

Flapjack

2oz. Sherry, 1oz. Double Cream, 1/2oz. Gomme Syrup.
Shake and strain into a martini glass.

Free Silver

2oz. Gin, 3/4oz. Dark Rum, 1/2oz. Lemon Juice, 1 dash Gomme Syrup,
1/2oz. Milk, Soda.
Shake and strain all but the soda into an ice-filled highball glass.
Top with the soda.

French Kiss

1oz. Vodka, 1oz. Crème de Mûre, 1/2oz. White Crème de Cacao,
1oz. Double Cream.
Shake and strain into a martini glass.

Frostbite

1oz. Silver Tequila, 1oz. White Crème de Menthe, 1oz. Double Cream.
Shake and strain into a martini glass.

Galway Grey

2oz. Vodka, 1oz. White Crème de Cacao, 1oz. Cointreau, 2oz. Lime Juice,
1oz. Double Cream.
Stir all but the cream and strain into an old-fashioned glass.
Float the cream on top.

Gentle Bull

1oz. Tequila, 1oz. Kahlúa, 1oz. Double Cream.

Build into an old-fashioned glass, floating the cream on top.

Goat's Cocktail

2oz. Cognac, 1oz. Kirschwasser, 1 dash Orgeat, 1 dash Anisette, 1/2oz. Double Cream.

Shake and strain into a martini glass.

Godchild

1oz. Amaretto, 1oz. Vodka, 1oz. Double Cream.

Shake and strain into a martini glass.

Golden Cadillac

1 1/2oz. White Crème de Cacao, 1 1/2oz. Galliano, 1oz. Double Cream.

Shake and strain into a martini glass.

Golden Dream

1oz. Galliano, 1oz. Cointreau, 1/2oz. Orange Juice, 1oz. Double Cream.

Shake and strain into a martini glass.

Grasshopper

1oz. Green Crème de Menthe, 1oz. White Crème de Cacao, 1oz. Double Cream.

Shake and strain into a martini glass.

Green Jade

1oz. Gin, 1oz. Green Crème de Menthe, 1oz. Double Cream, 1 Egg White.

Shake and strain into a martini glass.

Green Russian

1oz. Vodka, 1oz. Midori Melon Liqueur, 1oz. Double Cream.

Shake and strain into a martini glass.

Hair of the Dog

2oz. Scotch, 1oz. Clear Honey, 1oz. Double Cream.

Shake and strain into a martini glass.

Harvey Cowpuncher

2oz. Galliano, 6oz. Milk.

Build into a highball glass.

Hot Shot 2

1oz. Kahlúa, 1oz. White Crème de Cacao, 1oz. Amaretto, 2oz. Double Cream.

Shake and pour into an old-fashioned glass.

Ichbien

1oz. Cognac, 1oz. Grand Marnier, 1 Egg Yolk, 4oz. Milk.

Shake and pour into a highball glass. Sprinkle grated nutmeg over drink.

Irish Eyes

2oz. Irish Whiskey, 1oz. Green Crème de Menthe, 1oz. Double Cream.

Shake and pour into an old-fashioned glass.

Irish Frost

2oz. Bailey's, 1/2oz. Sweetened Coconut Cream, 1oz. Double Cream.

Shake and strain into a martini glass.

Iron Lady

1oz. Noix de Coco, 1oz. White Crème de Cacao, 1oz. Crème de Cassis, 2oz. Double Cream.

Shake and pour into a highball glass.

Italian Fascination

2oz. Vodka, 1oz. Galliano, 1oz. Strega, 3oz. Single Cream.

Shake and pour into a highball glass.

Italian Sombrero

2oz. Amaretto, 3oz. Double Cream.

Shake and strain into a champagne flute.

Italian Stallion

1 1/2oz. Amaretto, 1oz. Crème de Noyaux, 1oz. White Crème de Cacao, 2oz. Double Cream.

Shake and pour into an old-fashioned glass.

Itza Bitza

1oz. Amaretto, 1oz. Kahlúa, 1/2oz. Frangelico, 1oz. Double Cream.

Shake and strain into a martini glass.

Jamaica Hop

1oz. Tia Maria, 1oz. White Crème de Cacao, 1oz. Double Cream.

Shake and strain into a martini glass.

Jamaican Cow

1oz. Dark Jamaican Rum, 1oz. Kahlúa, 6oz. Milk, 1 dash Gomme Syrup.

Shake and pour into a highball glass.

Japanese Egg-Nog

1oz. Midori Melon Liqueur, 1oz. Cointreau, 1 Egg, 6oz. Milk.

Shake and pour into a highball glass. Sprinkle grated nutmeg over drink.

Joker

1/2oz. Anisette, 1/2oz. Crème de Violette, 1/2oz. Benedictine, 1/2oz. Double Cream.

Layer into a pousse-café glass.

Kahlúa Alexander

1oz. Kahlúa, 1oz. Gin, 1oz. Double Cream.

Shake and strain into a martini glass.

Kentucky Coffee

1oz. Bourbon, 1oz. Kahlúa, 1oz. Double Cream.

Shake and strain into a martini glass.

Lady Jade

1 1/2oz. Midori Melon Liqueur, 1 1/2oz. White Crème de Cacao, 3oz. Double Cream.

Shake and pour into an old-fashioned glass.

Lady Lion

1oz. Kahlúa, 1oz. Cognac, 1oz. Bailey's, 2oz. Double Cream.

Shake and pour into an old-fashioned glass.

Lady Love Fizz

2oz. Gin, 1/2oz. Gomme Syrup, 1oz. Lemon Juice, 1oz. Single Cream,, 1 Egg White, Soda Water.

Shake and strain into an ice-filled highball glass. Top with the soda.

L'aird

1oz. Scotch, 1oz. Kahlúa, 1/4oz. Maraschino Liqueur, 1/4oz. Ginger Wine, 1oz. Double Cream.

Stir all but the cream and strain into a champagne flute.
Float the cream on top and sprinkle ground coffee over drink.

Lalla Rookh

1 1/2oz. Cognac, 1oz. Dark Rum, 1/2oz. Galliano, 1/2oz. Gomme Syrup, 1/2oz. Double Cream.

Shake and strain into a martini glass.

Lamborghini

1oz. Kahlúa, 1oz. Galliano, 1oz. Green Chartreuse, 1oz. Double Cream.

Layer into a martini glass.
Ignite the chartreuse and pour the cream on top.

Lamborghini International

1oz. Kahlúa, 1oz. Galliano, 1oz. Sambuca, 1oz. Double Cream.

Layer into a martini glass and pour the cream on top.

Last Straw

1oz. Bailey's, 1oz. Cointreau, 1/2oz. Crème de Cassis, 2oz. Double Cream.

Shake and strain into a martini glass.

Lillian Russell

1oz. Crème de Rose, 1oz. Crème de Violette, 1oz. Double Cream.

Layer into a martini glass.

Lonely Bull

1oz. Tequila, 1oz. Kahlúa, 1oz. Double Cream.

Build into an old-fashioned glass.

Long Whistle

3oz. Cognac, 5oz. Milk, 1/2oz. Gomme Syrup.

Shake and strain into a highball glass. Sprinkle grated nutmeg over drink.

Long White Russian

1oz. Kahlúa, 1oz. Vodka, 3oz. Cola, 1oz. Double Cream.

Build into a highball glass, floating the cream on top.

Magic Moon

1oz. Kahlúa, 1oz. Cognac, 1/2oz. White Crème de Menthe, 1oz. Double Cream.

Stir the Kahlúa and cognac into an ice-filled old-fashioned glass. Stir the menthe into the cream and float this mixture on top of the drink.

Magic Wand

2oz. Kahlúa, 3oz. Stout, 1oz. Double Cream.

Build into a champagne flute, floating the cream on top.

Magnolia Blossom

2oz. Gin, 1/2oz. Lemon Juice, 1/2oz. Double Cream.

Shake and strain into a martini glass.

Marnier Madness

1oz. Grand Marnier, 1oz. Crème de Grand Marnier, 1/2oz. Cognac, 1/2oz. Double Cream.

Shake and strain into a martini glass.

Maureen

2oz. Cognac, 1/2oz. Tia Maria, 1oz. Double Cream.

Shake and strain into a martini glass.

Meadowbank

1oz. Midori Melon Liqueur, 1oz. Green Chartreuse, 1/4oz. Green Crème de Menthe, 1oz. Double Cream.

Shake and strain into a martini glass.

Midori Alexander

1oz. Midori Melon Liqueur, 1oz. White Crème de Cacao, 1oz. Double Cream.
Shake and strain into a martini glass.

Midori Ito

1oz. Midori Melon Liqueur, 1oz. Advocaat, 1oz. Apricot Juice, 1oz. Double Cream.
Shake and pour into a medium goblet.

Midori Spice

1 1/2oz. Midori Melon Liqueur, 1oz. Malibu, 4oz. Pineapple Juice, 1oz. Double Cream.
Pour into a large goblet half filled with crushed ice.
Float the cream on top.

Mikado 2

(RAY HOPGOOD)

1 1/2oz. Midori Melon Liqueur, 1/2oz. Kahlúa, 3oz. Double Cream.
Shake and pour into an old-fashioned glass.

Mona Lisa

1oz. Amer Picon, 1oz. Orange Curaçao, 1oz. Benedictine, 1/4oz. Double Cream.
Shake and strain into a martini glass.

Mother's Milk

1oz. Vodka, 1/2oz. Gin, 1 dash Tia Maria, 3/4oz. Orgeat, 4oz. Milk.
Shake and strain into an ice-filled old-fashioned glass.

Mother's Milk 2

(RAY HOPGOOD)

1oz. Frangelico, 1/2oz. Midori Melon Liqueur, 1/2oz. Kahlúa, 1/2oz. Bailey's, 3oz. Double Cream.
Shake and strain into a brandy balloon.

Mudslide

1oz. Vodka, 1oz. Kahlúa, 1oz. Bailey's, 2oz. Milk.
Shake and pour into a highball glass.

Multiple Orgasm

1oz. Kahlúa, 1oz. Bailey's, 1/2oz. Amaretto, 1/2oz. Tequila, 1oz. Double Cream.

Shake all but the tequila and pour into an old-fashioned glass. Pour the tequila on top.

New Orleans Gin Fizz

2oz. Gin, 1/2oz. Cointreau, 1/4oz. Kirschwasser, 1oz. Lemon Juice, 1/2oz. Single Cream, 1 Egg White, Soda Water.

Shake all but the soda and strain into a highball glass. Top with the soda.

Nineteen-Fourteen

1oz. Orange Curaçao, 1oz. Gin, 1oz. Double Cream.

Shake and strain into a martini glass.

North Pole

2oz. Gin, 1oz. Maraschino Liqueur, 1oz. Lemon Juice, 1 Egg White, 1/2oz. Double Cream.

Shake and strain into a martini glass. Float the cream on top.

Nutty Banana

1oz. Crème de Banane, 1oz. Amaretto, 1oz. Double Cream.

Shake and strain into a martini glass.

Nutty Hon'

1oz. Frangelico, 1oz. Tia Maria, 1oz. Clear Honey, 3oz. Single Cream.

Shake and pour into a highball glass.

Nutty Russian

1oz. Kahlúa, 1oz. Vodka, 1oz. Frangelico, 1oz. Double Cream.

Shake and strain into a martini glass.

Oak Tree

1oz. Tia Maria, 1oz. Cognac, 1oz. Amaretto, 4oz. Milk.

Shake and pour into a highball glass.

Olson

2oz. Bourbon, 1oz. Double Cream, 1/2oz. Honey.

Shake and strain into an ice-filled old-fashioned glass.

One For The Road

1oz. Benedictine, 1/2oz. Van der Hum, 1/2oz. Double Cream.

Stir and strain into a liqueur glass.

Orange Cadillac

1oz. Galliano, 1oz. White Crème de Cacao, 1/2oz. Cointreau, 1/2oz. Orange Juice, 1oz. Double Cream.

Shake and strain into a martini glass.

Orgasm

2oz. Bailey's, 1oz. Cointreau, 1oz. Double Cream.

Shake and strain into a martini glass.

Panama

1oz. Cognac, 1oz. White Crème de Cacao, 1oz. Double Cream.

Shake and strain into a martini glass.

Paradise Flip

(CHRISTABEL WARREN)

1oz. Midori Melon Liqueur, 1/2oz. Kirschwasser, 1/2oz. Green Crème de Menthe, 1oz. Double Cream.

Shake and strain into a martini glass.

Sprinkle grated chocolate over drink and serve with an After Eight mint.

Parisian Blend

1oz. Dark Rum, 1oz. Orange Curaçao, 1oz. Double Cream.

Shake and strain into a martini glass.

Parisian Blonde

1oz. Dark Rum, 1oz. Cointreau, 1oz. Double Cream.

Shake and strain into a martini glass.

Passion in Paradise

(LEONIE BERRIMAN)

1oz. Advocaat, 1/2oz. Crème de Banane, 1/2oz. Midori Melon Liqueur, 3/4oz. Double Cream.

Shake and strain into a martini glass.
Float 1 tsp. passion-fruit flesh on top.

Peach Bunny

1oz. Crème de Pêche, 1oz. White Crème de Cacao, 1oz. Double Cream.

Shake and strain into a martini glass.

Peach Cadillac

1oz. White Crème de Cacao, 1oz. Galliano, 1oz. Crème de Pêche, 1oz. Double Cream.

Shake and strain into a martini glass.

Peach Dream

1oz. Peach Schnapps, 1oz. Vodka, 3oz. Peach Nectar, 2oz. Single Cream.

Shake and pour into a highball glass.

Penguin

2oz. Kahlúa, 1oz. Cold Black Coffee, 1/2oz. White Crème de Cacao, 1oz. Double Cream.

Pour the Kahlúa and coffee into an ice-filled old-fashioned glass.
Mix the crème de cacao and cream and float this mixture on top.

Peppermint Paddy

1oz. Irish Whiskey, 1oz. White Crème de Menthe, 1oz. Double Cream.

Shake and strain into a martini glass.

Peppermint Stick

2oz. Green Crème de Menthe, 1oz. Vodka, 2oz. Double Cream.

Shake and strain into an old-fashioned glass.

Peridot

1oz. Gin, 1oz. White Crème de Menthe, 1oz. Double Cream.

Shake and strain into a martini glass. Garnish with a mint leaf.

Pink Cadillac

1oz. White Crème de Cacao, $^3/_4$oz. Galliano, $^1/_2$oz. Grenadine, 1oz. Double Cream, 1 dash Orange Juice.

Shake and strain into a martini glass.

Pink Lady 2

2oz. Gin, $^1/_2$oz. Single Cream, $^1/_4$oz. Grenadine, 1 Egg White.

Shake and strain into a martini glass.

Pink Panther

1oz. Tequila, 1oz. White Crème de Menthe, 2 dashes Grenadine, 4oz. Milk.

Shake and pour into a highball glass.

Pink Rose

2oz. Gin, $^1/_2$oz. Lemon Juice, $^1/_2$oz. Single Cream, 2 dashes Grenadine, 1 Egg White.

Shake and strain into a martini glass.

Pink Squirrel

2oz. Crème de Noyaux, $^3/_4$oz. White Crème de Cacao, $^1/_2$oz. Double Cream.

Shake and strain into a martini glass.

Platinum Blonde

1oz. Golden Rum, 1oz. Triple Sec, 1oz. Double Cream.

Shake and strain into a martini glass.

Polar Bear

2oz. Brown Crème de Cacao, 6oz. Cola, 1oz. Double Cream.

Build into a highball glass, floating the cream on top.

Port Egg-Nog

2oz. Port, $^3/_4$oz. Gomme Syrup, 1 Egg, 5oz. Milk.

Shake and pour into a highball glass. Sprinkle grated nutmeg over drink.

Princess

1$^1/_2$oz. Apricot Brandy, $^1/_2$oz. Double Cream.

Layer into a liqueur glass.

Pussy Foot

2oz. White Rum, 1oz. Orange Juice, 1oz. Pineapple Juice, 1oz. Lime Juice, 2 dashes Grenadine, 1/2oz. Double Cream.

Shake and pour into a highball glass.

Ramos Fizz

2oz. Gin, 2 dashes Cointreau, 2 dashes Orange Flower Water, 1oz. Lemon Juice, 1 Egg White, 2 dashes Single Cream, 1/4oz. Gomme Syrup, Soda Water.

Shake and strain into a highball glass. Top with the soda.

Ram-Raider

1oz. Galliano, 1oz. Noix de Coco, 4oz. Orange Juice, 1oz. Double Cream.

Shake and pour into a highball glass.

Renaissance

2 1/4oz. Gin, 3/4oz. Dry Sherry, 1/2oz. Single Cream.

Shake and strain into a martini glass.

Sprinkle grated nutmeg over drink.

Road Streaker

1oz. Vodka, 1oz. Crème de Pêche, 1/2oz. Frangelico, 1/4oz. Tia Maria, 2oz. Double Cream.

Shake and strain into an ice-filled old-fashioned glass.

Roasted Almond

1oz. Cognac, 1oz. Amaretto, 1/2oz. Kahlúa, 1oz. Double Cream.

Pour the cognac into a brandy balloon and ignite. While burning, pour in the remaining ingredients, this will extinguish the flames. Stir and sprinkle grated almonds over the drink.

Romance

(DAVID WILSON)

3/4oz. Kahlúa, 3/4oz. Bailey's, 3/4oz. Brown Crème de Cacao, 1oz. Double Cream.

Shake and strain into a martini glass.

Roman Toga

1oz. Cointreau, 1oz. White Crème de Cacao, 1oz. Strawberry Vodka (Uncoloured), 4oz. Milk.

Shake and pour into a highball glass.

Royal Blush

1oz. Vodka, 1oz. Crème de Framboise, 1oz. Double Cream, 2 dashes Grenadine.

Shake and strain into a martini glass.

Royal Mint

1oz. Royal Mint Chocolate Liqueur, 1/2oz. Cointreau, 1oz. Vodka, 1/2oz. Double Cream.

Shake and strain into a martini glass.

Royal Temptation

(GEORGE LIDDLE)

2oz. Amaretto, 1 1/2oz. Kahlúa, 1oz. Midori Melon Liqueur, 1/2oz. Double Cream.

Shake and strain into a deep-dish champagne saucer.
Garnish with orange zest and chocolate flakes.

Rum Alexander

1oz. Dark Rum, 1oz. Brown Crème de Cacao, 1oz. Double Cream.

Shake and strain into a martini glass. Sprinkle grated nutmeg over drink.

Rum Egg-Nog

2oz. Dark Rum, 1oz. Gomme Syrup, 5oz. Milk, 1 Egg.

Shake and pour into a highball glass. Sprinkle grated nutmeg over drink.

Rum Milk Punch

2oz. Dark Rum, 1oz. Gomme Syrup, 5oz. Milk.

Shake and pour into a highball glass.

Russian Bear

2oz. Vodka, 1oz. White Crème de Cacao, 1oz. Double Cream.

Shake and strain into a martini glass.

Santos Surprise

(SANTOS EZCARAY)

1/2oz. Midori Melon Liqueur, 1/2oz. Suntory Mango Liqueur, 1/2oz. Kahlúa, 1/2oz. Cognac, 1/2oz. Gin, 1/2oz. Bailey's, 3oz. Double Cream.

Shake and pour into a large goblet.

Scooter

1oz. Cognac, 1oz. Amaretto, 1oz. Single Cream.

Shake and strain into a martini glass.

Scotch Bird Flyer

2oz. Scotch, 1/2oz. Triple Sec, 1 Egg Yolk, 1oz. Double Cream, 1/4oz. Gomme Syrup.

Shake and strain into a champagne flute.

Scotch Milk Punch

2oz. Scotch, 6oz. Milk, 1oz. Gomme Syrup.

Shake and pour into a highball glass. Sprinkle grated nutmeg over drink.

Sherry Egg-Nog

2oz. Dry Sherry, 1 Egg, 1/2oz. Gomme Syrup, 6oz. Milk.

Shake and pour into a highball glass. Sprinkle grated nutmeg over drink.

Sherry Milk Punch

2oz. Cream Sherry, 1/2oz. Gomme Syrup, 6oz. Milk.

Shake and pour into a highball glass. Sprinkle grated nutmeg over drink.

Silk Stockings

1oz. Tequila, 1oz. White Crème de Cacao, 1oz. Double Cream, 1 dash Grenadine.

Shake and strain into a martini glass.

Smith & Wesson

2oz. Kahlúa, 1oz. Double Cream, 4oz. Soda Water.

Build into a highball glass.

Snowball 2

2oz. Gin, 3/4oz. Anisette, 1oz. Double Cream.
Shake and strain into a martini glass.

Sombrero

1oz. Kahlúa, 1oz. Bailey's, 1oz. Double Cream.
Shake and strain into a martini glass.
Sprinkle grated nutmeg over drink.

Sombrero 2

2oz. Kahlúa, 1oz. Double Cream.
Layer into an ice-filled old-fashioned glass.

Strawberry Blonde

2oz. Crème de Fraises, 1oz. White Crème de Cacao, 1oz. Double Cream.
Shake and strain into a martini glass.

Strawberry Fields

2oz. Crème de Fraises, 1oz. Midori Melon Liqueur, 2oz. Double Cream.
Shake and pour into a highball glass.

Summer Breeze

(STEPHEN FRANCIS)

3/4oz. Midori Melon Liqueur, 3/4oz. Cointreau, 3/4oz. Double Cream.
Layer into a pousse-café glass.

Tap Dancer

1oz. Grand Marnier, 1oz. White Crème de Cacao, 4oz. Milk,
1oz. Double Cream, 1/2 tsp. Chocolate Powder.
Shake and pour into a highball glass.

Toasted Almond 2

2oz. Kahlúa, 1oz. Amaretto, 1oz. Double Cream.
Build into an old-fashioned glass.

Tobacco

1oz. Kahlúa, 1oz. Bourbon, 1oz. Double Cream, 1 tsp. grated Coconut.
Shake all but the coconut and strain into a martini glass.
Sprinkle the coconut over the drink and stir.

Toreador

2 1/4oz. Tequila, 3/4oz. White Crème de Cacao, 1oz. Double Cream.
Shake and strain into a martini glass.
Sprinkle chocolate powder over drink.

Tree Climber

1oz. White Crème de Cacao, 1oz. Amaretto, 1oz. Double Cream.
Shake and pour into a medium goblet.

Triple M

1oz. Midori Melon Liqueur, 1oz. Suntory Mango Liqueur, 1/2oz. Malibu, 1oz. Double Cream, 1oz. Pineapple Juice.
Shake and strain into an ice-filled highball glass.

Van der Hum Cocktail

1oz. Van der Hum, 1oz. Grand Marnier, 1 dash Grenadine, 1oz. Double Cream.
Shake and strain into a martini glass.

Van der Hum Egg-Nog

2oz. Van der Hum, 1oz. Cognac, 3/4oz. Gomme Syrup, 1 Egg, 4oz. Milk.
Shake and pour into a highball glass.
Sprinkle grated chocolate orange over drink.

Velvet Hammer

2oz. Vodka, 1/4oz. White Crème de Cacao, 1/4oz. Double Cream.
Shake and strain into a martini glass.

Velvet Hammer 2

1oz. Kahlúa, 1oz. Apricot Brandy, 1oz. Cointreau, 1oz. Double Cream.
Shake and strain into an ice-filled old-fashioned glass.

Velvet Hammer 3

2oz. Strega, 1oz. White Crème de Cacao, 1/4oz. Double Cream.
Shake and strain into a martini glass.

Velvet Hammer 4

1oz. Cointreau, 1oz. Tia Maria, 1oz. Double Cream.
Shake and strain into a martini glass.

Velvet Hue

1oz. Cointreau, 1oz. Kahlúa, 1oz. Cognac, 1oz. Double Cream.
Shake and pour into an old-fashioned glass.
Sprinkle grated chocolate over drink.

Velvet Nut

2oz. Amaretto, 1oz. White Crème de Cacao, 1oz. Double Cream.
Shake and pour into an old-fashioned glass.

Vodka Egg-Nog

1oz. Vodka, 1oz. Grand Marnier, 1/2oz. Gomme Syrup, 1 Egg, 5oz. Milk.
Shake and strain into a highball glass.
Sprinkle grated nutmeg over drink.

Wet Dream

1oz. Galliano, 1oz. Cointreau, 1/2oz. Orange Juice, 1oz. Double Cream.
Shake and strain into a martini glass.

Whiskey Egg-Nog

1oz. Bourbon or Rye Whiskey, 1oz. Grand Marnier, 1/2oz. Gomme Syrup, 1 Egg, 5oz. Milk.
Shake and strain into a highball glass.
Sprinkle grated nutmeg over drink.

Whiskey Milk Punch

2oz. Bourbon or Rye Whiskey, 6oz. Milk, 1oz. Gomme Syrup.
Shake and pour into a highball glass. Sprinkle grated nutmeg over drink.

Whisky Egg-Nog

1oz. Scotch Whisky, 1oz. Grand Marnier, 1/2oz. Gomme Syrup, 1 Egg, 5oz. Milk.

Shake and strain into a highball glass. Sprinkle grated nutmeg over drink.

Whisky Milk Punch

2oz. Scotch, 6oz. Milk, 1oz. Gomme Syrup.

Shake and pour into a highball glass. Sprinkle grated nutmeg over drink.

White Beach

2oz. Vodka, 1oz. White Crème de Cacao, 1oz. Double Cream.

Shake and pour into an old-fashioned glass.

White Cadillac

1oz. Galliano, 3/4oz. White Crème de Cacao, 3/4oz. Cointreau, 1oz. Double Cream.

Shake and strain into a martini glass.

White Elephant

2oz. Gin, 1/2oz. Sweet Vermouth, 1 Egg White, 1/4oz. Double Cream.

Shake and strain into a martini glass.

White Kiss

1 1/2oz. Amaretto, 1/2oz. Double Cream.

Layer into a liqueur glass.

White Knight

2oz. Cointreau, 1oz. White Crème de Cacao, 3oz. Milk.

Shake and pour into a highball glass. Garnish with grated orange rind.

White Label

2oz. Vodka, 1/4oz. Anisette, 1/4oz. Kümmel, 1/2oz. Single Cream.

Shake and strain into a martini glass.

White Lantern

1oz. Irish Whiskey, 1oz. Frangelico, 3/4oz. Bailey's, 1oz. Double Cream.

Shake and strain into an ice-filled brandy balloon.

White Orange

2oz. Cointreau, 1oz. Single Cream, 1 Egg White.
Shake and strain into a martini glass.

White Pirate

1oz. Vodka, 1oz. Peach Schnapps, 1oz. Lime Juice, $\frac{1}{2}$oz. Gomme Syrup, 1 Egg White, 1 dash Single Cream,
Shake and strain into a martini glass.

White Plush

2oz. Bourbon, 1oz. Gomme Syrup, 6oz. Milk.
Shake and pour into a highball glass.

White Russian

2oz. Vodka, 1oz. Kahlúa, 1oz. Double Cream.
Shake and strain into a martini glass.

White Russian 2

$1\frac{1}{2}$oz. Vodka, $1\frac{1}{2}$oz. Kahlúa, 1oz. Double Cream.
Layer into an ice-filled old-fashioned glass.

White Satin

1oz. Tia Maria, 1oz. Galliano, 1oz. Double Cream.
Shake and strain into a martini glass.

White Stain

1oz. Calvados, $\frac{1}{2}$oz. Tequila, $\frac{1}{2}$oz. Grenadine, 1oz. Pineapple Juice, 1 dash Double Cream.
Shake all but the cream and strain into a martini glass.
Float the dash of cream on top to create the stain.

White Wedding

$\frac{3}{4}$oz. Grand Marnier, $\frac{1}{2}$oz. White Crème de Cacao, 1oz. Noix de Coco, 4oz. Milk.
Shake and pour into a highball glass.

Whiz Doodle

1oz. Gin, 1oz. Scotch, 1oz. Brown Crème de Cacao, 1oz. Double Cream, 1/4oz. Gomme Syrup.

Shake and pour into an old-fashioned glass.

Widow's Dream

2oz. Benedictine, 1 Egg, 1 tsp. Double Cream.

Shake the Benedictine and egg and strain into a martini glass. Float the cream on top.

X-Ray

1oz. Green Crème de Menthe, 1oz. Blue Curaçao, 1oz. Double Cream.

Shake and strain into a martini glass.

Yankee Doodle

2oz. Gin, 2 dashes Crème de Violette, 2 dashes Single Cream, 2 dashes Lemon Juice, 1/4oz. Gomme Syrup.

Shake and strain into a martini glass.

Yellow Fingers

1oz. Gin, 1oz. Crème de Mûre, 1/2oz. Crème de Banane, 1/2oz. Double Cream.

Shake and strain into a martini glass.

Yellow Monkey

1oz. Galliano, 1oz. White Crème de Cacao, 1/2oz. Crème de Banane, 1/2oz. White Rum, 1oz. Double Cream.

Shake and strain into a martini glass.

Zoom

1 1/2oz. Any Spirit, 1 tbsp. Honey, 1oz. Double Cream.

Dissolve the honey in boiling water then add to the remaining ingredients. Shake and strain into a martini glass.

WINE & CHAMPAGNE COCKTAILS

▼

A wine cocktail is one that contains Port, Sherry, Madeira or Wine. A champagne cocktail can be made not only with champagne but with any sparkling wine, whether *methode traditionelle* or not. I have provided many dozens of champagne recipes in addition to demonstrating the versatile use of all these wines.

Adonis

2oz. Dry Sherry, 1oz. Sweet Vermouth, 1 dash Orange Bitters.

Stir and strain into a martini glass.

Ambrosia

1oz. Calvados, 1oz. Cognac, 1 dash Curaçao, Chilled Champagne.

Shake and strain all but the champagne into a champagne saucer, top with champagne and serve.

Aphrodisiac

5oz. Port, 1 dash Cointreau.

Heat the ingredients in a pan and pour into a small wineglass. Sprinkle grated nutmeg and garnish with a lemon slice.

Archbishop Punch

2oz. Port, Juice of 1 Lime, 2oz. Water, 1 tsp. Gomme Syrup, 1oz. Overproof Dark Rum.

Shake and strain all but the rum into a martini glass. Float the rum on top and serve.

Arise My Love

1/2oz. Green Crème de Menthe, Chilled Champagne.

Put the menthe into a champagne flute and top with the champagne.

B & B Royale

1/2oz. Cognac, 1/2oz. Benedictine, Chilled Champagne.

Pour the brandy and Benedictine into a champagne saucer and top with the chilled champagne.

Balm

3oz. Dry Sherry, 1/4oz. Cointreau, 1 dash Orange Juice, 2 dashes Orange Bitters.

Shake and strain into a martini glass.

Bamboo

2oz. Sherry, 1oz. Dry Vermouth, 2 dashes Orange Bitters, 2 dashes Angostura Bitters.

Shake and strain into a martini glass.

Bamboo 2

2oz. Sherry, 1oz. Dry Vermouth, 1oz. Sweet Vermouth.

Shake and strain into a martini glass.

Barbara

2oz. Gin, 1oz. Sherry, 1/2oz. Lemon Juice, 1 dash Orange Bitters.

Shake and strain into a martini glass.

Barracuda

1oz. White Rum, 1oz. Galliano, 1oz. Pineapple Juice, 1/2oz. Lime Juice, 1/2oz. Grenadine, Chilled Champagne.

Build into a highball glass and top with the champagne.

Bellini

3oz. White Peach Purée (or Peach Nectar), 1 drop Grenadine, Chilled Champagne.

Mix the peach purée and grenadine together in a champagne flute then top with the champagne.

Betsy Ross

1½oz. Cognac, 1½oz. Port, 1 dash Cointreau.

Shake and strain into a martini glass.

Bishop

2oz. Dark Rum, 1oz. Red Bordeaux, 1oz. Lime Juice, 1oz. Gomme Syrup.

Shake and strain into a martini glass.

Black Velvet

4oz. Chilled Stout (Guinness), 4oz. Chilled Champagne.

Pour directly into a champagne flute.

Bosom Caresser

1oz. Cognac, 1oz. Madeira, ½ Cointreau, 1 dash Grenadine, 1 Egg Yolk.

Shake and strain into a martini glass.

Boston Flip

2oz. Bourbon, 1oz. Madeira, ½oz. Gomme Syrup, 1 Egg Yolk.

Shake and strain into a martini glass.

Brazil

1½oz. Dry Sherry, 1½oz. Dry Vermouth, 1 dash Angostura bitters, 1 dash Anisette.

Stir and strain into a martini glass.

Broken Spur

1oz. White Port, 1oz. Gin, 1oz. Anisette, 1 Egg Yolk.

Shake and strain into a martini glass.

Buck's Fizz

2oz. Orange Juice, Chilled Champagne.

Pour the orange juice into a champagne flute and top with the champagne.

Burgundy Bishop

2oz. White Rum, 1/2oz. Lemon Juice, 1 tsp. powdered Sugar, Red Wine.

Build into a highball glass and top with the red wine.

Caprilia

2oz. Vodka, 1oz. Port, 1oz. Cherry Brandy, 1 dash Grenadine.

Shake and strain into a martini glass.

Cardicus

1oz. White Port, 1oz. Cointreau, 1oz. White Rum.

Shake and strain into a martini glass.

Cardinal

See chapter three, The Classics under Kir, (pp 54–5).

Caribbean Royale

1/4oz. White Rum, 1/4oz. Crème de Banane, Chilled Champagne.

Build without ice into a champagne flute, topping with the champagne.

Champagne Cobbler

4 dashes Cointreau, Chilled Champagne.

Fill a large goblet with crushed ice and three-quarters fill with the champagne. Stir in the Cointreau and garnish with fruits in season and a sprig of mint.

Champagne Cocktail (Classic)

1oz. Cognac, 1 Sugar-Cube, 4 dashes Angostura Bitters, Chilled Champagne.

Place the sugar-cube into a champagne flute and soak with the bitters. Cover with the cognac and top with the chilled champagne. Garnish with a maraschino cherry.

Champagne Cooler

1oz. Grand Marnier, 1/2oz. Cognac, 2 dashes Angostura Bitters, Chilled Champagne.

Build into a napoli grande glass, topping with the champagne. Garnish with a slice of orange.

Champagne Cup

1 bottle Chilled Champagne, 3oz. Grand Marnier, 3oz. Cognac, 2oz. Maraschino Liqueur.

Mix together in a large jug with 10–15 ice-cubes. Stir in sliced fruits in season and fresh mint leaves. Serve in champagne flutes.

Champagne Julep

6 fresh Mint leaves, 1 tsp. powdered Sugar, 1 dash Cognac, Chilled Champagne.

Muddle the mint and sugar together with the cognac in a deep-dish champagne saucer. Top with champagne and serve.

Champagne Velvet

See Black Velvet, above (p. 324).

Chocolate Cocktail

2oz. Port, 1oz. Yellow Chartreuse, 1/2oz. Gomme Syrup, 1 Egg Yolk.

Shake and strain into a martini glass.

Chocolate Daisy

1oz. Port, 1oz. Cognac, 1oz. Lemon Juice, 1 dash Gomme Syrup.

Shake and strain into an ice-filled old fashioned glass. Garnish with fruits in season.

Claret Cobbler

3oz. Claret, 1oz. Soda Water, 1 tsp. powdered Sugar.

In a highball glass, dissolve sugar in water, fill with ice and stir in the claret. Garnish with seasonal fruits.

Claret Sangaree

3oz. Claret, 1oz. Lemon Juice, 1 tsp. powdered Sugar.

Fill a medium goblet with crushed ice and stir in the ingredients. Garnish with a slice of orange and sprinkle grated nutmeg over drink.

Clove

2oz. Sweet Vermouth, 1oz. Sloe Gin, 1oz. Muscat Wine.

Shake and strain into a martini glass.

Cocomacoque

2oz. White Rum, 2oz. Orange Juice, 1oz. Pineapple Juice, 1oz. Lemon Juice, Red Wine.

Shake all but the wine and pour into a highball glass. Top with the wine and serve.

Coffee Flip

1oz. Cognac, 1oz. Port, 1 Egg Yolk, 1/2oz. Gomme Syrup.

Shake and strain into a martini glass. Sprinkle grated nutmeg over drink.

Cognac Coupling

2oz. Cognac, 1oz. Port.

Swill together in a brandy balloon.

Continental Sour

2oz. Cognac, 1oz. Lemon Juice, 1/2oz. Gomme Syrup, 1oz. Red Bordeaux.

Shake all but the wine and pour into an old-fashioned glass. Float wine on top.

Creole Lady

1 1/2oz. Madeira, 1 1/2oz. Bourbon, 1 dash Grenadine.

Stir and strain into a martini glass.

Crimson

2oz. Gin, 1oz. Port, 1/2oz. Lemon Juice, 1 dash Grenadine.

Stir and strain into a martini glass.

Daredevil Flip

2oz. Port, 1 dash Triple Sec, 1 dash Gomme Syrup,
1 dash Angostura Bitters, 1 Egg Yolk.
Shake and strain into a martini glass.

Devil's Cocktail

1 1/2oz. Port, 1 1/2oz. Dry Vermouth, 1 dash Lemon Juice.
Stir and strain into a martini glass.

Diamond Fizz

2oz. Gin, 1oz. Lemon Juice, 1 tsp. powdered Sugar, Chilled Champagne.
Shake all but the champagne and pour into a sugar-rimmed highball glass. Top with the champagne and serve.

Dog's Nose

4oz. Port, 2oz. Gin.
Stir into an ice-filled highball glass.

Dolores

2oz. Dry Sherry, 1oz. Dark Rum, 1/2oz. Dubonnet, 1/2oz. Orange Juice.
Shake and strain into a martini glass.

Dry As A Bone

2oz. Dry Sherry, 1oz. Dry Vermouth, 5oz. Tonic Water.
Build into a highball glass.

Duke

1 Egg, 1 dash Triple Sec, 1 dash Maraschino Liqueur,
1 dash Lemon Juice, 1 dash Orange Juice, Chilled Champagne.
Shake all but the champagne and strain into a flute.
Top with the champagne.

Duke of Marlborough

1oz. Dry Sherry, 1oz. Sweet Vermouth, Juice of 1 Lime,
1 dash Orange Bitters, 1 dash Raspberry Syrup.
Shake and strain into a martini glass.

Dunhill

1oz. Dry Sherry, 1oz. Dry Vermouth, 1oz. Gin, 1 dash Orange Curaçao, 1 dash Pernod.

Stir and strain into a martini glass.

Dunlop

2oz. Rum, 1oz. Dry Sherry, 1 dash Orange Bitters.

Shake and strain into a martini glass.

Duty Free

1oz. Crème de Framboise, 1/2oz. Bourbon, 1 dash Angostura Bitters, 2oz. White Wine, 6oz. Soda.

Build into a napoli grande glass.

Dynamite

1/2oz. Cognac, 1/2oz. Grand Marnier, 1oz. Orange Juice, Chilled Champagne.

Build into a champagne flute topping with the champagne.

Eaglet

1/2oz. Mandarine Napoléon, Chilled Champagne.

Build in a champagne flute topping with the champagne.

East India 2

1 1/2oz. Dry Sherry, 1 1/2z. Dry Vermouth, 1 dash Orange Bitters.

Stir and strain into a martini glass.

Elk's Own

2oz. Scotch, 1oz. Port, 1/2oz. Lemon Juice, 1/2oz. Gomme Syrup, 1 Egg White.

Shake and strain into a martini glass.

English Bolo

4oz. Dry Sherry, 2 tsp. powdered Sugar, 1/2oz. Lemon Juice, 1 tsp. Ground Cinnamon.

Muddle the sugar, lemon and cinnamon together in an old-fashioned glass. Fill with ice and stir in the sherry.

Épernay Dream

1/2oz. Crème de Framboise, 1 dash Midori Melon Liqueur, Chilled Champagne.

Build into a champagne flute. Top with the champagne.

Erection

1oz. Green Crème de Menthe, Chilled Champagne.

Build into a champagne flute. Top with the Champagne.

Fino Mac

2oz. Fino Sherry, 2oz. Ginger Wine.

Stir and strain into an ice-filled old-fashioned glass.

Fino Martini

See chapter three, The Classics, (pp 57–62).

Substitute fino sherry for the dry vermouth in the dry martini recipe. Serve with a twist of lemon.

Flag

1oz. Apricot Brandy, 1/2oz. Crème Yvette, 1/2oz. Orange Curaçao, 2oz. Red Bordeaux.

Shake the apricot brandy and curaçao and strain into a martini glass which already contains the Crème Yvette. Top with the claret and serve.

Fog Cutter

2oz. White Rum, 1oz. Cognac, 1/2oz. Gin, 2oz. Orange Juice, 1/2oz. Lemon Juice, 2 dashes Orgeat, 1/2oz. Sweet Sherry.

Shake and strain into an ice-filled highball glass. Float the sherry on top.

French '75'

1oz. Gin, 1/2oz. Lemon Juice, Chilled Champagne.

Mix the gin and lemon together in a champagne flute and top with the champagne. Serve with a twist of lemon.

French '125'

1oz. Cognac, 1/2oz. Lime Juice, Chilled Champagne.

Mix the cognac and the lime together in a champagne flute and top with the champagne. Serve with a twist of lime.

French Sherbet

1/4oz. Cognac, 1/4oz. Kirschwasser, Lemon Water-Ice, Chilled Champagne.
Stir the spirits together with the water ice in a deep-dish champagne saucer. Top with the champagne.

Gin Sangaree

2oz. Gin, 1/2oz. Gomme Syrup, Soda, 1oz. Port.
Build into a highball glass. Top with the soda and float the port on top. Sprinkle grated nutmeg over drink.

Golden Girl

2oz. Gin, 1oz. Sherry, 2 dashes Orange Bitters, 1 dash Angostura Bitters.
Shake and strain into a martini glass.

Golden Heath

1oz. White Rum, 1oz. Dry Sherry, 1oz. Drambuie.
Shake and strain into a martini glass.

Golden Screw

1/2oz. Cognac, 1/2oz. Crème de Pêche, 1oz. Orange Juice, Chilled Champagne.
Build into a highball glass and top with the champagne.

Grand Mimosa

1/2oz. Grand Marnier, 1oz. Orange Juice, Chilled Champagne.
Build into a champagne flute without ice and top with the champagne.

Greenbriar

2oz. Dry Sherry, 1oz. Dry Vermouth, 2 dashes Peach Bitters.
Stir and strain into a martini glass. Garnish with a sprig of mint.

Happy Youth

1/2oz. Cherry Brandy, 1oz. Orange Juice, 1 Sugar-Cube, Chilled Champagne.
Place the sugar-cube into a champagne flute and cover with the cherry brandy and orange.
Top with the champagne and garnish with a cherry.

Havana 2

1½oz. Sweet Sherry, 1½oz. White Rum, ½oz. Lemon Juice.
Shake and strain into a martini glass.

Hemingway

1oz. Pernod, Chilled Champagne.
Build without ice into a champagne flute and top with the champagne.

High Life

1oz. Cognac, 1oz. Port, 1 Egg White, ½oz. Gomme Syrup.
Shake and strain into a martini glass.

Hi Ho

2oz. Gin, 1oz. White Port, 1 dash Angostura Bitters.
Shake and strain into a martini glass.

Hock & Seltzer

4oz. German Rhine Wine, 4oz. Soda.
Build into a highball glass.

Honeymoon Paradise

1¼oz. Blue Curaçao, ¾oz. Cointreau, 1oz. Lemon Juice, Chilled Champagne.
Build into a highball glass and top with the champagne.

Hot Springs

2oz. White Wine, 1oz. Pineapple Juice, ¼oz. Maraschino Liqueur, 1 dash Angostura Bitters.
Shake and strain into a martini glass.

Hurricane 4

2oz. Gin, 1oz. Dry Sherry.
Stir and strain into a martini glass. Serve with a twist of lemon.

IBF

½oz. Cognac, ¼oz. Orange Curaçao, ¼oz. Madeira, Chilled Champagne.
Build without ice into a champagne flute and top with the champagne.

Imperial 2

1oz. Cognac, 1oz. Port, 1oz. Orange Curaçao.
Shake and strain into a martini glass.

Imperial Delight

3/4oz. Cognac, 1 dash Fernet Branca, 1/4oz. Grand Marnier, Chilled Champagne.
Build without ice into a champagne flute and top with the champagne.

Imperial Fizz 2

1oz. Bourbon, 1/2oz. Lemon Juice, Chilled Champagne.
Build without ice, into a deep-dish champagne saucer and top with the champagne.

Inca

1oz. Gin, 1oz. Sherry, 3/4oz. Dry Vermouth, 3/4oz. Sweet Vermouth, 1 dash Angostura Bitters, 1 dash Orgeat.
Stir and strain into a martini glass.

Independence Cocktail

1 1/2oz. Cognac, 1oz. Port, 1oz. Tia Maria.
Build into an old-fashioned glass.

Iris

1oz. Gin, 1oz. Sherry, 1oz. Dry Vermouth, 1 dash Angostura Bitters, 1 dash Orgeat.
Stir and strain into a martini glass.

Izzadora

2oz. Cognac, 1 dash Cointreau, 1 dash Port, 1 dash Dubonnet.
Stir together in a brandy balloon.

Jabberwocky

1oz. Gin, 1oz. Dry Sherry 1oz. Caperitif, 1 dash Orange Bitters.
Stir and strain into a martini glass.

Jamaica Glow

2oz. Gin, 1/2oz. Claret, 1/4oz. Dark Jamaican Rum, 1/4oz. Orange Juice.

Shake and strain into a martini glass.

James Bond

1oz. Vodka, 1 Sugar-Cube, 3 dashes Angostura Bitters, Chilled Champagne.

Place the sugar-cube in a champagne flute and soak with the bitters. Pour on the vodka and top with the champagne.

Japanese Fizz

2oz. Bourbon, 1/4oz. Port, 1oz. Lemon Juice, 1/4oz. Gomme Syrup, 1 Egg White, Soda Water.

Shake all but the soda and strain into a highball glass. Top with the soda.

Jumping Jelly Bean

1oz. Tequila, 1oz. Grand Marnier, 1oz. Lemon Juice, Chilled Champagne.

Shake all but the champagne and strain into a martini glass. Top with the champagne.

Jungle

1oz. Gin, 1oz. Sweet Sherry, 1oz. Sweet Vermouth.

Shake and strain into a martini glass.

Kerry Cooler

2oz. Irish Whiskey, 1oz. Dry Sherry, 1/2oz. Gomme Syrup, 1/2oz. Lemon Juice, Soda Water.

Shake and pour into a highball glass and top with the soda.

King's Pet

1oz. Cognac, Chilled Champagne.

Build with one ice-cube into a champagne flute and top with the champagne.

Kir

See chapter three, The Classics, (pp 54–5).

Kir Royale

See chapter three, The Classics, (pp 54–5).

La Pirouette

2oz. Dry Vermouth, 2oz. Dry Sherry, 2 dashes Angostura Bitters.

Stir and strain into a medium wineglass. Serve with a twist of lemon.

Last Resort

2oz. Port, 1oz. Cognac, 1/4oz. Gomme Syrup, 1 Egg Yolk.

Shake and strain into a martini glass. Sprinkle grated nutmeg over drink.

Laura

2 1/2oz. Gin, 1oz. Sherry, 1/2oz. Midori Melon Liqueur, 1oz. Mandarin Juice.

Shake and strain into a martini glass.

Locomotive

5oz. Port, 1 dash Grand Marnier, 1 tsp. Clear Honey, 1 Egg Yolk.

Shake and pour into an old-fashioned glass.

London Special

2 dashes Angostura Bitters, 1 twist of Orange, Chilled Champagne.

Place the twist and bitters into a champagne flute and top with the champagne.

Loving Cup

1 bottle Claret, 6oz. Cognac, 4oz. Cointreau, 2oz. Grand Marnier, 4 tbsp. Sugar, 10oz. Sparkling Mineral Water.

Stir together in a large punch bowl.
Add seasonal fruits and lots of fresh mint.

Luxury

3oz. Cognac, 3oz. Chilled Champagne, 3 dashes Angostura Bitters.

Build without ice into a champagne flute.

Maggie May

1oz. Crème de Mûre, 6oz. Sparkling Lambrusco.

Pour together into a large wineglass.

Malmaison

2oz. White Rum, 1oz. Cream Sherry, 1oz. Lemon Juice.
Shake and strain into a martini glass.

Marco Polo

2oz. Cognac, 2oz. Port, Juice of 1/2 Lemon.
Shake and strain into a wineglass.

Marie Antoinette

1oz. Cognac, 1oz. Grand Marnier, 1 dash Dry Vermouth, 1 dash Port, Juice of 1/4 Ruby Orange.
Shake and strain into a martini glass.

Mary Rose

2oz. Port, 1oz. Gin, 2 dashes Grenadine.
Stir and strain into a martini glass.

Maurice

2oz. Port, 1oz. Cognac.
Pour into a brandy balloon.

Melon Mimosa

2oz. Midori Melon Liqueur, 4oz. Chilled Champagne.
Pour together in a champagne flute.

Mexican Hat

1oz. Tequila, 1oz. Crème de Cassis, 1oz. Champagne.
Pour into an old-fashioned glass three-quarters filled with crushed ice.

Midori Mist

2oz. Midori Melon Liqueur, 1oz. Chilled Champagne.
Stir Midori into an old-fashioned glass half filled with crushed ice. Add the champagne.

Midsummer Night

2oz. Campari, 1oz. Apricot Brandy, 1oz. Orange Juice, Chilled Sparkling Wine.
Build into a highball and top with the sparkling wine.

Mimosa

3oz. Orange Juice, 3oz. Chilled Champagne.

Pour together into a champagne flute.

Mint Gin

1oz. Gin, 1oz. White Crème de Menthe, 1oz. White Port.

Stir and strain into a martini glass.

Montana

1oz. Cognac, 1oz. Port, 1oz. Dry Vermouth.

Stir and strain into a martini glass.

Monte Carlo Cooler

1/2oz. Cointreau, 1/2oz. Cognac, 4oz. Red Wine, 4oz. Lemonade.

Build into a highball glass. Garnish with two slices of orange.

Monte Carlo Highball

2oz. Gin, 1/2oz. White Crème de Menthe, 1oz. Lemon Juice, Chilled Champagne.

Shake all but the champagne and pour into a highball glass. Top with the champagne.

Napoléon 4

1oz. Armagnac, 1/2oz. Dry Vermouth, 2 dashes Cointreau, Chilled Champagne.

Build without ice into a champagne flute and top with the champagne.

New Yorker

2oz. Dry Vermouth, 3/4oz. Gin, 3/4oz. Dry Sherry, 1 dash Triple Sec.

Shake and strain into a martini glass.

New York Sour

2oz. Scotch, 1oz. Lemon Juice, 1/2oz. Gomme Syrup, 1oz. Claret.

Shake and strain into a sour glass, floating the claret on top.

Nightmare

2oz. Gin, 1/2oz. Madeira, 1/2oz. Cherry Brandy, 1 dash Orange Juice, 1 dash Grenadine.

Shake and strain into a martini glass.

Nineteenth Hole

1oz. Scotch, 1oz. Dry Sherry, 1oz. Dry Vermouth.

Stir and strain into a martini glass.

Oaky

1oz. Cointreau, Red Burgundy Wine.

Build into a wineglass and top with the burgundy.

Pimm's Royal

1oz. Pimm's No.1, 5oz. Chilled Champagne.

Build without ice into a champagne flute.

Pimm's Royale

See chapter three, The Classics, (pp 66–7).

Substitute champagne for the lemonade in the Pimm's cocktail.

Poinsettia

1/2oz. Cointreau, Chilled Champagne.

Pour into a champagne flute and top with the champagne. Serve with a twist of orange.

Poop Deck

1oz. Cognac, 1oz. Crème de Mûre, 1oz. Port.

Stir and strain into a martini glass.

Poppy

2oz. Gin, 1oz. Dry Sherry, 2 dashes Orange Bitters.

Shake and strain into a martini glass.

Port & Brandy

2oz. Port, 1oz. Cognac.

Pour into a brandy balloon.

Port Cobbler

3oz. Port, 1 tsp. powdered Sugar, 1oz. Soda Water.

Dissolve the sugar in the water then add to a medium goblet three-quarters filled with crushed ice.
Stir in the port and garnish with seasonal fruits.

Port Flip

2oz. Port, 1/2oz. Gomme Syrup, 1 Egg Yolk.

Shake and strain into a martini glass.
Sprinkle grated nutmeg over drink.

Port Sangaree

2oz. Port, 1/2oz. Gomme Syrup.

Stir into an old-fashioned glass three-quarters filled with crushed ice.
Garnish with lemon slices.

Princeton 2

2oz. Gin, 3/4oz. Port, 3 dashes Orange Bitters.

Stir and strain into a martini glass.

Quarter Deck

2oz. White Rum, 1oz. Cream Sherry, 1/2oz. Lime Juice.

Shake and strain into a martini glass.

Quarter Deck 2

2oz. White Rum, 1oz. Dry Sherry, 1/4oz. Lemon Juice.

Shake and strain into a martini glass.

Queen Bee

2oz. Lime Vodka, 1oz. Tia Maria, 1/2oz. Dry Sherry.

Shake and strain into a martini glass.

Queen Charlotte

2oz. Claret, 1oz. Grenadine, 5oz. Lemonade.

Build into a highball glass and garnish with orange slices.

Raja

1oz. Cognac, 1oz. Chilled Champagne.

Stir and strain into a martini glass.

Rattle Skull

1oz. Port, 1oz. Cognac, 4oz. Red Wine.

Build into a highball glass.

Red Devil

1oz. Campari, 1/2oz. Red Curaçao, 1 dash Lemon Juice, Chilled Sparkling Wine.

Build into a large goblet, topping with the sparkling wine. Garnish with a slice of kiwi fruit and a cherry.

Red Kiss

(DAVIDE CAMPARI MILANO)

1/2oz. Campari, Chilled Champagne.

Build without ice into a champagne flute and top with the champagne.

Red Passion

1 dash Campari, 1 dash Crème de Pêche, Chilled Sparkling Wine.

Build without ice into a champagne flute and top with the sparkling wine. Garnish the edge of the glass with a marzipan heart.

Reform

2oz. Dry Sherry, 1/2oz. Dry Vermouth, 2 dashes Orange Bitters.

Stir and strain into a martini glass.

Rhine Cup

1 Bottle of Liebfraumilch, 2oz. Cognac, 2oz. Cointreau, 1/2oz. Anisette, 2oz. Gomme Syrup, 6oz. Soda Water.

Stir together in a punch bowl with 20 ice-cubes. Garnish with slices of seasonal fruits.

Ritz Fizz

1/2oz. Amaretto, 1/2oz. Blue Curaçao, 1 dash Lemon Juice, Chilled Champagne.

Build without ice into a deep-dish champagne saucer and top with the champagne.

Rosy

2oz. Gin, 1oz. Claret, 1oz. Orange Juice.

Shake and strain into a martini glass.

Royal Wedding

1/4oz. Kirschwasser, 1/4oz. Crème de Pêche, 1/4oz. Orange Juice, Chilled Champagne.

Build without ice into a champagne flute and top with the champagne.

Sangria

1 Bottle Red Wine, 2oz. Cognac, 2oz. Cointreau, 1/2oz. Anisette, 3oz. Gomme Syrup, 8oz. Soda Water.

Stir together in a large jug with 10–15 ice-cubes.
Add lots of sliced citrus fruits and stir again. Serve in medium goblets.

Sherry Cobbler

2oz. Sweet Sherry, 1/4oz. Orange Curaçao, 2 dashes Gomme Syrup.

Pour ingredients into an ice-filled wineglass.
Stir and garnish with seasonal fruit.

Sherry Cocktail

3oz. Dry Sherry, 2 dashes Angostura Bitters.

Stir and strain into a martini glass.

Sherry Cocktail 2

1oz. Sherry, 1oz. Gin, 1oz. Lemon Juice.

Shake and strain into a martini glass.

Sherry Flip

2oz. Cream Sherry, 1 Egg Yolk, 1/2oz. Gomme Syrup.

Shake and strain into a martini glass.

Sicilian Delight

(VITO SCADUTO)

1oz. Campari, 1/2oz. Mandarine Napoléon, 2 dashes Maraschino Liqueur, 1oz. Mandarin Juice, 1 dash Grenadine, Chilled Moscato di Sicilia.

Shake all but the Moscato and strain into a champagne flute.
Top with the Moscato and garnish with a slice of orange and a cherry.

Soixante-Neuf

1oz. Gin, 1/2oz. Lemon Juice, Chilled Champagne.

Shake the gin and lemon and strain into a deep-dish champagne saucer.
Top with the champagne and serve with a twist of lemon.

Soviet

2oz. Vodka, 3/4oz. Amontillado Sherry, 1/2oz. Dry Vermouth.

Shake and pour into an old-fashioned glass. Serve with a twist of lemon.

Spritzer

4oz. White Wine, 4oz. Soda Water.

Build into a highball glass. Garnish with a slice of lemon.

Stoli-Bolli

('ABSOLUTELY FABULOUS')

1oz. Stolichnaya Vodka, Chilled Bollinger Champagne.

Pour into a champagne flute, topping with the Bollinger.

Stone Cocktail

2oz. Dry Sherry, 1oz. White Rum, 1/2oz. Sweet Vermouth.

Stir and strain into a martini glass.

Tawny Cobbler

3oz. Tawny Port, 1/4oz. Orange Curaçao, 1 dash Gomme Syrup.

Pour the port into an ice-filled wineglass.
Stir in the sugar and curaçao and garnish with seasonal fruits.

Tawny Flip

2oz. Tawny Port, 1oz. Cognac, 1 Egg Yolk.

Shake and strain into a medium wineglass.
Sprinkle grated nutmeg over drink.

Tawny Owl

1oz. Tawny Port, 1oz. Cognac, 1oz. White Crème de Cacao.

Stir and strain into a martini glass.

Tawny Sangaree

3oz. Tawny Port, 1oz. Gomme Syrup.

Stir into an old-fashioned glass three-quarters filled with crushed ice.
Sprinkle grated nutmeg over drink and garnish with a slice of lemon.

Tawny Sour

2oz. Scotch, 1oz. Lemon Juice, 1/2oz. Gomme Syrup, 1oz. Tawny Port.

Shake all but the port and pour into an old-fashioned glass.
Float the port on top.

Tempter

2oz. Port, 1oz. Apricot Brandy.

Stir and strain into a martini glass.

Tinton

2oz. Calvados, 1oz. Port.

Shake and strain into a martini glass.

Typhoon

1oz. Gin, 1 dash Anisette, 1/2oz. Lime Juice, Chilled Champagne.

Shake all but the champagne and strain into an ice-filled highball glass.
Top with the champagne.

Up To Date

1oz. Bourbon, 1oz. Sherry, 1/4oz. Grand Marnier,
2 dashes Angostura Bitters.

Shake and strain into a martini glass.

Valencia Royale

1oz. Apricot Brandy, 1/2oz. Orange Juice, Chilled Champagne.

Build without ice into a champagne flute and top with the champagne.

Wally

3/4oz. Cognac, 1/4oz. Benedictine, 2 dashes Lemon Juice, Chilled Champagne.

Build without ice into a champagne flute and top with the champagne.

West End Girl

1oz. Calvados, 2oz. Dry White Wine, 2 dashes Angostura Bitters, 3oz. Perrier Water.

Build into a highball glass. Garnish with a slice of lime.

White Cargo

1oz. Gin, 1oz. Sauterne, 1 scoop Vanilla Ice-Cream.

Shake and pour into an old-fashioned glass.

White Wine Cooler

1oz. Grand Marnier, 4oz. Dry White Wine, 1 dash Orange Bitters, Soda Water.

Build into a highball glass.

Windowlene

1oz. Blue Curaçao, 1/2oz. White Rum, 1/4oz. Gin, 1/4oz. Vodka, 4oz. Chilled Champagne.

Build into a highball glass. Garnish with a spiral of lemon peel.

Wine Sangaree

3oz. Red or White Wine, 1 dash Lemon Juice, 3/4oz. Gomme Syrup.

Stir into an old-fashioned glass three-quarters filled with crushed ice. Sprinkle grated nutmeg over drink.

Wine Spritzer

4oz. Dry White Wine, 4oz. Soda Water.

Build into a highball glass. Garnish with a slice of lemon.

Wonder

1oz. Red Bordeaux, 1oz. Gin, 1oz. Lemon Juice, 1/2oz. Gomme Syrup.

Shake and strain into a martini glass.

Xeres

3oz. Dry Sherry, 1 dash Orange Bitters.

Stir and strain into a martini glass.

Zaza 3

1 1/2oz. Dry Sherry, 1 1/2oz. Dubonnet, 1 dash Orange Bitters.

Stir and strain into a martini glass. Serve with a twist of orange.

SHOOTERS

▼

Despite its diminutive stature (usually no more than 2–2½oz. volume), the shooter plays a fundamentally important role in the cocktail world of the 'nineties. No bartender's repertoire is complete unless it includes a wide selection of shooters. This lilliputian tipple has evolved from the chaser, the concept of drinking a beer and chasing it down with a dram of whisky or schnapps in one shot. However, the inspiration behind many of today's innovative shooters has meant that its uninspiring ancestor has been condemned to obscurity. Shooters are dispensed in a variety of vessels, the purpose-built shot glass being the predominant choice. I give a selection of older recipes, all of which are identifiable by the stipulation of a liqueur glass. The tiny shooter is a drink of fleeting existence, which can result in excess. As a safeguard, I find it is advisable to set a limit on the number you are going to drink before you start drinking.

Angel's Kiss

½oz. White Crème de Cacao, ½oz. Sloe Gin, ½oz. Cognac, ½oz. Double Cream.

Layer into a shot glass.

Angel's Kiss 2

1oz. Benedictine, 1oz. Double Cream.

Layer into a shot glass.

Angel's Lips

1½oz. Benedictine, ½oz. Double Cream.

Layer into a shot glass.

Angel's Tip

1½oz. White Crème de Cacao, ½oz. Double Cream.

Layer into a shot glass.

Angel's Tit

1½oz. Maraschino Liqueur, ½oz. Double Cream.

Layer into a shot glass.

Angel's Wing

¾oz. Brown Crème de Cacao, ¾oz. Cognac, ½oz. Double Cream.

Layer into a shot glass.

Baby Kitty

¾oz. Anisette, ¾oz. Crème de Violette, ½oz. Double Cream.

Layer into a shot glass.

Baby's Own

1oz. Cointreau, 1oz. Double Cream, 1 drop Angostura Bitters.

Layer into a shot glass. Drop bitters on the top.

Brain Tumour

1oz. Peach Schnapps, 1oz. Bailey's, 1 dash Grenadine.

Layer the schnapps and Bailey's into a shot glass.
Drop the grenadine into create the tumour effect.

Cherry Bomb Shooter

1½oz. Cherry Brandy, ¼oz. Polish Pure Spirit.

Shake and strain into a shot glass.

Cocaine

1oz. Galliano, 1oz. Tequila.

Layer into a shot glass.

Dead Rat Shooter

1 1/2oz. Scotch, 1/2oz. Green Chartreuse.

Shake and strain into a shot glass.

Deep Throat

1oz. Kahlúa, 1oz. Vodka.

Layer into a shot glass and shoot drink without using your hands. (Warning: Hold the glass between your lips and not between your teeth, the latter could result in the glass breaking.)

Depth Charge 2

Fill a shot glass with any flavoured schnapps and drop it into a glass of beer.

Devil's Breath

2oz. Drambuie, 5 dashes Tabasco Sauce.

Shake and strain into a shot glass.

Donkey's Kick

2oz. Gold Tequila, 3 dashes Tabasco Sauce, 1 dash Clamato Juice.

Shake and strain into a shot glass.

Dragon's Breath

1oz. Absolut Pepper Vodka, 1/2oz. Drambuie, 4 dashes Tabasco Sauce.

Stir and strain into a shot glass.

Dutch Courage

2oz. Genever, 2 dashes Angostura Bitters.

Shake and strain into a shot glass.

E.T.

3/4oz. Vodka, 3/4oz. Midori Melon Liqueur, 3/4oz. Bailey's.

Layer into a shot glass.

F–16

3/4oz. Kahlúa, 3/4oz. Bailey's, 3/4 Overproof Rum.

Layer into a shot glass.

Flaming Blue Bahoona Shooter

$^{3}/_{4}$oz. White Crème de Cacao, $^{3}/_{4}$oz. Blue Curaçao, $^{3}/_{4}$oz. Peppermint Schnapps, 1 dash Overproof Rum.

Layer into a shot glass. Ignite, extinguish and drink through straw.

Flaming Flamingo

$^{3}/_{4}$oz. Green Crème de Menthe, $^{3}/_{4}$oz. Triple Sec, $^{3}/_{4}$oz. Cognac.

Layer into a shot glass, ignite the cognac and drink through a straw.

Flaming Lamborghini

$^{1}/_{2}$oz. Grenadine, 1oz. Galliano, 1oz. Sambuca, $^{1}/_{2}$oz. Green Chartreuse, 1oz. Kahlúa, 1oz. Blue Curaçao, Ground Cinnamon.

Layer the first four ingredients into a martini glass. Pour the Kahlúa and curaçao into individual shot glasses. To cunsume the drink you will require an assistant. Ignite the chartreuse and start to drink the flaming concoction through 2 long straws (long straws prevent you from singeing your eyebrows). While you are drinking, your assistant slowly pours the contents of the shot glasses into the martini and then sprinkles the cinnamon into the flames to create a sparkling effect. Although this is not technically a shooter, the idea is to drink the whole mixture in one go.

Flaming Sambuca

2oz. Sambuca, 3 Coffee Beans.

Pour the sambuca into a liqueur glass, add the beans and ignite. Extinguish after 5–10 seconds, allow the glass to cool and then drink.

Flaming Star

$^{3}/_{4}$oz. White Crème de Menthe, $1^{1}/_{2}$oz. Bourbon, 1 dash Overproof Rum.

Layer into a shot glass. Ignite, extinguish and drink through a straw.

Gallstone Shooter

$^{3}/_{4}$oz. Crème de Noyau, $^{3}/_{4}$oz. White Crème de Cacao, $^{1}/_{2}$oz. Vodka.

Layer into a shot glass.

Golden Shot

$^{3}/_{4}$oz. Drambuie, $^{1}/_{2}$oz. Bailey's, $^{3}/_{4}$oz. Vodka.

Layer into a shot glass.

Good & Plenty Shooter

1oz. Pernod, 1oz. Kahlúa.

Layer into a shot glass.

Half Gram

1oz. Grand Marnier, 1oz. Crème de Grand Marnier.

Layer into a shot glass.

Harbour Light

$^1/_2$oz. Tequila, $^1/_2$oz. Kahlúa, $^1/_2$oz. Cognac, 1 dash Overproof Rum.

Layer into a shot glass. Ignite drink, extinguish flame, allow glass to cool then shoot drink.

Hard Dick

1oz. Amaretto, Chilled Champagne.

Build into an old-fashioned glass and top with the Champagne. Drink in one shot.

Honeysuckle

1$^1/_2$oz. White Rum, $^1/_4$oz. Gomme Syrup, $^1/_4$oz. Lime Juice.

Stir and strain into a shot glass.

Hot Shot

$^1/_2$oz. Hot Sweet Black Coffee, $^3/_4$oz. Galliano, $^1/_2$oz. Double Cream.

Layer into a shot glass.

Iguana

1oz. Vodka, $^1/_2$oz. Tequila, $^1/_2$oz. Kahlúa.

Shake and strain into a shot glass.

Illusion

$^3/_4$oz. Peach Schnapps, $^3/_4$oz. Vodka, 1 dash Cranberry Juice, 1 dash Orange Juice.

Shake and strain into a shot glass.

Italian Flag

$^3/_4$oz. Crème de Fraise, $^3/_4$oz. Green Crème de Menthe, $^3/_4$oz. Cointreau.

Layer into a shot glass.

Jamaican Duster

1oz. Dark Rum, 1oz. Tia Maria, 1 dash Pineapple Juice.

Stir and strain into a shot glass.

Jaw Breaker

2oz. Schnapps, 4 dashes Tabasco Sauce.

Stir and strain into a shot glass.

Jelly Bean

1oz. Sambuca, 1oz. Crème de Mûre.

Shake and strain into a liqueur glass.

Jelly Fish

1oz. Kahlúa, 1oz. Bailey's, 1 dash Grenadine.

Layer into a shot glass. Drop the grenadine in the middle and use a cocktail stick to create the grenadine tentacles.

Jersey Cocktail

1oz. Cognac, 1oz. Green Chartreuse.

Layer into a liqueur glass.

Jersey Lily

1oz. Cognac, 1oz. Green Chartreuse, 10 dashes Angostura Bitters.

Layer into a liqueur glass and drop the bitters on the top.

Katinka

1oz. Gin, 1 dash Green Chartreuse, 1 dash Angostura Bitters.

Stir and strain into a liqueur glass.

King Alphonse Shooter

$1^1/_2$oz. White Crème de Cacao, $^1/_2$oz. Double Cream.

Stir and strain into a shot glass.

La Créole

1/2oz. Raspberry Syrup, 1/2oz. Maraschino Liqueur, 1/2oz. Yellow Chartreuse, 1/2oz. Green Chartreuse.

Layer into a pousse-café glass.

Lafitte

1/2oz. Gin, 1/2oz. Pernod, 1/2oz. Dry Vermouth, 1/2oz. White Crème de Menthe.

Shake and strain into a liqueur glass.

Landslide

1/2oz. Crème de Banane, 3/4oz. Amaretto, 3/4oz. Bailey's.

Layer into a shot glass.

Leg Spreader

1oz. Kahlúa, 1oz. Galliano.

Shake and strain into a shot glass.

Lighthouse

1oz. Kahlúa, 1oz. Bacardi 151 proof Rum.

Layer into a shot glass. Ignite, extinguish flame, allow glass to cool and shoot drink.

Lillian Waldorf

1oz. Maraschino Liqueur, 1oz. Crème Yvette.

Layer into a liqueur glass.

Mae West

2oz. Cognac, 1/2oz. Gomme Syrup, 1 Egg Yolk.

Shake and strain into a martini glass. Sprinkle cayenne pepper over drink.

Mexican Flag

1/2oz. Grenadine, 3/4oz. White Crème de Menthe, 3/4oz. Green Chartreuse.

Layer into a shot glass.

Mind Eraser

1 1/2oz. Kahlúa, 1 1/2oz. Vodka, 2oz. Soda.

Shake and strain into an old-fashioned glass. Drink in one go with a straw.

Nashville Shooter

1½oz. Vodka, 1 dash Lemon Juice, 1 dash Lime Juice, 1 dash Cranberry Juice.

Shake and strain into a shot glass.

Peaches & Cream

1½oz. Peach Schnapps, ½oz. Double Cream.

Layer into a shot glass.

Peck

1oz. Gin, ½oz. Apricot Brandy, ½oz. Dry Vermouth.

Stir and strain into a liqueur glass.

Petit Pois

1oz. Green Curaçao, 2 dashes Green Crème de Menthe, 1 dash Blue Curaçao.

Stir and strain into a liqueur glass.

Petroleum

1½oz. Mescal, 2 dashes Worcestershire Sauce, 2 dashes Tabasco Sauce, 1 Lime Wedge, Salt.

Stir and strain into a shot glass.

Lick the salt, bite the lime and shoot the drink.

Pink Nipple

1oz. Crème de Mûre, 1oz. Bailey's, 1 dot Grenadine.

Layer into shot glass. Drop grenadine on the top to create the nipple.

Polo

1oz. Gin, ¼oz. Orange Juice, ¼oz. Lemon Juice.

Shake and strain into a liqueur glass.

Polo 2

1oz. Gin, ¼oz. Orange Juice, ¼oz. Grapefruit Juice.

Shake and strain into a liqueur glass.

Port & Starboard
$^1/_2$oz. Grenadine, 1oz. Green Crème de Menthe.
Layer into a liqueur glass.

Pousse-Café
Equal Parts: Grenadine, Crème de Cassis, Galliano, Cointreau, Cognac, Green Chartreuse.
Layer into a pousse-café glass.

Pousse-Café 2
Equal Parts: Grenadine, Yellow Chartreuse, Green Crème de Menthe, Kümmel, Gold Tequila.
Layer into a pousse café-glass.

Pousse-Café (Green Fly)
Equal Parts: Midori Melon Liqueur, Green Crème de Menthe, Green Chartreuse.
Layer into a shot glass.

Pousse-Café (Rainbow)
Equal Parts: Grenadine, Brown Crème de Cacao, Crème de Cassis, White Crème de Menthe, Drambuie, Green Chartreuse.
Layer into a pousse-café glass.

Pousse L'Amour
$^1/_4$oz. Maraschino Liqueur, 1 Egg Yolk (Unbroken), $^1/_2$oz. Benedictine, $^1/_2$oz. Cognac.
Layer into a liqueur glass.

Prairie Fire Shooter
$1^1/_2$oz. Mescal, 5 dashes Tabasco Sauce.
Stir and strain into a shot glass.

Red Hot Shooter
1oz. Absolut Pepper Vodka, $^1/_2$oz. Orange Juice, 2 dashes Tabasco Sauce.
Stir and strain into a shot glass.

Regional Shooter

1/2oz. Grappa, 1/2oz. Sake, 1/2oz. Underberg, 1/2oz. Peach Nectar.

Stir and strain into a shot glass.

Roberto's Ruin

(DAVID WILSON)

1/4oz. Midori Melon Liqueur, 1/4oz. Crème de Fraises, 1 1/2oz. Vodka.

Layer into a shot glass.

Rocky Mountain Shooter

1oz. Bourbon, 1/2oz. Amaretto, 1/2oz. Orange Juice.

Stir and strain into a shot glass.

Saucy Sue

2oz. Calvados, 1 dash Apricot Brandy, 1 dash Anisette.

Stir and strain into a liqueur glass.

Sherry Egg Cocktail

2oz. Dry Sherry, 1 Egg.

Place the egg in a martini glass without breaking the yolk.
Pour the sherry over the egg. Drink in one gulp.

Slippery Nipple

1oz. Sambuca, 1oz. Bailey's.

Layer into a shot glass.

Stoli Buster

1oz. Stolichnaya Vodka, 1oz. Bailey's.

Stir and strain into a shot glass.

Tequila Shot

2oz. Tequila, 1 Lime Wedge, 1/4 tsp. Salt.

Sprinkle salt along the back of the left hand.
Hold shot glass of tequila in the same hand and the lime in the other.
Lick the salt, shoot the tequila then bite into the lime.

Tequila Slammer

1oz. Tequila, 1oz. Chilled Champagne.

Pour into an old-fashioned glass. Cover glass with hand. Slam on the table and shoot drink whilst effervescing.

Test-Tube Baby

1oz. White Crème de Menthe, 1oz. Schnapps, 1 dash Single Cream.

Layer the first two ingredients. Pick up the cream with a straw and hold it in place by covering one end with your finger. Put the straw into the drink so that the open end is level with the liqueur layer and release the cream into the drink. It will suspend in the centre.

Texas Whore

1oz. Tequila, 1/2oz. Crème de Cassis, 1/2oz. Bourbon.

Stir and strain into a shot glass.

Thriller

1oz. Brown Crème de Cacao, 1/2oz. Cognac, 1/2oz. Bunderberg Australian Overproof Rum.

Layer into a shot glass. Ignite, extinguish flame, allow glass to cool and shoot drink.

Tic-Tac

1oz. White Crème de Menthe, 1oz. Ouzo.

Stir and strain into a shot glass.

Tiger's Bite

1oz. Brown Crème de Cacao, 1/2oz. Wood's 100 Dark Rum, 1/2oz. Wild Turkey 101 Bourbon.

Stir and strain into a shot glass.

Top Banana Shooter

3/4oz. Vodka, 1/2oz. Crème de Banane, 1/2oz. White Crème de Cacao, 1 dash Kahlúa.

Shake and strain into a shot glass.

Union Jack Shooter

$^{3}/_{4}$oz. Grenadine, $^{3}/_{4}$oz. Maraschino Liqueur, $^{3}/_{4}$oz. Green Chartreuse.
Layer into a shot glass.

Universal Shooter

1oz. Vodka, 1oz. Midori Melon Liqueur, 1oz. Grapefruit Juice.
Shake and strain into an old-fashioned glass.

Ward Eight Shooter

1$^{1}/_{2}$oz. Bourbon, 1 dash Grenadine, 2 dashes Lime Juice.
Shake and strain into a shot glass.

Warped Willy

$^{3}/_{4}$oz. Vodka, $^{3}/_{4}$oz. Amaretto, 2 dashes Rose's Lime Cordial.
Shake and strain into a shot glass.

Watermelon Shooter

1oz. Southern Comfort, $^{1}/_{4}$oz. Crème de Noyaux, $^{1}/_{4}$oz. Vodka, $^{1}/_{4}$oz. Pineapple Juice.
Shake and strain into a shot glass.

White Light

1oz. White Crème de Menthe, 1oz. Sambuca.
Layer into a shot glass. Ignite drink, extinguish flame, allow glass to cool then shoot drink.

White Mite

$^{1}/_{4}$oz. White Crème de Cacao, $^{1}/_{4}$oz. White Crème de Menthe, $^{1}/_{4}$oz. Triple Sec, $^{1}/_{4}$oz. Vodka, $^{3}/_{4}$oz. Double Cream.
Shake and strain into a shot glass.

RICKEYS, HIGHBALLS, FIZZES AND SWIZZLES

▼

Rickeys, highballs and fizzes are all cousins within the same family of cocktails. The fizz is most closely related to the Collins, the primary distinction being that a Collins is built in the glass, whereas the fizz is always shaken. Both drinks feature here. The highball is a long drink, generally of spirit or liqueur base topped with an effervescent beverage of some kind, creating a stimulating thirst-quencher. In the case of the rickey the juice of a lime is used and the spent lime shell is always added to the drink. Finally I have included the swizzle, a style of cocktail similar to both the fizz and the rickey. It is named after the West Indian tradition of serving with a dried sprig of a tropical plant, which is used to blend the drink by rapidly rubbing one end between the palms of the hands. The swizzle is served with a swizzle stick, allowing the customer to perform the final mix.

Addington Highball

1oz. Dry Vermouth, 1oz. Sweet Vermouth.

Stir and strain into an ice-filled highball glass.

Top with soda or ginger ale and serve with a twist of orange.

Admiral Highball

2oz. Bourbon, 1oz. Pineapple Juice, 1 dash Lemon Juice, Soda Water.

Stir and strain into an ice-filled highball glass.

Top with soda or ginger ale and serve.

Alabama Fizz

2oz. Gin, Juice of 1 Lemon, 2 tsp. powdered Sugar, Soda Water, Sprig of fresh Mint.

Shake and pour into a highball, topping with the soda water. Add the sprig of mint and serve.

Albemarle Fizz

2oz. Gin, Juice of 1 Lemon, 2 tsp. powdered Sugar, Soda Water, 1/4oz. Raspberry Syrup.

Shake and pour into a highball, topping with the soda water. Add the raspberry syrup and serve.

Amaretto Rose

2oz. Amaretto, 1oz. Rose's Lime Cordial, Soda Water.

Build the Amaretto and Rose's into a highball glass, top with the soda, stir and serve.

American Fizz

1 1/2oz. Bourbon or Rye Whiskey, 2oz. Lemon Juice, 1/2oz. Gomme Syrup, Soda Water.

Shake all but the soda and strain into a sugar-rimmed, ice-filled highball glass. Top with the soda and garnish with a slice of lemon.

American Glory Highball

2oz. Champagne, 2oz. Orange Juice.

Build into a highball glass, top with ginger ale and serve.

Americano

2oz. Campari, 2oz. Sweet Vermouth, Soda Water.

Shake and pour into a highball glass, top with soda, stir and serve.

American Swizzle

2oz. Bourbon or Rye Whiskey, 1oz. Lime Juice, 3/4oz. Gomme Syrup, 2 dashes Angostura Bitters, Soda Water.

Build into a highball glass, topping with the soda. Serve with a swizzle stick.

American Whiskey Collins

See chapter three, The Classics, (p. 52).
Substitute bourbon or rye whiskey for the gin in the Collins.

American Whiskey Highball

2oz. Bourbon or Rye Whiskey, Ginger Ale.
Build into a highball glass, topping with the ginger ale.
Serve with a twist of lemon.

American Whiskey Rickey

2oz. Bourbon or Rye Whiskey, 1/2 Lime, Soda Water.
Squeeze lime juice into a highball glass.
Fill with ice and drop in the spent lime shell.
Stir in the bourbon or rye whiskey and top with the soda.

Amer Picon Highball

2oz. Amer Picon, 1oz. Grenadine.
Stir and strain into an ice-filled highball glass.
Top with soda or ginger ale and serve.

Apple Blow Fizz

2oz. Calvados, 1oz. Lemon Juice, 2 tsp. powdered Sugar, 1 Egg White.
Shake and strain into an ice-filled highball glass, top with soda water and serve.

Apple Brandy Rickey

2oz. Calvados, Juice of 1/2 Lime, Soda Water.
Build the gin and lime in a highball glass, drop in the 1/2 lime shell, top with soda and serve.

Applejack Highball

2oz. Applejack, 1oz. Cognac, 1 dash Lemon Juice.
Stir and strain into an ice-filled highball glass, top with soda or ginger ale and serve.

Apple Rum Rickey

1oz. Calvados, 1oz. Dark Rum, Juice of 1/2 Lime, Soda Water.

Build the gin, rum and lime into a highball glass, drop in the 1/2 lime shell, top with soda and serve.

Après Ski

1oz. Vodka, 1oz. White Crème de Menthe, 1oz. Anisette, Soda Water.

Shake and strain all but the soda into an ice-filled highball glass. Top with soda and stir in a sprig of mint.

Apricot Rickey

2oz. Apricot Brandy, Juice of 1/2 Lime, Soda Water.

Build the apricot brandy and lime into a highball glass, drop in the 1/2 lime shell, top with soda and serve.

Armagnac Rickey

2oz. Armagnac, Juice of 1/2 Lime, Soda Water.

Build the armagnac and lime into a highball glass, drop in the 1/2 lime shell, top with soda and serve.

Bermuda Highball

1oz. Gin, 1oz. Apricot Brandy, 1oz. Dry Vermouth, Ginger Ale.

Build into a highball glass and top with the ginger ale.

Bourbon Highball

2oz. Bourbon, Soda or Ginger Ale.

Pour the bourbon into an ice-filled highball glass. Top with the soda or ginger ale and serve with a twist of lemon.

Brandy Swizzle

2oz. Cognac, 1 1/2oz. Lime Juice, 1/2oz. Gomme Syrup, 1 dash Angostura Bitters.

Build into a highball glass half-filled with crushed ice. Top with soda and serve with a swizzle stick.

Cablegram

2oz. Scotch, 1oz. Lemon Juice, 1/2oz. Gomme Syrup, Ginger Ale.

Build into a highball glass, topping with the ginger ale.

California Root Beer

1oz. Kahlúa, 1oz. Galliano, 6oz. Cola.

Build into a highball glass.

Catfish

2oz. White Rum, 1oz. Blue Curaçao, Lemonade.

Build into a highball glass, topping with the lemonade.

Charleston

1oz. Mandarine Napoléon, 1oz. Cherry Brandy, Lemonade.

Build into a highball glass, topping with the lemonade.

Cherry Fizz

2oz. Cherry Brandy, 1oz. Lemon Juice, 1/2oz. Grenadine, Soda.

Shake the first three ingredients and pour into a highball glass.
Top with soda and garnish with a Maraschino cherry.

City Lights

2oz. Glayva, 1oz. Orange Juice, 1oz. Lemon Juice, Soda.

Build into a highball glass, topping with the soda.

Cliff-Hanger

2oz. Silver Tequila, Bitter Lemon.

Build into a highball glass, topping with the bitter lemon.

Cognac Highball

2oz. Cognac, Soda or Ginger Ale.

Build into a highball glass and garnish with a lemon peel spiral.

Comfortable Fizz

2oz. Southern Comfort, 1oz. Lemon Juice, 1/2oz. Gomme Syrup, Soda.

Shake all but the soda and pour into a highball glass.
Top with the soda and stir.

Cuba Libra

2oz. White Rum, Juice of 1/2 Lime, Cola.

Squeeze the lime juice into a highball glass and add the lime shell. Fill with ice and pour in the rum and cola. Stir and serve.

Derby Fizz

2oz. Scotch, 1oz. Lemon Juice, 1/2oz. Gomme Syrup, 1 Egg, Soda.

Shake all but the soda and pour into a highball glass. Top with the soda and stir.

Drambuie Swizzle

2oz. Drambuie, 1oz. Lime Juice, 1/2oz. Gomme Syrup, Soda.

Build into a highball glass and serve with a swizzle stick. Garnish with a sprig of mint.

Dubonnet Fizz

2oz. Dubonnet, 1/2oz. Gin, 1oz. Lemon Juice, 1oz. Orange Juice, Soda.

Shake all but the soda and pour into a sugar-rimmed highball glass. Top with the soda.

Dubonnet Highball

2oz. Dubonnet, Ginger Ale or Soda.

Pour the Dubonnet into an ice-filled highball glass. Top with the soda or ginger ale and serve with a twist of lemon.

El Diablo

2oz. Tequila, 1/2oz. Crème de Cassis, 1/2oz. Lime Juice, Ginger Ale.

Build into a highball glass, topping with the ginger ale.

Ellise Highball

1oz. Cognac, 1/4oz. Strega, 1 dash Angostura Bitters, Ginger Ale.

Build into a highball glass, topping with the ginger ale. Garnish with a spiral of lemon peel.

Emerald Fizz

2oz. Midori Melon Liqueur, 1oz. Lime Juice, 6oz. Soda.

Build into a highball glass and stir.

English Highball

$^3/_4$oz. Gin, $^3/_4$oz. Sweet Vermouth, $^3/_4$oz. Cognac, Ginger Ale.

Build into a highball glass, topping with the ginger ale.
Serve with a twist of orange.

Eton Blazer

2oz. Plymouth Gin, $^3/_4$oz. Kirschwasser, 1oz. Lemon Juice, 1 dash Gomme Syrup, Soda.

Shake all but the soda and strain into an ice-filled highball glass.
Top with the soda.

Fog Horn

1$^1/_2$oz. Gin, Juice of $^1/_2$ Lime, Ginger Ale.

Build into a highball glass, topping with the ginger ale.

Forth Flyer

1oz. Glayva, $^1/_2$oz. Galliano, $^1/_2$oz. Blue Curaçao, 6oz. Ginger Ale.

Build into a highball glass.

Gable's Collins

2oz. Vodka, $^3/_4$oz. Crème de Noyau, $^1/_4$oz. Lemon Juice, $^1/_4$oz. Pineapple Juice, Soda.

Build into a highball glass, topping with the soda.

Gin Buck

2oz. Gin, 1oz. Lemon Juice, Ginger Ale.

Build into a highball glass, topping with the ginger ale.

Gin Fizz

2oz. Gin, 1oz. Lemon Juice, $^1/_2$oz. Gomme Syrup, Soda Water.

Shake all but the soda and strain into a sugar-rimmed highball glass.
Add ice, top with the soda and stir.

Gin Highball

2oz. Gin, Ginger Ale.

Build into a highball glass, topping with the ginger ale.
Serve with a twist of lemon.

Gin Rickey

2oz. Gin, Soda, 1/2 Lime.

Build the gin and lime juice into an old-fashioned glass.
Drop in the spent lime shell and stir in the soda.

Gin Swizzle

2oz. Gin, 1oz. Lime Juice, 1/2oz. Gomme Syrup, 2 dashes Angostura Bitters, Soda Water.

Build into a highball glass, topping with the soda.
Serve with a swizzle stick.

Gin Thing

2oz. Gin, 1/2oz. Lime Juice, Ginger Ale.

Build into a highball glass, topping with the ginger ale.

Golden Fizz

2oz. Gin, 1oz. Lemon Juice, 1/2oz. Gomme Syrup, 1 Egg Yolk, Soda.

Shake and strain into an ice-filled highball glass, topping with the soda.

Green Fizz

2oz. Gin, 1oz. Lemon Juice, 1/2oz. Gomme Syrup, 1 dash Green Crème de Menthe, Soda Water.

Shake all but the soda and strain into a sugar-rimmed highball glass.
Add ice, top with the soda and stir.

Green Swizzle

2oz. Gin, 1oz. Lime Juice, 1 dash Green Crème de Menthe, 1/2oz. Gomme Syrup, 2 dashes Angostura Bitters, Soda Water.

Build into a highball glass, topping with the soda.
Serve with a swizzle stick.

Grove Cooler

1 1/2oz. Campari, 1/2oz. Vodka, 1 dash Orange Bitters, Ginger Ale.

Build into a highball glass, topping with the ginger ale.

Headless Horseman

2oz. Vodka, 4 dashes Angostura Bitters, Ginger Ale.

Build into a highball glass, topping with the ginger ale.

Hong Kong Gin Fizz

1oz. Gin, 1/2oz. Vodka, 1/4oz. Tequila, 1/4oz. White Rum, 1/4oz. Orange Curaçao, 1/4oz. Benedictine, 1/4oz. Yellow Chartreuse, 1/4oz. Green Chartreuse, 1oz. Lemon Juice, Soda.

Shake and pour into a highball glass, topping with the soda.

Horse's Neck

2oz. Scotch, Ginger Ale, 1 Lemon.

Peel the entire lemon skin in one continuous spiral. Hang one end over the rim of a highball glass and allow the rest to hang into the glass. Fill with ice, add the whisky and top with the ginger ale.

Imperial Fizz

1oz. White Rum, 1oz. Scotch, 1oz. Lemon Juice, 1/2oz. Gomme Syrup, Soda Water.

Shake all but the soda and pour into a highball glass. Top with the soda.

Irish Rickey

2oz. Irish Whiskey, 4oz. Soda Water, 1/2 Lime.

Squeeze the lime juice into a highball glass and drop in the spent lime shell. Add ice and build in the remaining ingredients.

Irish Whiskey Highball

2oz. Irish Whiskey, Ginger Ale.

Build into a highball glass, topping with the ginger ale. Serve with a twist of lemon.

John Collins

See chapter three, The Classics, (p. 52).

Kaiser Bill

1oz. Schnapps, 1oz. Lime Juice, Soda Water.

Build into a highball glass, topping with the soda.

Key Largo

1oz. Campari, 1oz. Cointreau, 2oz. Grapefruit Juice, Soda Water.
Shake and pour into a highball glass, topping with the soda.
Garnish with a slice of grapefruit.

Kirsch Highball

2oz. Kirschwasser, 1oz. Grenadine, Soda Water.
Build into a highball glass, topping with the soda.
Serve with a twist of lemon.

Leap Frog

2oz. Gin, 1oz. Lemon Juice, 6oz. Ginger Ale.
Build into a highball glass.

Long Blonde

1 1/2oz. Dubonnet Blonde, 1 1/2oz. Gin, Soda Water.
Build into a highball glass, topping with the soda.

Mamie Gilroy

2oz. Scotch, 1oz. Lime Juice, 6oz. Ginger Ale.
Build into a highball glass.

Mamie's Sister

2oz. Gin, 1 Lime, 6oz. Ginger Ale.
Add the juice and peeled rind of the lime to a highball glass.
Fill with ice and stir in the gin and ginger ale.

Manhattan Skyscraper

2oz. Bourbon, 1/2oz. Sweet Vermouth, 1/2oz. Dry Vermouth,
1 dash Angostura Bitters, 5oz. Ginger Ale.
Build into a highball glass, topping with the ginger ale.

May Blossom Fizz

2oz. Swedish Punsch, 1oz. Lemon Juice, 1 dash Grenadine, Soda Water.
Shake all but the soda and pour into a highball glass. Top with the soda.

Merry Widow Fizz

2oz. Sloe Gin, 1/2oz. Gomme Syrup, 1oz. Lemon Juice, 1 Egg White, Soda Water.

Shake all but the soda and strain into an ice-filled highball glass. Top with the soda.

Morning Glory Fizz

2oz. Scotch, 1/4oz. Anisette, 1oz. Lemon Juice, 1/2oz. Gomme Syrup, 1 Egg White, Soda Water.

Shake all but the soda and pour into a highball glass. Top with the soda.

New Orleans Buck

2oz. White Rum, 1 1/2oz. Orange Juice, 1oz. Lemon Juice, 4oz. Ginger Ale.

Build into a highball glass.

Northern Lights

2oz. Bourbon, 1oz. Aquavit, 1 dash Angostura Bitters, 2 dashes Grenadine, 6oz. Soda Water.

Build into a highball glass.

Orange Buck

2oz. Gin, 1 1/4oz. Orange Juice, 1/4oz. Lime Juice, Ginger Ale.

Shake and pour into a highball glass, topping with the ginger ale.

Peach Fizz

1oz. Peach Schnapps, 1oz. Vodka, 1oz. Lemon Juice, 1/2oz. Gomme Syrup, Soda Water.

Shake all but the soda and pour into a sugar-rimmed highball glass. Top with the soda.

Picon Cocktail 2

2oz. Amer Picon, 1oz. Grenadine, 6oz. Soda Water.

Build into a highball glass.

Pineapple Fizz

2oz. Gin, 1oz. Pineapple Juice, 1/2oz. Gomme Syrup, Soda Water.

Shake all but the soda and pour into a sugar-rimmed highball glass. Top with the soda.

Raspberry Fizz

2oz. Chambord Black Raspberry Liqueur, 1oz. Lemon Juice, 1/2oz. Gomme Syrup, Soda Water.

Shake all but the soda and pour into a highball glass. Top with the soda.

Red Gin Rickey

2oz. Gin, 1/2 Lime, 2 dashes Grenadine, Soda Water.

Squeeze the lime juice into a highball glass and fill with ice. Add the spent lime shell and the gin. Top with soda and stir in the grenadine.

Red Swizzle

2oz. Gin, 1oz. Lime Juice, 1/2oz. Gomme Syrup, 1oz. Grenadine, 1 dash Angostura Bitters, Soda Water.

Pour into a highball glass filled with crushed ice and top with the soda. Serve with a swizzle stick.

Royal Gin Fizz

2oz. Gin, 1oz. Lemon Juice, 1/2oz. Gomme Syrup, 1 Egg Yolk, Soda Water.

Shake all but the soda and strain into an ice-filled, sugar-rimmed highball glass. Top with the soda.

Rum Highball

2oz. Dark Rum, Ginger Ale.

Build into a highball glass, topping with the ginger ale. Serve with a twist of lemon.

Rum Rickey

2oz. White Rum, 1/2 Lime, Soda Water.

Squeeze the lime juice into an ice-filled highball glass. Drop in the spent lime shell and add the rum. Top with the soda.

Rum Swizzle

2oz. White Rum, 1oz. Lime Juice, 3/4oz. Gomme Syrup, 2 dashes Angostura Bitters, Soda Water.

Pour into a highball glass filled with crushed ice, topping with the soda. Serve with a swizzle stick.

Rye Collins

2oz. Rye Whiskey, 1oz. Lemon Juice, 1/2oz. Gomme Syrup, Soda Water.

Build into a highball glass and top with the soda.

Rye Highball

2oz. Rye Whiskey, Ginger Ale.

Build into a highball glass, topping with the ginger ale. Serve with a twist of lemon.

Scotch Collins

2oz. Scotch, 1oz. Lemon Juice, 1/2oz. Gomme Syrup, Soda Water.

Build into a highball glass, topping with the soda.

Scotch Highball

2oz. Scotch, Ginger Ale.

Build into a highball glass, topping with the ginger ale. Serve with a twist of lemon.

Scotch Rickey

2oz. Scotch, 1/2 Lime, Soda Water.

Squeeze the lime juice into an ice-filled highball glass. Drop in the spent lime shell and add the Scotch. Top with the soda and stir.

Silver Fizz

2oz. Gin, 1oz. Lemon Juice, 1/2oz. Gomme Syrup, 1 Egg White, Soda Water.

Shake all but the soda and pour into a sugar-rimmed highball glass. Top with the soda.

Sloe Comfortable Fizz

1oz. Sloe Gin, 1oz. Southern Comfort, 1oz. Lemon Juice, 1/2oz. Gomme Syrup, Soda Water.

Shake all but the soda and pour into a highball glass. Top with the soda.

Sloe Gin Fizz

2oz. Sloe Gin, 1oz. Lemon Juice, 1/2oz. Gomme Syrup, Soda Water.

Shake all but the soda and pour into a sugar-rimmed highball glass. Top with the soda.

Sloe Gin Rickey

2oz. Sloe Gin, 1/2 Lime, Soda Water.

Squeeze the lime juice into an ice-filled highball glass. Add the spent lime shell and the sloe gin. Top with the soda.

Sloe Swizzle

2oz. Sloe Gin, 1 1/2oz. Lime Juice, 1/4oz. Gomme Syrup, 1 dash Angostura Bitters, Soda Water.

Pour into a highball glass three-quarters filled with crushed ice, topping with the soda. serve with a swizzle stick.

Strawberry Fizz

2oz. Crème de Fraises, 1oz. Lemon Juice, 1/2oz. Gomme Syrup, Soda Water.

Shake all but the soda and pour into a highball glass. Top with the soda.

Tequila Collins

2oz. Tequila, 1oz. Lemon Juice, 1/2oz. Gomme Syrup, Soda Water.

Build into a highball glass, topping with the soda.

Tequila Fizz

2oz. Tequila, 1oz. Lemon Juice, 1/2oz. Gomme Syrup, 7Up.

Shake all but the 7Up and pour into a sugar-rimmed highball glass. Top with the 7Up.

Tequila Fizz 2

2oz. Tequila, 1oz. Lime, 1/4oz. Grenadine, 1 Egg White, Ginger Ale.

Shake all but the ginger ale and pour into a highball glass. Top with the ginger ale.

Tequila Highball

2oz. Tequila, 1oz. Pineapple Juice, Ginger Ale.

Build into a highball glass, topping with the ginger ale.

Tequila Rickey

2oz. Tequila, 1/2 Lime, Soda Water.

Squeeze the lime juice into an ice-filled highball glass. Drop in the spent lime shell, add the tequila and top with the soda.

Tequila Swizzle

2oz. Tequila, 1oz. Lime Juice, 1/2oz. Gomme Syrup, 1 dash Angostura Bitters, Soda Water.

Build into a highball glass three-quarters filled with crushed ice, topping with the soda. Serve with a swizzle stick.

Tom Collins

See chapter three, The Classics, (p. 52).

Uncle Sam

2oz. Bourbon, 1oz. Peach Schnapps, Soda Water.

Build into a highball glass, topping with the soda. Serve with a twist of lemon.

Upstairs

2oz. Dubonnet, 1oz. Lemon Juice, Soda Water.

Build into a highball glass, topping with the soda. Serve with a slice of orange.

Vermouth Curaçao Highball

1oz. Dry Vermouth, 1oz. Orange Curaçao, Ginger Ale.

Build into a highball glass, topping with the ginger ale. Serve with a twist of lemon.

Victory Highball

2oz. Pernod, 1/2oz. Grenadine, Soda Water.

Build into a highball glass, topping with the soda.

Vodka Collins

See chapter three, The Classics, (p. 52).

Substitute vodka for the gin in the Collins.

Vodka Fizz

1 1/2oz. Vodka, 2oz. Lemon Juice, 1/2oz. Gomme Syrup, Soda Water.

Shake all but the soda and strain into a sugar-rimmed, ice-filled highball glass. Top with the soda and garnish with a slice of lemon.

Vodka Highball

2oz. Vodka, Ginger Ale.

Build into a highball glass, topping with the ginger ale.
Serve with a twist of lemon.

Vodka Swizzle

2oz. Vodka, 1oz. Lime Juice, 3/4oz. Gomme Syrup, 2 dashes Angostura Bitters, Soda Water.

Build into a highball glass, topping with the soda.
Serve with a swizzle stick.

Whisky Collins

See chapter three, The Classics, (p. 52).

Substitute Scotch whisky for the gin in the Collins.

Whisky Fizz

1 1/2oz. Scotch Whisky, 2oz. Lemon Juice, 1/2oz. Gomme Syrup, Soda Water.

Shake all but the soda and strain into a sugar-rimmed, ice-filled highball glass. Top with the soda and garnish with a slice of lemon.

Whisky Highball

2oz. Scotch, Ginger Ale.

Build into a highball glass, topping with the ginger ale.
Serve with a twist of lemon.

Whisky Rickey

2oz. Scotch, 1/2 Lime, Soda Water.

Squeeze lime juice into a highball glass.
Fill with ice and drop in the spent lime shell.
Stir in the Scotch whisky and top with the soda.

Whisky Swizzle

2oz. Scotch, 1oz. Lime Juice, 3/4oz. Gomme Syrup,
2 dashes Angostura Bitters, Soda Water.

Build into a highball glass, topping with the soda.
Serve with a swizzle stick.

Yodel

2oz. Fernet Branca, 1oz. Orange Juice, 6oz. Soda Water.

Build into a highball glass.

HOT DRINKS

▼

In this section is the full range of liqueur coffee cocktails, the most familiar of which is Irish coffee. In addition to these there are recipes for drinks heated by the *flambé* method, some hot punch recipes and a variety of other warm alcoholic concoctions guaranteed to enliven a harsh winter evening.

American Coffee

1oz. Bourbon, Hot Black Coffee, 2 tsp. Demerara Sugar, 1oz. Double Cream.

Build into a liqueur coffee glass and float the cream on top.

American Grog

2oz. Dark Rum, 1/2oz. Lemon Juice, 1 Sugar-Cube.

Place all the ingredients into a medium goblet, top with hot water, stir and serve.

(Place a teaspoon in the glass prior to pouring the hot water. This will absorb the heat and prevent the glass from cracking.)

American Whiskey Skin

2oz. Bourbon or Rye Whiskey, 1 Sugar-Cube, 1 piece of Lemon Peel, 3oz. Boiling Water.

Stir together in an old-fashioned glass.

Baked Apple

2oz. Calvados, 1oz. Dark Rum, 4oz. Apple Juice, 1 dash Crème de Cassis, 1 Cinnamon Stick.

Pour the calvados, cassis and rum into a medium heat-proof goblet. Heat the apple juice until hot but not boiling and pour into the spirit mixture. Serve with the cinnamon stick as a stirrer.

Belgian Coffee

1oz. Elixir d'Anvers, Hot Black Coffee, 2 tsp. Demerara Sugar, 1oz. Double Cream.

Build into a liqueur coffee glass and float the cream on top.

Café Gates

1oz. Tia Maria, 1oz. Brown Crème de Cacao, 1oz. Grand Marnier, Hot Black Coffee, 1oz. Double Cream.

Build into a liqueur coffee glass and float the cream on top.

Café Normandie

1oz. Calvados, Hot Black Coffee, 2 tsp. Demerara Sugar, 1oz. Double Cream.

Build into a liqueur coffee glass and float the cream on top.

Café Religeux (Monk's Coffee)

1oz. Benedictine, Hot Black Coffee, 2 tsp. Demerara Sugar, 1oz. Double Cream.

Build into a liqueur coffee glass and float the cream on top.

Café Royale

1oz. Cognac, Hot Black Coffee, 2 tsp. Demerara Sugar, 1oz. Double Cream.

Build into a liqueur coffee glass and float the cream on top.

Calypso Coffee

1oz. Tia Maria, Hot Black Coffee, 2 tsp. Demerara Sugar, 1oz. Double Cream.

Build into a liqueur coffee glass and float the cream on top.

Canadian Coffee

1oz. Canadian Club Whiskey, Hot Black Coffee, 1oz. Gomme Syrup, 1oz. Double Cream.

Build into a liqueur coffee glass and float the cream on top.

Caribbean Coffee

1oz. White Rum, Hot Black Coffee, 2 tsp. Demerara Sugar, 1oz. Double Cream.

Build into a liqueur coffee glass and float the cream on top.

Dutch Coffee

1oz. Genever, Hot Black Coffee, 2 tsp. Demerara Sugar, 1oz. Double Cream.

Build into a liqueur coffee glass and float the cream on top.

Fragile Baby

1oz. Frangelico, 1/2oz. Bailey's, 1oz. Hot Coffee, 1oz. Double Cream.

Build into a liqueur coffee glass and float the cream on top.

Gaelic Coffee

1oz. Scotch, Hot Black Coffee, 2 tsp. Demerara Sugar, 1oz. Double Cream.

Build into a liqueur coffee glass and float the cream on top.

German Coffee

1oz. Kirschwasser, Hot Black Coffee, 2 tsp. Demerara Sugar, 1oz. Double Cream.

Build into a liqueur coffee glass and float the cream on top.

Grog

2oz. Dark Rum, 1oz. Gomme Syrup, 1/2oz. Lemon Juice, 6 Cloves, 1 Cinnamon Stick, 1 Lemon Wheel.

Stud the lemon wheel with the cloves and place in a heatproof tankard. Add the remaining ingredients, top with boiling water and stir.

Hot Brandy Flip

2oz. Cognac, 1/2oz. Gomme Syrup, 1 Egg Yolk, Hot Milk.

Mix the first three ingredients together in a highball glass then stir in the hot milk. Sprinkle grated nutmeg over drink.

Hot Buttered Rum

2oz. Dark Rum, 1oz. Gomme Syrup, 1 1/4 oz. lump Butter.

Three-quarters fill a heat proof glass with boiling water. Stir in the sugar and butter, add the rum and sprinkle grated nutmeg over drink.

Hot Egg-Nog

1oz. Dark Rum, 1oz. Cognac, 1oz. Gomme Syrup, 1 Egg, 6oz. Hot Milk.

Shake all but the milk and strain into a highball glass.
Stir in the hot milk. Sprinkle grated nutmeg over drink.

Hot Eskimo

2oz. Grand Marnier, Hot Chocolate, 1oz. Double Cream.

Build into an old-fashioned glass, floating the cream on top.

Hot Gold

3oz. Amaretto, 6oz. Orange Juice.

Heat the orange until very warm, then build with the amaretto into a highball glass.

Hot Toddy

1 1/2oz. Scotch, 1oz. Lemon Juice, 1 Cinnamon Stick, 6 Cloves, 1 tsp. Brown Sugar, 1/2oz. Orgeat, 1 Lemon Wheel.

Stud the lemon with the cloves and place into a heat proof goblet with the remaining ingredients.
Top with boiling water and stir with the cinnamon stick.

Indian Summer

2oz. Apple Schnapps, 6oz. Hot Apple Cider.

Build without ice into an old-fashioned glass rimmed with ground cinnamon.

Irish Coffee

1oz. Irish Whiskey, Hot Black Coffee, 2 tsp. Demerara Sugar, 1oz. Double Cream.

Build into a liqueur coffee glass and float the cream on top.

Italian Coffee

1oz. Strega, Hot Black Coffee, 2 tsp. Demerara Sugar, 1oz. Double Cream.

Build into a liqueur coffee glass and float the cream on top.

Mexican Coffee

1oz. Kahlúa, Hot Black Coffee, 2 tsp. Demerara Sugar, 1oz. Double Cream.

Build into a liqueur coffee glass and float the cream on top.

Midnight Snowstorm

1oz. White Crème de Menthe, 7oz. Hot Chocolate, 1oz. Double Cream.
Build without ice into a highball glass and float the cream on top.

Monte Cristo

1oz. Kahlúa, 1oz. Grand Marnier, 3oz. Hot Black Coffee, 1oz. Double Cream.
Build without ice into a heat-proof mug and float the cream on top.

Mulled Wine

1 Bottle Claret, 4oz. Port, Rind of 1 Lemon & 1 Orange, 4 tbsp. Sugar, 10 Cloves, 2 Whole Cinnamon Sticks, 1 tsp. Grated Nutmeg.
Heat all the ingredients together in a pan for a minimum of 15 minutes. Serve very hot. Serve in heat-proof mugs.

Navy Brew

2oz. Captain Morgan's Dark Overproof Rum, 1oz. Cointreau, 1 tsp. Demerera Sugar, 6 Cloves, 1 Cinnamon Stick, 4oz. Boiling Water.
Place ingredients into a heat-proof mug and stir in the boiling water.

Nightcap

2oz. Dark Rum, 1/2oz. Gomme Syrup, 6oz. Hot Milk.
Mix together in a heat proof mug. Sprinkle grated nutmeg over drink.

Paint Thinner

1oz. Dark Rum, 1oz. Bailey's, 4oz. Hot Black Coffee.
Pour into a heat-proof mug.

Paraffin

2oz. Parfait Amour, 1oz. Tequila, 1/2oz. Overproof Rum.
Stir the first two ingredients and strain into a brandy balloon. Float the rum on top. Ignite the rum, swill drink until flame is extinguished, allow glass to cool, then drink.

Prince Charles Coffee

1oz. Drambuie, Hot Black Coffee, 2 tsp. Demerara Sugar, 1oz. Double Cream.
Build into a liqueur coffee glass and float the cream on top.

Rum Toddy

2oz. Dark Rum, 1oz. Lime Juice, 1 Cinnamon Stick, 6 Cloves, 1 tsp. Demerera Sugar, 1 dash Orgeat Syrup, 1 Lime Wheel.

Stud the lime wheel with the cloves and combine with the remaining ingredients in a heat-proof mug. Fill with boiling water and serve.

Russian Coffee

1oz. Vodka, Hot Black Coffee, 2 tsp. Demerara Sugar, 1oz. Double Cream.

Build into a liqueur coffee glass and float the cream on top.

Scandinavian Coffee

1oz. Aquavit, Hot Black Coffee, 2 tsp. Demerara Sugar, 1oz. Double Cream.

Build into a liqueur coffee glass and float the cream on top.

Toasted Almond

1½oz. Amaretto, 1½oz. Cognac.

Pour into a brandy balloon. Ignite and allow to burn for 3–5 seconds. Extinguish flame, allow glass to cool and drink.

Tom & Jerry

2oz. Dark Rum, 1oz. Cognac, 1 Egg, 1 tsp. powdered Sugar, Hot Milk.

Preparation: Separate the yolk and white and thoroughly beat, independently. Stir them together and add the sugar and ½oz. of the rum. This will preserve the mixture.

When creating the drink, place 1 tbsp. of the mixture in the bottom of a heat-proof mug, add the remaining rum and stir in enough hot milk to fill to the three-quarters point. Finally pour on the cognac and serve.

Velvet Coffee

1oz. Bailey's, 1oz. Brown Crème de Cacao, Hot Black Coffee, 1oz. Double Cream.

Pour into a heat-proof glass, floating the cream on top.

Whisky Toddy

2oz. Scotch, 4oz. Boiling Water, ¼ Lemon, 1 tsp. granulated Sugar.

Mix together in a heat-proof mug. Sprinkle grated nutmeg over drink.

FLIPS AND PICK-ME-UPS

▼

At first glance these two styles of cocktail appear unrelated. However, I have decided to combine them in one section, as one or more of their ingredients (for instance the egg yolk in the flip) is considered to have remedial properties. Fernet Branca and Underberg are said to have medicinal and restorative qualities. Indeed, it was for this reason that Fernet Branca was the only legitimate alcohol available in the USA during Prohibition. In addition, many of the recipes feature menthe, angostura, pastis, vermouth and cognac, all of which are alleged to have medicinal powers. In all seriousness, the hair-of-the-dog approach is inadvisable when dealing with the effects of over-indulgence. However, all the cocktails in this section are marvellous aperitifs or digestifs.

Absinthe

2oz. Absinthe (Pernod or Ricard, absinthe is not in production), 1/2oz. Anisette, 1/4oz. Orgeat, 2 dashes Angostura Bitters.

Stir and pour into an old-fashioned glass and serve with a twist of lemon.

Absinthe Swiss

2oz. Pernod, 1/2oz. Anisette, 1/2oz. White Crème de Menthe, 1 Egg White, 2 dashes Orange Flower Water.

Shake and strain into a martini glass.

Ale Flip

3oz. Ale, 1 Whole Egg, 1 tsp. powdered Sugar.

Shake and strain into a wineglass and serve with a sprinkling of grated nutmeg.

American Whiskey Flip

1oz. Bourbon or Rye Whiskey, 1oz. Cointreau, 1 Egg Yolk.

Shake and strain into a martini glass. Sprinkle grated nutmeg over drink.

Apothecary

2oz. Gin, 1oz. Cognac, 1oz. Fernet Branca.

Stir and strain into a martini glass.

Bloodshot

2oz. Vodka, 3oz. Tomato Juice, 3oz. Beef Bouillon, 1 dash Lemon Juice, Worcestershire Sauce, Tabasco and Celery Salt to taste.

Shake and pour into a highball glass.

Bloody Caesar

2oz. Vodka, 5oz. Clamato Juice, 1 dash Lemon Juice, Worcestershire Sauce, Tabasco and Celery Salt to taste.

Shake and pour into a highball glass.

Bloody Maria

2oz. Tequila, 5oz. Tomato Juice, 1 dash Lemon Juice, Worcestershire Sauce, Tabasco and Celery Salt to taste.

Shake and pour into a highball glass.

Bloody Mary

See chapter three, The Classics, (pp 50–1).

Brandy Flip

2oz. Cognac, 1 Egg Yolk, 1/2oz. Gomme Syrup.

Shake and strain into a martini glass.
Sprinkle grated nutmeg over the drink.

Bronx Golden

2oz. Gin, 1oz. Sweet Vermouth, 1oz. Dry Vermouth, Juice of 1/4 Orange, 1 Egg Yolk.

Shake and strain into a martini glass.

Bullshot

2oz. Vodka, 4oz. Beef Bouillon, 1 dash Worcestershire Sauce, pinch Salt and Pepper.

Shake and strain into an ice-filled old-fashioned glass.

Cherry Flip

2oz. Cherry Brandy, 1 Egg Yolk, 1/2oz. Gomme Syrup.

Shake and strain into a martini glass.
Sprinkle grated nutmeg over drink.

Chocolate Flip

1oz. Cognac, 1oz. Brown Crème de Cacao, 1 Egg Yolk, 1/2oz. Gomme Syrup.

Shake and pour into an old-fashioned glass.

Comfortable Flip

2oz. Southern Comfort, 1/2oz. Gomme Syrup, 1 Egg Yolk.

Shake and strain into a martini glass.

Corpse Reviver

1oz. Cognac, 1oz. Fernet Branca, 1oz. Green Crème de Menthe.

Shake and strain into a martini glass.

Corpse Reviver 2

1oz. Cognac, 1oz. Sweet Vermouth, 1oz. Calvados.

Shake and strain into a martini glass.

Corpse Reviver 3

1 1/2oz. Gin, 1/2oz. Dry Vermouth, 1oz. Lemon Juice, 1oz. Anisette.

Shake all but the anisette and strain into a martini glass.
Float the anisette on top.

Corpse Reviver 4

2oz. Gin, 1/2oz. Triple Sec, 1oz. Lemon Juice, 1oz. Pastis.
Shake all but the pastis and strain into a martini glass.
Float the pastis on top.

Fernet Branca Cocktail

1oz. Fernet Branca, 1oz. Gin, 1/2oz. Sweet Vermouth.
Stir and strain into a martini glass.

Fernet Cocktail

2oz. Fernet Branca, 1oz. Cognac, 1oz. Gomme Syrup.
Shake and pour into an old-fashioned glass.

Fernet Menthe

1 1/2oz. Fernet Branca, 1 1/2oz. Green Crème de Menthe.
Build into an old-fashioned glass.

Gin Flip

2oz. Gin, 1/2oz. Gomme Syrup, 1 Egg Yolk.
Shake and strain into a martini glass. Sprinkle grated nutmeg over drink.

Golden Slipper

2oz. Eau de Vie de Danzig, 1oz. Yellow Chartreuse, 1 Egg Yolk.
Stir and strain into a martini glass and float the unbroken yolk on the top.

Guggenheim

2oz. Dry Vermouth, 1/4oz. Fernet Branca, 3 dashes Angostura Bitters.
Shake and strain into a martini glass.

Hanky-Panky 2

1oz. Gin, 1oz. Sweet Vermouth, 1/4oz. Fernet Branca.
Shake and strain into a martini glass.

Ice-Cream Flip

1oz. Cointreau, 1oz. Maraschino Liqueur, 1 Egg Yolk,
1 small Scoop Vanilla Ice-Cream.
Shake and strain into a medium goblet. Sprinkle grated nutmeg over drink.

Italian Cocktail

2oz. Sweet Vermouth, 1oz. Fernet Branca, 1/4oz. Gomme Syrup, 1 dash Pastis.

Stir and strain into a martini glass.

Mountain Oyster

1oz. Cognac, 1oz. Tomato Juice, 2 dashes Tabasco Sauce, 2 dashes Worcestershire Sauce, Salt and Pepper, 1 Egg Yolk.

Stir all the ingredients together in a martini glass and drop the whole egg yolk in the centre. Drink in one gulp.

Orange Flip

2oz. Orange Curaçao, 1/2oz. Gomme Syrup, 1 Egg Yolk.

Shake and strain into a martini glass. Sprinkle grated nutmeg over drink.

Peach Flip

2oz. Peach Schnapps, 1 Egg Yolk.

Shake and strain into a martini glass. Sprinkle grated nutmeg over drink.

Pick-Me-Up

1oz. Fernet Branca, 1/2oz. Sweet Vermouth, 2 dashes Angostura Bitters.

Build into an old-fashioned glass.

Pick-Me-Up 2

1oz. Fernet Branca, 1oz. Bourbon, 1/2oz. Pernod.

Stir and strain into a martini glass.

Pick-Me-Up 3

1oz. Green Crème de Menthe, 1oz. Fernet Branca, 1/4oz. Pernod, 1/4oz. Lemon Juice.

Shake and strain into a martini glass.

Pick-Me-Up 4

1oz. Pernod, 1oz. Cognac, 3 dashes Grenadine, 3 dashes Angostura Bitters.

Shake and strain into a martini glass.

Prairie Chicken

1oz. Gin, 1 Egg, 1 dash Worcestershire Sauce, 1 dash Tabasco Sauce, Salt and Pepper.

Crack the egg into a wineglass without breaking the yolk.
Pour the remaining ingredients on top and drink in one gulp.

Prairie Hen

1oz. Vodka, 1 Egg, 1 dash Worcestershire Sauce, 1 dash Tabasco Sauce, Salt and Pepper.

Crack the egg into a wineglass without breaking the yolk.
Pour the remaining ingredients on top and drink in one gulp.

Prairie Oyster

1oz. Cognac, 1oz. Tomato Juice, 1 dash Worcestershire Sauce, 1 dash Tabasco Sauce, Salt and Pepper, 1 Egg Yolk (unbroken).

Stir all but the egg together in a martini glass.
Add the egg to the centre and drink in one gulp.

Raspberry Flip

2oz. Crème de Framboise, 1/2oz. Gomme Syrup, 1 Egg Yolk, 4 fresh Raspberries.

Crush the raspberries and combine them with the remaining ingredients in the shaker.
Shake and strain into a martini glass.

Red Eye

4oz. Tomato Juice, Beer.

Mix together in a tall pilsner glass, topping with the beer.

Red Head

2oz. Tomato Juice, Chilled Stout.

Pour the tomato juice into a highball glass and top with the stout.

Reviver

1oz. Gin, 1oz. Pernod, 1/2oz. Dubonnet, 1/2oz. Underberg, 2 dashes Angostura Bitters.

Shake and strain into a martini glass.

Rum Flip

2oz. Dark Rum, 1/2oz. Gomme Syrup, 1 Egg Yolk.

Shake and strain into a martini glass.
Sprinkle grated nutmeg over drink.

Sloe Comfortable Flip

1oz. Sloe Gin, 1oz. Southern Comfort, 1/2oz. Gomme Syrup, 1 Egg Yolk.

Shake and strain into a martini glass.

Sloe Gin Flip

2oz. Sloe Gin, 1 Egg Yolk, 1/2oz. Gomme Syrup.

Shake and strain into a martini glass.

Stomach Reviver

1oz. Kümmel, 1oz. Cognac, 1oz. Fernet Branca, 4 dashes Angostura bitters.

Stir and strain into a martini glass.

Strawberry Flip

*2oz. Crème de Fraises, 1/2oz. Gomme Syrup, 1 Egg Yolk,
4 fresh Strawberries.*

Crush the Strawberries and combine them with the remaining ingredients in the shaker.
Shake and strain into a martini glass.

Tequila Flip

1 1/2oz. Tequila, 1oz. Cointreau, 1 Egg Yolk.

Shake and strain into a martini glass. Sprinkle grated nutmeg over drink.

Triple Flip

1oz. Cognac, 1/2oz. Grand Marnier, 1/2oz. Cointreau, 1 Egg Yolk.

Shake and strain into a martini glass. Sprinkle grated nutmeg over drink.

Van der Hum Flip

2oz. Van der Hum, 1/2oz. Grenadine, 1 Egg Yolk.

Shake and strain into a martini glass. Sprinkle grated nutmeg over drink.

Vodka Flip

1oz. Vodka, 1oz. Cointreau, 1 Egg Yolk.

Shake and strain into a martini glass. Sprinkle grated nutmeg over drink.

Whisky Flip

1oz. Scotch, 1oz. Cointreau, 1 Egg Yolk.

Shake and strain into a martini glass. Sprinkle grated nutmeg over drink.

Zero Mist

2oz. Green Crème de Menthe, 1oz. Water.

Chill in a freezer until viscous but not solid (approximately 1–2 hours). Serve in a frosted martini glass.

Index

INDEX

▼